RELIGIONS OF THE
ANCIENT NEAR EAST

RELIGIONS OF THE ANCIENT NEAR EAST

Helmer Ringgren

Translated by John Sturdy

THE WESTMINSTER PRESS
Philadelphia

Translation © John Sturdy 1973

This book is a translation of *Främre Orientens Religioner i Gammal Tid,* published by Svenska Bokförlaget/Bonniers (Stockholm 1967), with subsequent additions and alterations by the author

Second printing, 1974

PUBLISHED BY
THE WESTMINSTER PRESS®
PHILADELPHIA, PENNSYLVANIA

PRINTED IN THE UNITED STATES OF AMERICA

Library of Congress Cataloging in Publication Data

Ringgren, Helmer, 1917–
    Religions of the ancient Near East.

    Translation of Främre Orientens religioner i gammal tid.
    Bibliography: p.
    1.   Semites—Religion.   I.   Title.
BL1600.R513   1973   299.9   72–8587
ISBN 0–664–20953–X

Contents

Translator's Note

In accordance with the usual convention, in passages quoted from ancient texts square brackets indicate words or parts of words conjecturally restored, which have been lost in the original. Round brackets indicate words supplied by the translator of the text to fill out the sense, which have never stood in the original.

Quotations from ancient works which in the Swedish edition were translated from a German rendering have been for this edition translated direct from the German into English.

Preface

The study of the religions of the Ancient Near East is of interest both for its own sake and as a background to the study of the Old Testament. It is, however, important that the latter aspect should not take the form of an unplanned search for parallels to Old Testament usages and ideas, but that the ideas of the Ancient Near East should be studied in the context of their function and of the culture to which they belong.

This book attempts to meet both these needs. It is intended to represent the religions of the Ancient Near East in their context, but at the same time to emphasize certain elements which are of special interest for the study of the Old Testament. It makes no claim to offer new and original results, but rather to draw together and set out the positions at present held by scholarship. As regards Sumerian and West Semitic religion this has necessitated a comprehensive study of articles in periodicals and of monographs to make the presentation up to date. In the Swedish edition certain Ugaritic texts which at the time were unpublished could be included, thanks to the kindness of Professor C. Schaeffer, who permitted the use of the proofs of *Ugaritica* v. In the English edition references have been provided to this material, and other minor corrections and additions have been made.

Helmer Ringgren   June 1972
Uppsala

1
Sumerian Religion

INTRODUCTION

The religious history of ancient Mesopotamia does not display a smooth and unitary development. The political history of the country, which we can follow for three thousand years, is stormy and full of changes. It exhibits both conflict among the land's own inhabitants and hostile invasions with periods of foreign domination.

There are two groups of peoples in particular which have left their mark on the cultural development of Mesopotamia, the Sumerians and the Semitic peoples, the Babylonians and Assyrians. But it is not simply the case that the former were the original inhabitants of the country, who were gradually displaced by the invading Semites. On the contrary, all the signs are that the earliest inhabitants of the land were neither Sumerians nor Semites, that the Sumerians settled there in the course of the centuries immediately before 3000 B.C., and that they already had close contact, at least intermittently, with Semitic tribes at that time.

We do not know where the Sumerians came from, but there is much to suggest that it was from the east or north-east. Their language cannot be assigned to any known family of languages. The earliest records (about 3000 B.C.) are written in a very primitive pictorial script. This gradually developed into cuneiform, in which from then on both Sumerian and the Semitic languages were written.

The Sumerians were from the beginning organized into a number of city-states, consisting of a city with surrounding villages and countryside, and only gradually does a Sumerian state develop. The interesting document which is called 'the Sumerian king-list' speaks first of eight kings in five different cities with a total length of reigns of 241,200 years, and then adds: 'the flood swept over (the land)'. These details are of course entirely legendary, but are strikingly reminiscent of the accounts in the Bible of the high ages of the men before the flood.

In the period immediately after the flood the king-list shows one city after another having the government of the whole country, but no doubt in fact several dynasties existed at the same time. Among the first rulers we hear of Etana, Gilgamesh, and Dumuzi, who later appear in myths and legends.

Sumerian history acquires firmer outlines from about 2500 B.C., when the city of Lagash is dominant under such kings as Mesilim, Eannatum (whose victory monument, the 'Stele of the vultures', is well known), Entemena, Urukagina (known as a social reformer), and Lugalzaggesi. This last succumbed about 2350 to an attack by a Semitic prince, Sargon, who founded a powerful kingdom and built his capital at Agade. His dynasty also included the vigorous Naramsin, who called himself 'king of the four points of the compass' and 'the mighty god of Agade (Akkad)'.

The kingdom of Akkad fell before an invasion from the north about 2150. The invaders were the Gutians ('the people from Gutium', Central Kurdistan), who made themselves a name for all time as the hostile nation *par excellence*. An interesting composition, the 'Curse on Agade', interprets this event as meaning that the goddess Inanna had left her city and her temple in consequence of a sin which Naramsin had committed. This is an interesting example of an interpretation of history with a religious bias.

The Gutians seem to have been gradually assimilated, and about 2100 Lagash succeeded in recovering its independence, under such kings as Gudea, who is especially known for his great temple-building activity. The inscription in which he tells how he had the city's temples restored on the instructions of the goddess Baba is the classical record of the Sumerian language, and an important religious document. Somewhat later the third dynasty of Ur came to power, and, under such kings as Urnammu, Shulgi, Shusin, and Ibbisin, Sumerian culture experienced a renaissance. Other peoples, however, the Amorites and Elamites, appeared on the stage now. Ur was weakened, and about 2000 B.C. the city was captured and destroyed, an event which was perpetuated in a magnificent song of lamentation.

Sumerian power lasted a couple of centuries longer, but this was a period of decline. The centre of power was now at Isin (under

Ishmedagan and Lipitishtar) and at Larsa (under Rimsin and others), but the rulers could no longer hold the state together, and the city-states made themselves largely independent again. The Semitic peoples gradually made their presence more and more felt. It is characteristic that the last Sumerian rulers have Semitic names, which suggests that Sumerian was dying out as a living language. In Mari on the upper Euphrates an Amorite (West Semitic) kingdom had its capital, and around Nineveh the kingdom of Assyria began to take shape. The position of primacy, however, was soon taken by Babylon under an Amorite dynasty, the most famous ruler of which, the great legislator Hammurabi (1728–1686), brought the whole land under his sway.

This marked the end of the independent existence of Sumerian culture. It is noteworthy that it is precisely in these last centuries that most works of Sumerian literature seem to have been written down.[1] It is probable that they existed earlier (and recent discoveries of texts have produced examples of this[2]), but were transmitted often in oral form. It looks as if the Sumerian men of learning, having noticed that knowledge of the language was on the decline among the people, wished to save as much as possible of their literary heritage for posterity.

We have therefore as sources for our knowledge of Sumerian religion a rich store of myths, epic, hymns, lamentations, proverbs, and 'wisdom literature' at our disposal. For the most part this material, some of which comes from excavations as long ago as the turn of the century, has become known, and been classified and examined, in these last decades. Among those to whom credit is due for this work S. N. Kramer of Philadelphia should be mentioned first. By his unremitting work in the cuneiform collections of different museums he has succeeded in reconstructing a large number of Sumerian texts of different sorts. Other leading Sumerian scholars, among them A. Falkenstein of Heidelberg and T. Jacobsen of Chicago (now at Yale), have made important contributions to the interpretation of the texts, but there still remains much work to be done before our picture of Sumerian religion is complete.

We are in a significantly poorer position as regards the religion of the oldest period. For this we are almost completely thrown back on the evidence of archaeology. For the pre-Sumerian period almost all that we have is female figurines of a type that is found over large parts of the world, and is assumed to represent a mother-goddess.

In the earliest Sumerian period it can be observed that in the southern parts of the land the temples are located in groups of two. This suggests that a pair of deities were worshipped, probably the mother-goddess and her consort, later known under the names of Inanna and Dumuzi.

An important source for our knowledge of this period are the cylinder-seals, which were used to make impressions on clay for the same purpose as our seals. These seals were usually decorated with mythological pictures, perhaps intended to place what was sealed under the protection of the gods. Common scenes include two animals facing one another, probably a symbol of the activity of the god Dumuzi in encouraging fertility, and two animals on either side of a human figure, a scene also connected by many with the Dumuzi cult. The mother-goddess and her symbols occur frequently, as also do ritual and cultic scenes.

Of particular interest is a metre high alabaster vase from Uruk with various cultic scenes, including one of a woman who is standing in front of two mother-goddess symbols and is receiving a man behind whom sacrificial offerings are being carried. This could perhaps be the king coming to the temple of Inanna to celebrate the sacred marriage. A large cattle-trough has a different scene: a hut with the symbols of the mother-goddess, which is certainly connected with rites to promote the fertility of herds of cattle.

What has been said applies primarily to the southern part of the country, where an urban culture was developed very early. Further north this development took longer, and the religion seems in part at least to have taken other forms. For instance, the temples are not found grouped in pairs; apparently several gods were worshipped, arranged in a pantheon. This was later the case in the whole country.

THE GODS

In classical Sumerian literature the gods (Sumerian *dingir*, of uncertain derivation) appear, as S. N. Kramer says, as 'a group of living beings, manlike in form, but superhuman and immortal . . . invisible to the mortal eye', who guide and control the world so that it does not fall into chaos. Jacobsen believes he can show that it was not always so, but that at first the gods were the active principle or force in certain occurrences and situations: there is a goddess of reeds, of beer, etc., and they are all more or less identical with the phenomenon which they represent. The same is true of the 'great' gods: Utu is the sun and the power of the sun, Nanna is the moon and the power of the moon, An is heaven and the god of heaven. It is only later, Jacobsen thinks, that the gods were separated off from these phenomena and assumed human form.[3]

It is not easy to form a judgement on Jacobsen's theory. It seems to depend on certain specific theories about the history of religion, but also to rest on some concrete evidence, which, however, is very difficult to interpret. It can, however, at least be said that in the religion of the classical period extremely few gods are limited to one single phenomenon; most have a many-sided field of activity (although this in its turn may be due to syncretism).

What is clearly attested, however, is the view that every phenomenon is controlled by an indwelling divine force (*me*) which determines its essential character and nature. There is a myth which tells how the goddess Inanna succeeded in wheedling out of the god Enki in Eridu all these *me*s and transferring them to her own city of Uruk. In this connection a list is given of a hundred or so cultural themes, of whose *me*s the goddess took possession. They include godship, the throne of kingship, the sceptre, kingship, various priestly offices, the flood, sexual intercourse, art, music, heroship, power, the destruction of cities, lamentation, the craft of the smith, the craft of the builder, wisdom, fear, peace, weariness, etc. It could almost be called a system of ideas, like those of Plato. The point, however, is that in this case Inanna, or in other cases other gods, are praised as the lords over these *me*s. In other words these are the indwelling laws of each phenomenon, as they are determined by the gods.

We know the names of hundreds of Sumerian deities through lists composed in schools, through lists of sacrifices, and through personal names in which the name of a god occurs ('theophoric names'). Many of these deities are clearly the theoretical creations of learned theologians, who wished to provide the gods with children, servants, and so on. Others are probably epithets of known gods, which we cannot now identify. The Sumerians thought that the gods were organized on the pattern of a council with a king at its head. The most important were the gods who 'fix the destinies', and a group of fifty who are called 'the great gods'. A distinction is also made between the creative and the non-creative gods; the first group includes especially the gods of heaven, earth, sea, and air.

Generally four deities stand first in the list of gods: An the god of heaven, Enlil the god of the atmosphere, Enki the god of water, and Ninḫursag the mother-goddess.

An, the god of heaven, is known from the oldest Sumerian period, and is regarded in theory as the highest god, but he does not play a correspondingly important role in myths, hymns, and the cult. His name is written with the same sign (a star) as indicates 'heaven' and 'god' in general. It looks as if An, like so many other sky-gods, was something of a *deus otiosus*. His principal seat of worship was Uruk.

Enlil is the god of the atmosphere, and especially of the wind. He is the active god, and in many respects the principal god in the Sumerian pantheon. He is 'the father of the gods', 'the king of heaven and earth', 'the king of all the lands'. He often has the epithet 'the great mountain', which is meant either to emphasize his strength or to connect him with the cosmic mountain, from which heaven and earth at one time came. According to a myth[4] it was he who separated heaven and earth—as would be natural for a god of the atmosphere, made seeds grow and provided all that was needful, created the day and determined the fate of the world, and created the pickaxe, and gave it to mankind ('the black-headed', as the Sumerians called themselves) to be used for farming and building. In the 'dispute between Summer and Winter' we meet Enlil as the god who provided all trees and all grains, produced abundance and prosperity in the land, and appointed Winter to be 'the farmer of the gods' and to have charge of the life-producing waters and of all that grows. Enlil, therefore, is a benefactor of mankind. It is he too who gives kings their authority and makes them successful in war and peace.

On the other hand Enlil also has a terrifying side to him. He is the devastating god of storm and tempest, and it is often told how his 'word' acts violently on the earth, breaks trees and destroys everything that comes in its way.

These characteristics also appear in the numerous hymns to Enlil, for instance in the following excerpts:

Enlil, whose command goes far, whose word is holy,
whose utterance is unchangeable, determines destinies for ever,
whose uplifted gaze sets all lands in commotion . . .
Father Enlil, who sits mighty upon his holy throne, on the high
    throne,
the respected, whose sovereignty and princeliness are in the
    highest degree perfect.
The gods of the earth bow themselves before him,
the gods of the heavens all hasten to him . . .
injustice and a hostile word, enmity and unseemliness . . .
evil, oppression . . . , violence, slander,
arrogance, the breaking of one's word . . .
such abomination the city does not allow to come before him . . .
No evil or wicked man escapes his hand . . .
Without Enlil, the great mountain,
no city is built, no settlement is founded,
no cowshed is built, no pen is made,
no king is enthroned, no *en*-priest is born . . .
the fish of the water do not spawn in the reeds,
the birds of the heaven build no nest on the wide earth . . .
grass and herbs, the pride of the steppe, do not grow,
no tree in the gardens bears any fruit.[5]

The strong you cast down, to the gate of heaven you tread,
the bolt of heaven you seize,
heaven's lock you tear off,
heaven's bolt you remove.
The land that does not submit you lay in ruins,
the rebellious land that does not submit, you do not let rise
    again.
Lord, how long will you turn against the land, that you have
    made of one mind?
Who can calm your angry heart?
The utterance of your mouth does not alter,
Who could rebel against it?[6]

The royal throne he has firmly founded,
Ur he has made to arise in splendour,
the shepherd Urnammu he has clothed in terrible splendour,
the king of Sumer he has let raise his head proudly to heaven.
This has been granted him by his king Enlil.[7]

Enki should from his name be 'the lord of the earth', but he is in fact the lord of Abzu, the ocean of sweet water which is under the earth (it is this water that appears in the springs and that gives the earth fertility). But Enki is also the god of wisdom and of the art of sorcery. In different contexts he appears as the one who in the beginning orders the world by his wise plans, or gives instructions for the creation of man. In both cases it is of course his wisdom that is manifested.

A good picture of his character is given by the following introductory section of a hymn of intercession:

Lord, of high mind, who has sure knowledge,
whose will is unsearchable, who knows all,
Enki, of far-reaching understanding, highest lord of the Anunna gods,
the clever, who pronounces the verdict, who gives the right word, who sees the decision,
who finds out the judgement, who from sunrise to sunset gives counsel,
Enki, lord of every true word, you will I ever praise.[8]

In the introduction to the long myth of Enki and the World Order (see below) he appears as the one who has all the *me*s in his hand (in other words determines the standards for the manner of being of all things), who brought skill in handicrafts to the earth; he is 'the ear and understanding of all lands', who with Enlil determines the fates 'in the mountain of wisdom' and 'at the place of sunrise'. The most important cult-centre of Enki is Eridu, which according to the king-list is the oldest city of Sumeria.

Ninḫursag, also called Ninmaḫ, 'the exalted lady', or Nintu, the goddess of birth, is the mother-goddess, the mother of all living creatures. We have already come across the part she played in the creation of man. Kings often boasted that they had been 'constantly nourished with her milk'.

Next after these four 'creating' deities come three astral divinities: the moon-god Nanna, the sun-god Utu, and the goddess Inanna.

That Nanna (sometimes also Su'en) is the god of the moon is almost the only simple thing that can be said about his nature. Almost all conceivable divine properties are applied to him in the hymns. These have recently been edited by Å. Sjöberg, and a

French scholar has given them the titles successively of 'the fruitful life of Su'en' (he furthers the well-being of the cattle), 'the lord of the fates' (he has secured all the highest *me* powers), 'Nanna, the wealth of Ur' (he has chosen Ur for his city, makes both men and beasts numerous), 'Nanna, the splendour of heaven' (the brilliant celestial body) and 'Nanna, the universal lord'.[9] His properties and functions are also largely indicated by this list.

Utu, the god of the sun, was regarded as the son of the moon-god. In the morning he climbs up between the hills in the east, in the evening he descends into the sea. Pictures on seals from the old Akkadian period show the sun-god with rays coming from his back setting foot on a mountain, while two gods open the gate of heaven before him; in his hands he holds a tool like a saw. It is a picture of sunrise. We have evidence already for the oldest period that Utu is described as a judge, and he is praised in a hymn as the god of justice, who regulates and supervises the world order.[10]

Utu does not, however, seem to have had the same significance in Sumerian religion as the later Akkadian sun-god had. A special type of prayer or 'incantation by Utu'[11] seems to have appeared so late that it must depend on Semitic influence.

Inanna or Innin (the original form of the name is disputed;[12] the variant Ninanna, 'mistress of heaven', also occurs sometimes) is perhaps the most important goddess in the Sumerian pantheon, but without doubt also the one that it is hardest to understand. In the picture our texts give of her it looks as if several traditions are united. Sometimes she is the daughter of An, sometimes of Nanna; even Enlil appears sometimes as her father. As an astral deity Inanna represents the planet Venus, the morning and evening star.

In the evening she is the 'strange' star, [the Venus star],
that [fills] the holy heaven with clear light.
To her, the lady of the evening, the hero[ine,
who alone] comes from heaven,
men in all lands [direct] their gaze . . .
The numerous beasts of Shakan, all the living creatures of the
    steppe,
all four-footed beasts under the wide heaven,
fruit-planting and garden, flower-beds and verdant reeds,
the fish of the pond, the birds of heaven,
all wait upon my lady, when it is quiet (at night),

all living creatures, men in their numbers bow the knee before
   her . . .
My lady looks down kindly from heaven;
they all come forward to the holy Inanna.[13]

Inanna's astral form is often connected with her functions in
war. She appears in hymns as the strong and terrible one who
strikes down all opposition.

My father has given me the heaven, has given me the earth; I
   am the lady of heaven.
Does any, even a god, compete with me?
. . .
Lordship he has given me, the position of lady he has given me,
the battle he has given me, the t[umult of bat]tle he has given
   me,
the hurricane he has given me, the whirlwind he has given me.
Heaven he has placed as a crown upon my head,
the earth he has set as a sandal upon my foot,
the shining cloak of the gods he has put around me,
given me the shining sceptre in my hand.[14]

In a myth which possibly contains an echo of victorious campaigns in the north and north-east[15] we are told how the personified mountain Ebeḫ, which threatened the land of the Sumerians
and filled it with terror, is attacked by Inanna:

The spear will I swing against it (Ebeḫ),
the boomerang, the weapon aim against it,
the forests around it I will set on fire,
against the evil (men) there I will swing the battle-axe,
the rivers I will dry up like the clean Gibil . . .
As a city which An has cursed it (Ebeḫ) will not rise up again,
as a city which Enlil has beheld in anger it will not again rise up.

Inanna is best known, however, as the goddess of love and of
fertility. As such she usually appears in connection with the god
Dumuzi, a figure who only acquires sharper outlines in the latest
Sumerian period. It was for a long time thought that he was a
typical representative of the type of gods who are usually characterized as dying and rising gods of fertility and vegetation, and he was
simply put in the same category as the Egyptian Osiris, the

Phoenician and Greek Adonis, and the Canaanite Baal. This view depended, however, on very late and disparate material, and later discoveries have shown that it is necessary to draw a much more complex picture of Dumuzi and of his cult.

Dumu-zi means roughly 'faithful son',[16] but the god is known also by other epithets, such as Ama-ushumgal-anna, which perhaps means 'the mother is the dragon of heaven',[17] or Damu, 'the child'. In the oldest sources he appears primarily as the shepherd, who protects the herds, in later texts he is also connected with corn and vegetation. This could mean that there was a development and adaptation of Dumuzi as the lord of sustenance and of vitality, but it is also conceivable that a fusion of originally separate divine figures has taken place.

For the oldest period Moortgat[18] has attempted to make use of cylinder-seals and other pictorial representations, and by these means he claims to have found three motifs which are connected with Dumuzi. The first is of a man who in a particular stylized, symbolic manner offers food to cattle, and since Dumuzi is the herdsman *par excellence*, it should be he or his cultic representative, the king, who is portrayed. The second theme consists of a man who stands between two symmetrically placed wild beasts, who seem to be attacking him; according to Moortgat this is Dumuzi, who is warding off an attack of wild beasts upon the herds. This identification, however, is dubious, since it lacks support in the texts; the man between the wild beasts was also identified long ago as Gilgamesh.[19] The third motif shows a god, who climbs out of a mountain with a 'saw' in hand, and this is regarded by Moortgat as pointing to Dumuzi's resurrection from the dead. It has, however, generally been interpreted as the rising of the sun-god from behind the mountain of the east, and since no allusions to such a situation have yet been found in the texts about Dumuzi, most scholars take a sceptical view of this interpretation.[20]

The myths about Dumuzi deal either with his love-relationship with Inanna or with his death. In the dispute between the shepherd Dumuzi and the farmer Enkimdu[21] both of these appear as suitors of Inanna and assert their own superiority. The goddess is at first inclined to prefer the farmer, but finally on the advice of the sun-god chooses Dumuzi. Another unfortunately very fragmentary text[22] tells how Dumuzi comes to Inanna's house with gifts of fat, milk, and beer, and is admitted after the goddess has

asked her mother's advice, and also describes Inanna's preparations and their union. This text[23] obviously has a cultic background
in the *hieros gamos* rite, to which we will return later.

The account of the death of the god is known in two somewhat
different versions, of which one is clearly connected with a myth of
Inanna's descent into the underworld.[24] The content of this cycle
is as follows: Inanna decides to descend into the underworld to
make herself its mistress, and dresses herself therefore in all her
finery and makes herself ready. She gives her vizier Ninshubur
instructions what he is to do if she does not return, and makes her
way to the 'land of no return', where her sister Ereshkigal reigns.
She goes through the seven gates of the underworld, and at each
one has to take off a garment or ornament, until finally she appears
naked before Ereshkigal. She and the judges of the underworld
fix the gaze of death upon her so that she dies, and her corpse is
hung up on a stake. After three days have passed, Ninshubur
begins to be suspicious, and starts to take the measures which the
goddess ordered him to. Enki creates two beings which are sexless,
and can therefore get admission to the land of the dead, and obtain
access to Inanna's dead body and bring her back to life. But the
goddess cannot return without first finding a substitute. Escorted
by a number of *galla*-demons she is sent back to earth to seek for
one. When they come to Dumuzi, Inanna's husband, who is king
of Kullab, he is holding a feast. Inanna is enraged, and chooses
him to be handed over to the underworld. Dumuzi turns to the
sun-god Utu with prayers for help against the *galla*-demons, and
succeeds in escaping from them twice. But the third time he is
surprised in the sheepfold and killed.

Another version, called the Death of Dumuzi,[25] tells of the bad
dreams which portend Dumuzi's death, and gives a somewhat
different description of the attack of the *galla*-demons. The death
of Dumuzi is described in the following words:

> The first *galla* enters the sheepfold,
> he smites Dumuzi on the cheek with a piercing nail;
> the second one enters the sheepfold,
> he strikes Dumuzi on the cheek with the shepherd's crook,
> the third one enters the sheepfold,
> of the holy churn the stand is removed;
> the fourth one enters the sheepfold,

the cup hanging from a peg, from the peg falls,
the fifth one enters the sheepfold,
the holy churn lies shattered, no milk is poured,
the cup lies shattered, Dumuzi lives no more,
the sheepfold is given to the wind.

With the resources which are at present at our disposal it is difficult to give a complete and reliable picture of the character and significance of Dumuzi. A large part of the material is still unedited, more is available only in antiquated or unsatisfactory editions. Falkenstein, who presented his view of the literary material at a meeting of Assyriologists in 1952, asserts that Dumuzi was originally a king, who for one reason or another came to be regarded as a god.[26] Jacobsen, who has for a long time been engaged on the Tammuz problem, has up to now published only a popularized summary of his views[27] in which only a portion of the material is presented. He sees four elements in the Dumuzi figure of the historical period, which were originally independent deities:

1. Ama-ushumgal-anna is properly the power in the yield of dates, it is with him that the *hieros gamos* rites are connected, and his cult is predominantly concerned with success in love and with a feeling of security.

2. Dumuzi, the herdsman, manifests himself primarily in milk, and it is with him that the ideas of death, sorrow, and mourning are connected. His mother's lamentation in the desert for his death is a basic motif.

3. Another Dumuzi is manifested in the grain. The harvesting and grinding are the death of the god, and feelings of guilt can be seen clearly in the texts.

4. Finally Damu, the 'child', is the rising waters of the spring-time, and especially the sap in trees and bushes.[28] There are a number of texts which speak of how lamentation is made for the dead god, how his mother looks for him among the trees and reeds and in the wilderness, and finally of how he is found, and returns in triumph 'from the river'.[29] Originally, according to Jacobsen, this last cult belonged in the southernmost part of the land with its horticulture, and later spread to the north and combined with the generally similar cult of the shepherd Dumuzi.

This identification is found, for instance, in the text 'in the early grass', which speaks of lamentation for the death of the god, of his mother's search for him among the reeds and in the desert. She tells how he was snatched away by *galla*-demons, and finally looks for him in the land of the dead. Here too there seems to be a suggestion of his return.[30]

It is not easy to form a judgement on this interpretation so long as the material on which it is based is not available in full. It is clear that the consistent 'nature mythology' view which Jacobsen presents cannot be the whole truth. Nor is it certain that we should prefer to speak of four originally independent deities rather than of four aspects or manifestations of one and the same god. In any case Jacobsen himself points out that the death motif is not connected only with Dumuzi. In the myth of Enlil and Ninlil ('the birth of the moon-god') Enlil is banished to the underworld as punishment for his sexual transgression, and another myth speaks of the disappearance of the god Ishkur to the underworld and of his rescue from there.[31] It can hardly be doubted that we have here different mythical expressions of the dying away of life in the hot and dry summer, and it is highly probable that these myths had their place in the rites connected with this. Different geographical distribution of food patterns then determines the more precise details of the motif: cattle-breeding, corn-growing, and fruit cultivation each have their own Dumuzi figure.

It has recently been denied that the texts contain anything about the 'resurrection' of Dumuzi. In the light of what has been said about Damu this must be described as an exaggeration. There is in fact a text which says: 'You (Dumuzi) half a year, your sister half a year', which in context means that Dumuzi was allowed to live on earth for half the year, while his sister Geshtinanna was in the underworld.[32]

In the litanies of lamentation Dumuzi is often identified with other deities,[33] among them Ningishzida, 'the lord of the good tree'. This is a chthonic deity, who appears, for example, also in the Babylonian Adapa myth together with Tammuz (Dumuzi). A long series of dead kings are also identified in the liturgies with Dumuzi, and this can be understood as a consequence of the conception of the king as the quintessence of the powers of fertility. In the celebration of the *hieros gamos* too each king no doubt played the part of Dumuzi. It would seem that here we have the connection between the king Dumuzi and the god of the same name, a combination which, as we have seen, has puzzled Falkenstein in particular.

The typical mark of the Dumuzi liturgies is their sentimental content: the expression of sympathy and compassion, of grief and distress.[34] The sense of despair and loss in his mother and his wife make a pathetic impression. Dumuzi's pitiable state is described in detail: he is bound and fettered, he lies beaten and bloody. In connection with this it is emphasized that life in the land similarly comes to a stop when he is away: the field does not yield grain and flax, the garden does not yield wine and honey, lettuce and cress, the woods yield no game, the river is not filled with fish, and in the palace the king's life is in danger.[35]

Some short quotations may give a picture of the character of the laments:

Woe for her husband! Woe for her son!
Woe for her house! Woe for her town!
For her captive husband, her captive son,
For her dead husband, her dead son,
For her husband lost for Uruk in captivity,
Lost for Uruk and Kullab in death;
Who no more bathes himself in Eridu,
Who no more rubs himself with soap in Enun,
As whose (loving) mother no guardian deity serves;
Who no more sweetens the work for the maidens of his town,
Who no more tussles with the lads of his town,
Who wields his sword no more among the guardsmen of his
    town,
The peer, who is shown honour no more![36]

. . . my husband dwells (here) no longer,
the shepherd, the lord Dumuzi dwells (here) no longer . . .
the lord of the stall dwells (here) no longer . . .
he that creates growth in the land dwells (here) no longer,
the lord of might dwells (here) no longer.
When he lies there, sheep and lambs also are still,
when he lies there, goat and kid also are still,
Yea, to the dwelling-place of the deep I will give heed,
to the dwelling-place of the mighty one I will give heed . . .

The mighty one, in the mountain is he shut in,
the mighty one, in the mountain is he vanquished.
For the sake of the mighty one, the lord,
I eat no meat for the lord's sake,
I drink no water for the lord's sake . . .[37]

A reed-pipe, (the instrument) of dirges!—My heart plays a
    reed-pipe, (the instrument) of dirges, for him in the desert,
I, the mistress of Eanna, who lay waste the mountains,
(And) I, Ninsur, mother of the lord.
(And) I, Geshtinanna, daughter-in-law of Heaven,
My heart plays a reed-pipe, (the instrument) of dirges, for him
    in the desert,
Plays where the lad dwelt,
Plays where Dumuzi dwelt,
In the underworld, on the Shepherd's Hill;
My heart plays a reed-pipe, (the instrument) of dirges, for him
    in the desert,
Where the lad dwelt, he who is captive,
Where Dumuzi dwelt, he who is bound,
Where the ewe surrendered the lamb.[38]

Ninurta ('the lord of the earth') was regarded as the son of
Enlil, and was worshipped together with him in Nippur. In
hymns he is praised because he gives fertility to the herds, fruitfulness to the fields, and abundance of fishes to the water. He is
called 'his father Enlil's farmer', and in a wisdom text[39] he gives
his son instructions on how the land is to be cultivated. But he also
shows typically warlike features. He wars against the 'rebellious'
hostile land which threatens Babylonia, especially the mountain
peoples. A large poetic cycle, which Kramer called 'the Deeds and
Exploits of Ninurta',[40] tells among other things of his fight against
the demon Asag high in the hill country. After the demon has been
killed, however, famine comes upon the land, and Ninurta piles
stones together to keep harmful water away, and to let sweet water
generate life. The description is broken off here and there by hymnic
elements, and ends with a curse on the stones which hindered
Ninurta and a blessing on those which helped him. There are
different views on the interpretation of the myth: Kramer sees it
as a fight against the powers of the underworld, others think of
historical enemies in the hill country,[41] while Jacobsen interprets

it as a nature myth which refers to the spring thunderstorms, Asag being the cold of winter and Ninurta the forces of spring. Since there is no complete modern edition, it is hard to reach a decision on the meaning.

In Lagash Ninurta appears to have been worshipped under the name Ningirsu (the lord of Girsu, a part of the city). He too has two aspects, as a fertility and vegetation god with such epithets as 'lord of the cultivated land', 'Enlil's chief tenant', and 'he who keeps field and canal in order', and as a warlike god who fills foreign peoples with terror.[42] In Gudea's temple-building hymn he appears also as a god who practises righteousness. He shows himself in dreams to Gudea 'with wings like the *imdugud*-bird, with the lower part of his body like a hurricane'. The lion-headed eagle Imdugud is his symbolic animal and emblem. The hymn of Gudea refers to his having subdued a series of mythological beasts, among them 'the six-headed wild sheep', 'the seven-headed lion', 'the good dragon', and 'the lion, the terror of the gods'. There is also a mention of his sacred marriage with the goddess of the city, Baba (or Bau).

The Sumerian pantheon also has a large number of other deities. Ishkur is the god of storm and thunder, who is worshipped primarily in his destructive aspect as the lord of hail and flood. Nerigal is the god of the underworld, but is also connected with the burning heat of the sun, with reed fires, and with fevers. His consort is Ereshkigal. Gibil is the god of fire in a double aspect, as bringer of light, and as the originator of conflagrations and of reed fires. His father is Nusku, who is also a god of fire and light. Ninazu is a god of the underworld who is also worshipped as a god of healing. Other deities with similar functions are the goddesses Gula and Nininsina. Nisaba is the goddess of corn and of the art of writing. Nanshe (Nazi) is a goddess who is mentioned in a hymn as guardian of righteousness.

Of special interest are the personal tutelary deities which certainly the king, and possibly all men, are thought of as having. This may be one of the inferior deities or a quite separate god. He is spoken of as 'my god', and it is expected that when necessary he will take the part of his protégé before the great gods, and make intercession for him. Pictures show him leading his protégé by the hand to one of the great gods. A poem which is sometimes called 'the Sumerian Job' speaks of how a suffering man after persistent

prayer to 'his god' is finally helped and restored. Jacobsen takes
the view that this personal tutelary deity was originally a personi-
fication of a man's 'luck', his capacity for thinking and acting,
which was only gradually identified with one of the minor deities
in the pantheon.[43] While this cannot perhaps be proved, it is
certain that it is the special tutelary deity of an individual and
family that we are dealing with. 'To acquire a god' is a phrase
which is used to describe a striking success. It is said also that
without a (personal) god man cannot earn his living or be courageous in battle,[44] and again:

> When thou dost plan ahead, thy god is thine,
> when thou dost not plan ahead, thy god is not thine.[45]

MYTHOLOGY

Sumerian literature is rich in mythological material. Unfortunately
until now only a small part of this has been published fully. For the
rest of it we must be content, meanwhile, with the various surveys
of contents which have been published by Professor Kramer,[46]
and which in certain cases have been criticized by other scholars.[47]
   Kramer believes that the Sumerian myths are not to be regarded
as ritual texts. 'Practically all the extant Sumerian myths are
literary and aetiological in character,' he says, but it does not
appear clearly on what he builds this judgement apart from an
insistence that the myths have often been erroneously classified
as the spoken part of a ritual. To say that the myths are aetiological, i.e. intended to explain the cause or origin of some
important phenomenon, is not an argument against their ritual
function. On the contrary, it is a feature of cultic myths that they
tell of the primeval event which underlies the phenomenon which
the rite is intended to promote. An argument for a cultic use of at
least some myths is the fact that they are introduced by, and end
with, hymnic sections. In the case of 'the Deeds and Exploits of
Ninurta' a ritual function was already assumed by Geller in his
very fragmentary edition of 1917,[48] but the same is true, for instance, of 'Enki and the World Order'. It has been pointed out by
van Dijk that the so-called disputes, in which two mythological
figures compete in emphasizing their own superiority, belong to the
New Year Festival after the celebration of the *hieros gamos*. This

is not to deny that a number of Sumerian myths give the impression of being more literary than cultic; but in many cases this is probably the result of a reworking of originally cultic myths.

Oddly enough we have no creation myth proper from the Sumerian period. On the other hand, other mythological texts contain allusions which make it possible to reconstruct in some measure the picture given of the origin of the world. The story of 'Gilgamesh, Enkidu, and the Underworld', for instance, alludes to the time when heaven and earth were separated from one another, clearly by Enlil, the god of the wind and the atmosphere (similar ideas are found, for instance, in Egyptian mythology). Another text clearly tells of how heaven and earth are united in a cosmic marriage, and how the earth in consequence brings forth herbs, wine, and honey. On the question how heaven and earth originated, however, no specific answer is given. A list of gods describes the goddess Nammu as 'the mother, who gave birth to heaven and earth'. Nammu appears to represent the sweet water ocean below the earth, or perhaps more concretely the swampland at the mouth of the Euphrates and of the Tigris, where new land is constantly created by the deposits of the two rivers.[49]

J. van Dijk, who has gone into this question in detail,[50] believes it is possible to establish the existence of two originally completely different representations of creation. According to the first, which has its home in the nomadic culture of the north, there was first an embryo-like universe (sometimes clearly treated as a mountain), from which the heaven An rose; heaven united with earth in a cosmic marriage, and then separated from earth, while gods and men grew up as the fruit of this marriage. The second basic type, which has its home at Eridu in the south, starts from the water of Abzu, or Nammu and Mother Earth, as representing the origin of life and of the world. In this system man was formed from earth. These two presentations were then conflated with one another.

When we look at the rest of the store of Sumerian myths, it is noticeable that two themes are strongly dominant, those of the ordering of the world, and of the struggle against evil powers. The myth of 'Enki and the World Order' is a good example of the first category.[51]

An introductory hymnic section praises Enki as the god who watches over the whole world and is responsible for the fertility of the land and the well-being of the cattle, insists how his word is

powerful to produce prosperity and abundance, and emphasizes
that it is he who governs all *me*s (divine laws or powers). After
certain rites in the sanctuary of the gods have been described, we
hear how Enki orders all things well in Sumer, makes its *me*
powers exalted, and determines the destiny of Ur. After this he
orders other lands and gives each of them its natural resources and
its character, fills the Tigris with water, creates the swamplands
and provides them with fish and reeds, arranges for rain, looks after
the fields and creates agricultural tools, and gives the plateau its
vegetation and livestock. He entrusts each phenomenon to a god
who is responsible for it. He fixes frontiers on earth and sets the
sun-god Utu 'over the whole universe'. (The final part of the
myth is somewhat obscure: it describes Inanna's discontent
with her part, and assigns her certain further tasks.) It is hard
to see reasons why this myth cannot have a background in the
cult.

The creation of man is dealt with by the myth of Enki and
Ninmaḥ.[52] This begins with the gods lamenting how difficult it is
for them to get food. They expect help from Enki, but he is lying
down asleep. His mother Nammu wakes him up, however, and
bids him stand up and create a servant for the gods. Enki decides
to grant her request and answers:

> O my mother, the creature whose name you uttered, it exists,
> bind upon it the image (?) of the gods;
> mix the heart of the clay that is over the abyss,
> the good and princely fashioners will thicken the clay.
> You, do you bring the limbs into existence;
> Ninmaḥ will work above you,
> the goddesses of birth will stand by you at your fashioning;
> O my mother, decree its (the newborn's) fate,
> Ninmaḥ will bind upon it the image (?) of the gods,
> it is man.

The poem goes on to describe how Ninmaḥ creates certain de-
formed and inferior types of man, who also have 'their destiny
decreed', this is, receive a function and their livelihood. It seems as
if this last is the point of the myth, but at the same time it does in
any case give a version of the conception held of man's creation
and destiny.

Another version exists in the introductory section of the didactic poem about the pickaxe. There it is said that after Enlil had separated heaven and earth, he created the pickaxe, and with it made a hole in the ground, so that men grew out of it. In a hymn on Enki's temple in Eridu we encounter a similar idea:

When everything created had its destiny determined,
when men in a year of abundance, created by An,
like grass broke through from the ground,
then the lord of Abzu, Enki, built . . .[53]

In other myths the motif is varied by the introduction of different cultural features. In the myth of Inanna and Enki[54] the goddess induces the god to become intoxicated and while he is drunk despoils him of all the *me*s to take them to her city Uruk. When Enki returns to his senses, he tries to prevent the goddess from getting home with her booty, but in vain. The point here is clearly the organization of culture in Uruk. This text is of special interest because it lists in passing all the *me*s that are stolen (cf. p. 5 above).

The myth of the pickaxe tells how at the beginning of time this tool, which is important both in agriculture and in the making of bricks, came into existence through a divine act. The dispute between cattle and grain looks back to a time when two important livelihoods arose through divine initiative. There was a time, it is said, when no lamb or goat gave birth to their young, when no grain grew, and the gods were not familiar with the use of clothes, and ate grass and drank water like wild beasts. Then Laḫar and Ashnan, the deities of cattle and of grain, were formed, and cattle-breeding and agriculture were founded. The introduction to another dispute, that between summer and winter, tells how the deities of these two seasons each originated a number of useful and necessary objects in the world of nature.

Behind all these myths lies the conviction that every phenomenon of nature and every cultural feature has its own intrinsic law (*me*), its given function in the running of the whole, and that this is the result of divine appointment.

We can perhaps include in this group of myths the so-called myth of Dilmun, which has often been described as the paradise myth of the Sumerians. On Kramer's interpretation[55] it begins with a description of the happy state of affairs in the land of Dilmun, where no beast of prey prowls and no illness is found. But there is no water, and since life cannot exist without it, the sun-god at Enki's request causes springs to break forth out of the earth. Dilmun thus becomes a fruitful garden with luxuriant vegetation and rich fruit. The goddess Ninhursag makes eight plants spring up in this paradise—here there is an involved process of birth involving several generations—but in spite of a prohibition Enki eats all eight of them. The goddess is angry and pronounces a curse on Enki, and disappears. But the curse is effective: eight or Enki's organs are attacked by illness, and the gods lament. Finally, they persuade the fox to bring the goddess back, and to cure the suffering god she now gives birth to eight healing deities.

There are obviously certain similarities between this myth and the biblical picture of paradise. We find the water that rises from the ground to water the earth again in Gen. 2.6, and the eating of the forbidden plants is distantly reminiscent of the tree of know-ledge in the garden of Eden. This is a question of the general background to the myth. But the text we are discussing clearly has a completely different function from the biblical story. It leads up to the creation of the eight healing deities, and it would not be surprising if it were intended to serve a magical, medicinal purpose. It is by no means unusual for incantations against illness to be connected with a mythical event, which forms a pattern for the healing which it is wished to bring about. It should also be mentioned that two French scholars[56] have argued strongly that the Dilmun myth is composed of a number of passages of different origin, and that in any case the introductory passage (where the translation of several words is uncertain) describes a primeval condition in general, before anything existed, or rather before any sort of activity took place. This is the way in which myths of origins often begin. (On the other hand, in a quite different context we come across the idea of a golden age at the beginning. In an epic text about king Enmerkar and the lord of Aratta there is a passage which speaks of a time when there was no snake or scorpion, no hyena, lion, or wolf, when man was without fear, and with one voice praised Enlil.[57] It seems, however, that Enki either in anger or in fear made an end of this happy state of affairs.)

To go on to the theme of struggle, we have already encountered this in the myth of the Deeds and Exploits of Ninurta. It should, however, be noticed that this myth also contains elements of creation, or perhaps more precisely of the ordering of the world: the god utters sentences over various sorts of stone which give them their character and nature.[58]

A myth in hymn form tells of Inanna's struggle against the mountain-god Ebeḫ and his victory over him.[59] It has been conjectured that the text reflects historical events, namely Utu-ḫegal's expulsion of the Gutians, an event which is also referred to specifically in a (perhaps late) poem about victory over 'the dragon of the mountain and highland, the enemy of the gods'.

Another myth of struggle tells of the hero Gilgamesh's struggle with the monster Ḫuwawa in the cedar wood. Kramer calls him the first St George. It is, however, doubtful whether this should be treated as a myth; it is rather a hero-saga.

The myth of Inanna and the gardener Shukalletuda is interesting.[60] It tells how Shukalletuda once found the goddess in a state of extreme weariness, and took advantage of this to have intercourse with her. The goddess sent three disasters upon Sumer for punishment: first she turned the water of the wells to blood (cf. Exod. 7.14–24), then she sent a destructive storm over the land, and finally a disaster the nature of which remains obscure because of the fragmentary state of the text. In spite of this the sinner succeeds in escaping. The text unfortunately breaks off just when the goddess is asking Enki for advice about what she should do now.

The so-called flood story also deals with a disaster sent by the gods.[61] Unfortunately it is only preserved in fragments, so that the context is not completely clear. But we do hear of a decision of the gods to destroy mankind through a flood, and of a pious and god-fearing man, Ziusudra, who is warned by the voice of a deity. It is clear that Ziusudra then built a boat to save himself, but in the text as preserved we read only of a flood which lasts for seven days and seven nights, and of the hero's sacrifice to the sun-god after it is ended. The last lines tell of how Ziusudra acquires 'life like (that of) a god', and comes to dwell in the land where the sun rises.

Lastly, there must be mentioned a myth which tells how Martu, the tutelary deity of the Semitic bedouin, wishes to find himself a wife.[62] By performing a heroic deed he evokes the admiration of the Sumerian deity Numushda, so that he promises him a rich reward. He says, however, that he wants no other reward than the god's daughter. This he obtains, although the daughter's friends try to dissuade her from marrying such a barbarian. Clearly historical and political circumstances are reflected in this myth, and it is open to question whether it should be regarded as a real cultic myth at all.

THE CULT

In Sumerian thought man was created to serve the gods. It was therefore of the greatest importance that this service of the gods should be carried out according to all the rules of the craft. We know unfortunately very little about the way in which the individual carried out this duty. Our documents witness only to the cult as performed by the community through its leaders and specialists.

The centre of the community's cultic action was the temple.[63] We know a large number of Sumerian temples through excavations, ranging from small primitive buildings to massive and splendid structures. Common to all of them is an inner room with a niche for the emblem or statue of the god, and a sacrificial altar. At an early date temples began to be built on a terrace or platform. In most of the larger cities there were also temple towers in the form of staircases, which were called *ziggurrat*. Their function has not been explained; probably there was a small sanctuary right at the top, and it is possible that the tower is intended to symbolize the cosmic mountain, or else to form a connecting link between heaven and earth.

The temple was not primarily a place for religious services in our sense, but rather the dwelling-place of the god, where he was thought of as being present in a special way among men. It was a place where men could fulfil the service to the god which was their first duty. A line in a hymn to the temple Ekur witnesses to a cosmic symbolism when it says that 'in its midst is the mountain of the aromatic cedar'. The mountain of the aromatic cedar is the mountain where the sun rises, and the whole temple area is regarded as a replica of the cosmic mountain.[64]

We get a picture of how a temple was erected in the account King Gudea of Lagash gives of his temple-building. The god Ningirsu showed himself in a dream to the king as a huge man with a divine crown on his head, wings like a bird's, and the lower part of his body 'like a floodwave'. He commanded Gudea to build a temple to him. Then a man appeared in the dream who drew on a tablet a plan of the future temple. After he had had the dream interpreted Gudea set to work. First, the city and its inhabitants had to be purified; no complaints, accusations, or punishments were allowed. The favour of the gods must be won by lavish sacrifices. Finally, Ningirsu's temple was ready. New rites of purification followed, and sacrifices were made. Temple officials were installed. Then Ningirsu and his consort Baba were united in a holy marriage, and a feast of seven days was celebrated, concluded by a banquet for the great gods.

The priests in the temples all had different functions. We have a whole series of different priestly titles, but we know very little of their functions. The highest spiritual position was held by the *en* priest, while the *sanga* was the administrative head. The priest called *ishib* seems to have had charge of drink-offerings and purifications, the *gala*-priests to have been singers and poets. Other classes of priests were called *guda*, *mah*, and *nindingir*, but their duties cannot at present be established. In the temples of Inanna there were eunuchs and hierodules (temple prostitutes), who took part in the cult of the goddess of love. Ancient pictorial representations show that the priests often performed their duties naked. Such ritual nakedness is known also elsewhere, but it is not clear how it is to be interpreted.

We do not know the daily routine of the temple in detail. We can assume that there were daily sacrifices of animals and vegetables, drink-offerings of wine and beer, and the burning of incense. The temple accounts also give us a picture of the deliveries and consumption of goods.

We know the names of a number of greater festivals, which vary with the different cultic centres, at which the greater ceremonies took place. Unfortunately we are as a rule very badly informed about the details of the ritual. About the greatest of the festivals, the New Year Festival, however, we know a great deal.[65] It is clear that a *hieros gamos* rite, a holy marriage between the king and the goddess of the city, represented by a priestess, was the centre of the festival. The texts show that there were significant local variations, but in large measure the course of the festival is clear.

The festival began with a procession up to the temple by boat

or cart. This was accompanied by general rejoicings in the city.
Then followed sacrifices of bulls, sheep, and goats, which were
clearly regarded as a sort of gift in kind for the wedding day. So a
text from the time of King Shulgi says:

> The true shepherd Shulgi, the beloved, dressed himself in *ma*-
> clothes,
> the charms of the crown and of the clothing were radiant on his
> head.
> Inanna was in raptures at it;
> a poem welled up from her emotion,
> she struck up a song.[66]

Clad in sacred attire, then, the king drew near to the sanctuary of
the goddess. It is perhaps just such a scene that is portrayed on the
very ancient Uruk vase. The goddess had already long since
prepared herself for the sacred marriage in the temple; she had
been bathed, anointed with sweet-smelling oils, and dressed in
special clothes and glittering crown. All this is described in another
text as follows:

> In the palace . . .
> the 'black-headed men', all of them together,
> have erected a throne for the 'mistress of the palace';
> the king, the god, abides there with her.
> So that she can decide the destiny of the lands . . .
> there was prepared on the New Year's Day, the day of the
> cultic celebrations
> for my mistress a couch,
> it was purified with (grass and plants) . . . cedar,
> it was made a couch for my mistress,
> a robe was made ready for her,
> so that she might delight in the robe, enjoy the couch.
> My mistress was bathed for the holy lap,
> bathed for the king's lap,
> bathed for Iddin-Dagan's lap . . .
> the floor was sprinkled with sweet-smelling cedar-resin.[67]

When the king draws near to the temple, the love song follows in
which the goddess (i.e. her priestess) welcomes her bridegroom
king. We quote again from the Shulgi text:

For the king, for the lord
when I have bathed,
when for the shepherd, the faithful son, I have bathed,
when my . . . is adorned,
and when my face glistens with amber,
when antimony has been put on my eyes,
when in his hand of sweetness
my waist is bent down,
when the lord who lies with the holy Inanna,
the shepherd Dumuzi has said:
'I shall open my lap' . . .
when he has caressed me upon the bed,
then I shall have caresses for the lord,
a good destiny I shall determine for him . . .
I shall caress his waist,
I shall determine as his fate
to be the shepherd of the lands. [68]

Another such song runs:

How luxuriant he is, he is the greenery of the garden, refreshed
by the dew of heaven!
You are mine, O orchard which gives shade to the pickers, the
joy of your mother,
my corn, full of charms in your furrows, the greenery of the
garden, refreshed by the dew of heaven,
my choice pomegranate tree, framed in foliage, the greenery of
the garden, refreshed by the dew of heaven!
honey man, honey man, he spreads his sweetness over me,
my *en*-priest, the honey man, he is a god, the joy of his mother;
his hands are honey, his feet are honey; he spreads his sweetness over me; . . .
you that are mine, the navel, since you are completely sweet,
the joy of your mother,
when you give pleasure to my private parts, and the arm is
brought down over . . . the greenery of the garden, refreshed
by the dew of heaven. [69]

We have several other examples of such songs, which show a
striking similarity to the poetry of the Song of Songs of the Bible.[70]
Sometimes the priestess's song of welcome grows into a dialogue

between her and the king. The following is an example of such a love song:

> Bridegroom, dear to my heart,
> Goodly is your beauty, honeysweet,
> Lion, dear to my heart,
> Goodly is your beauty, honeysweet.
> You have captivated me, let me stand tremblingly before you,
> Bridegroom, I would be taken by you to the bedchamber,
> You have captivated me, let me stand tremblingly before you,
> Lion, I would be taken by you to the bedchamber.
> Bridegroom, let me caress you,
> My precious caress is more savoury than honey,
> In the bed-chamber, honey-filled,
> Let me enjoy your goodly beauty,
> Lion, let me caress you,
> My precious caress is more savoury than honey . . .
> Your spirit, I know where to cheer your spirit,
> Bridegroom, sleep in our house until dawn,
> Your heart, I know where to gladden your heart,
> Lion, sleep in our house until dawn.[71]

After this the marriage rite itself followed. Most of the texts are silent on this point but in one case we have a quite explicit description:

> The king goes with head upright to the sacred bosom,
> goes with head upright to Inanna's bosom,
> Ama-ushumgal-anna lies with her,
> caresses her holy body . . .
> Her beloved consort she embraces,
> the holy Inanna embraces,
> is radiant on the throne, the great high seat, bright as day.
> The king, shining like the sun, takes his place on the throne at
>   her side,
> in abundance, in joy and gladness he comes before her,
> prepares her a banquet.
> The 'black-headed ones' come before her . . .
> The king refreshes himself with food and drink . . .
> The palace is (like) a feast, the king is full of joy,
> The people spend the day in luxury.[72]

It appears from these passages that the king plays the part of Dumuzi, the god of fertility, and that the priestess represents the goddess Inanna. It may therefore be correct to connect with this rite a number of mythological texts which tell of the love of these two deities for one another. One such text tells of how the two meet, and how Inanna is inflamed with such love for Dumuzi that she sends word to her father to set her house in order, so that she can bring her beloved there, and he 'can lay his hand in my hand, and lay his heart to my heart'. In another text Dumuzi comes on a visit to the goddess, who is advised by her mother to open her house for him, after which it is said that he brings her to 'his god's house'. A third text tells how the two lovers have to deceive her mother in order to be together. It has not yet been established what ritual functions these texts may have had.

All the sources, however, agree that the marriage rite leads up to the goddess determining a good destiny for the king. It is also quite clear what this consists in: the texts speak of prosperous government, good vegetation, abundant prosperity, victory and success. It is true that expressions connected with fertility predominate, and we must allow for a connection being made by analogy between the contents of the rite, and what it was hoped would result. In other words the king, by uniting with the life-giving goddess of love, ensures life and fertility to his land. But it is clear that 'a good destiny' includes much more too, in fact all that was expected from good government.

After the marriage rite itself there followed a banquet, in which the king and the priestess presided as representatives of the god and goddess. This was accompanied by music and various amusements. To this context belong a group of texts called in Sumerian *adaman-du-ga*. This is a sort of battle of words or disputation, e.g. between summer and winter, between farmer and shepherd, between copper and iron, or between pickaxe and plough, and the purpose of it is for each party to maintain so much as it can its own value and importance, and seek to depreciate those of the opponents. These poems generally consist of two main sections: (*a*) a narrative framework, which gives a mythological setting, often right back in primeval times, and reports the divine judgement which decides the dispute, and (*b*) the dialogue itself. Probably these controversy dialogues were dramatically performed. They seem, however, not to form an important and central part of the *hieros*

Sumerian Religion

gamos rite itself. It is possible that they served more as light relief.[73]

It is noteworthy that all the texts which speak explicitly of the *hieros gamos* come from just one period, exactly the same period at which the kings consistently provided their names with the determinative sign for a 'god' or 'deity'. It has therefore been supposed that the celebration of the divine marriage is in some way closely connected with the divinity of the king. On the other hand, it is clear that the *hieros gamos* was celebrated at other periods too in the history of the Sumerians.

There is also, however, an interesting text which connects the New Year Festival and the determination of destiny with the offering of the first fruits. It describes how the king brings offerings of first fruits to the temple of Nanna, and how the god delights in it.

> Enlil delighted in the feast, and determined for him a good fate,
> the mother who had put him in the world, the great queen Ninlil,
>   greeted him.
> Su'en spoke to Enlil and Ninlil:
> He prayed them to determine the fate of Siniddinam for a distant
>   future:
> May the life of the humble herd be prolonged through your
>   just word . . .
> May a life for ever be determined as his just fate,
> may a share of eternal life be given to him . . .
> may he make great the name of this year . . .
> Years of enjoyment, days of life, months of peace, let us
>   determine for him,
> in his palace you shall prepare for him in abundance the delights
>   of body and heart.[74]

We know the names of various other festivals, and we have lists of the sacrifices which were offered upon them. But we have no detailed information about their exact content. Names of months such as 'the month of the eating of the gazelles', or 'the month of the eating of barley of Ningirsu', 'the month in which Baba entered into his temple', 'the month of the house of sheep-shearing' give us some allusions, but unfortunately nothing more.[75] There are also statements that the new moon was celebrated with a feast of three days, and that a special sacrifice was offered at the full moon.

The myth of Dumuzi's death and return to life has already been discussed. There is every reason to assume that the texts which deal with it are in fact a ritual for an annual feast, the main theme of which was lamentation over the death of the god, the goddess's search for the missing god, and joy over his final return. There are signs that similar themes were also connected with other gods (at least with Enlil and Ishkur), and that these rites were carried out in summer, when the water was scarce, and the life of nature went through a critical period.[76] Jacobsen points out that in any case many of the Sumerian kings were identified with Dumuzi after their death, and that the litanies often show a special interest in the place where the dead god 'lies', i.e. where his grave is. He draws the conclusion that we have here the idea of the ruler as a magical source of fertility, the powers of which still pour out after his death from his grave.[77]

There is another group of laments which have sometimes been compared with the Dumuzi songs, and therefore need to be dealt with here. These are laments over the fact that a god has abandoned his sanctuary, and that the temple and the city have been destroyed.

The most explicit of these texts is the lamentation over the destruction of Ur.[78] This speaks despairingly of the catastrophe which has overtaken the city: the moon-god has left his temple, the city has been devastated by enemies (Elamites), the population laments bitterly, Ningal, the consort of the moon-god, bewails the destruction of the temple through the curse of An and Enlil. How can you live, the poet says to her, when your city lies in ruins and no offering is made in your temple, no feasts celebrated at your alter? Your city laments before you. You have left your house. How long will you stand aside? May Anu and Enlil soon decide that you may return to your city.

Another text from the time of King Ibbisin describes the devastation which befell Sumer through the wrath of the gods: public order has been destroyed, the enemy rules, and animals and crops fail.[79]

A lament over Nippur ends on a more hopeful note with the restoration of the city by Ishmedagan.[80]

A further development of this category is represented by the text which is called The Curse on Agade (cf. p. 2).[81] Here we first have a description of the rich and prosperous life of Agade, while the city was under the protection of Inanna. But then, it says, came disaster: the holy Inanna left her gifts untouched, the city was seized by fear, and finally the goddess abandoned her city and her temple, 'went from there like a maid who forsakes her chamber', and finally attacked her city with weapons of war. The cause is ascribed to King Naramsin's sins against Enlil.

We can perhaps assume that these songs were accompanied by special ceremonies of lamentation occasioned by historical events. In that case the lament for Agade in particular is of great interest, for it shows how historical catastrophes were interpreted as the result of the wrath of a deity.[82] In all the examples quoted it is also characteristic that the prosperity of the city is intimately connected with the presence of the god in his temple; this is why the destruction of his temple is so great a disaster. But there is a tendency towards the stereotyping of the lament theme, and the question has been raised whether the devastation of the city and temple is in some cases of a symbolic and ritual nature. This is especially the case where the lament deals primarily with the disappearance of the god; his return should then mark the restoration of good fortune. This was the decisive point for Witzel when he arranged a large number of such songs under the heading of Tammuz liturgies.[83] In a number of cases we find descriptions of how Enlil's word (or storm or tempest) gives rise to devastation. On Witzel's theory this devastation will have been represented symbolically in the cult each year, and regularly followed by the restoration of normal circumstances in the temple. Since the translations on which he builds are uncertain, and in many cases definitely wrong, it would be wise to await the results of future discussions of this question. The longer texts of which we have given an account are in fact treated by Kramer and Falkenstein as referring to historical events.[84]

Song and music were also part of the cult. A large number of hymns of varied form and content have been preserved, and are perhaps the best source we have for our knowledge of Sumerian religion. The style is generally somewhat long-winded for our taste, with many repetitions. This is no doubt connected with their liturgical use.

The Sumerians themselves distinguished between several different sorts of hymns and psalms, as far as we can tell by the different styles of performing them, or by the different musical instruments which were used to accompany the performance (cf. the psalm headings of the Old Testament). We are perhaps more interested ourselves in classifying the hymns by content. We find first of all a group which is by far the largest, which praises different gods and their properties. We have already given quotations from a number of such hymns. In a number of cases the hymn has attached to it a prayer for the reigning king. In these cases, therefore, praise of the attributes of the god forms a background for a prayer for certain gifts, and especially for strength for a good reign.

Another group of hymns is concerned with certain temples. They sing of the magnificence of the building, the beauty of the temple worship, and the greatness of the god. We know a number of such hymns, some of them of considerable length. Especially interesting is a collection of short hymns to all the most important temples in Sumer and Akkad. The text about Gudea's temple-building mentioned above also really belongs in this category. As an illustration some lines from a hymn to the temple of Enki in Eridu can be quoted:

With silver and lapis lazuli which shine like the day,
has the house in Abzu been adorned in all beauty,
its light, artistic form rises out of Abzu:
all (the gods) go to the lord Nudimmud.
Of silver he has built the house, adorned it with lapis lazuli,
splendidly covered it with gold,
in Eridu he has built the house on the shore (of the sea) . . .
Eridu, your shadow spreads over the middle of the sea,
the raging sea, which has no opponent,
the broad river, which inspires fear and stills the land . . .
At the side lies the reed-bed,
in its green garden which bears rich fruit
the birds sit on their eggs.
There the perch bring forth their young,
The carp in the low reeds move their long tails.
When Enki rises, all the fish rise with him in . . .
To everyone's amazement Enki comes to Abzu,
gives joy to the ocean.
Fear lies upon the sea before him,
he appears to the river in fearful splendour,
the Euphrates rises before him (as before) a strong south
    wind . . .
Because he has built a house of silver for Eridu,
Father Enki be praised![85]

There is an important group of hymns which have the king as
their subject. He can be praised in the third person, and often in
words which could equally well be applied to a god. Or the hymn
can have the king praise himself in very laudatory language (so-
called 'self-praise'). We will return to the royal hymns in connection with kingship ideology. Here we give only one example
to illustrate the I-style.

> I, the king, am a hero from my mother's womb,
> I, Shulgi, am from birth a mighty man.
> I am a lion with wild look, born of a dragon,
> am the king of the four regions of the world,
> am the watcher, the shepherd of the 'black-headed',
> am the hero, the god of all lands.
> The child that Ninsuna has born,
> the one whom the holy An has called in his heart,
> for whom Enlil has determined his fate,
> Shulgi, the beloved of Ninlil, am I . . .
> The wise writer of Nisaba am I,
> like my heroism, like my strength,
> is my knowledge complete,
> I rival his fixed word.
> The right I love,
> the evil I hate,
> hostile words I hate.
> I, Shulgi, am the mighty king, who precedes all.[86]

It is uncertain to what extent the royal hymns had a place in the
cult. Falkenstein believes he can show that they were not cultic in
the strict sense, and he regards this as obvious in the case of the
self-praise.[87] On the other hand, we have no information about
what other function they could have had.

Finally, something should be said about the incantations.
Admittedly they belong rather to magic than to religion, but it
should be remembered that the distinction between religion and
magic can be maintained strictly only on paper, and that the
Sumerian incantations in general call on the help of the gods. The
actions that accompany the incantations can perhaps therefore
not be called cultic, but they are still rites through which men wish
to make sure of the assistance of the gods, and the incantation

priests function with a commission from the gods. The frontier between religion and magic is therefore very fluid.

The incantation texts can be classed into several main types. One of these has the purpose of securing the safety of the man making the incantation while he carries out a difficult task; the concern is to provide him, as it were, with legitimation. One example in a somewhat abbreviated form runs like this:

Evil *udug*, mighty spirit of death of the land,
evil *udug*, that runs around in the land,
evil *udug*, that grinds the land as if to flour . . .
evil *udug*, that harasses the land,
evil *udug*, that takes captive the animals . . .
I am the incantation priest, the high-priest of Enki.
The lord has sent me.
Behind me shall you not roar,
behind me shall you not cry,
you shall not let me be seized by an evil man,
you shall not let me be seized by an evil *udug*.
By heaven be he conjured, by earth be he conjured![88]

A second type has the purpose of protecting not the man making the incantation but other people against demons. In most cases it is a question of illness, which is assumed to be caused by evil spirits. The incantation begins with a description of the harm done by the demon, and of the illness which it has caused. Then we hear how the god Asariluḫi turns to his father Enki, 'who knows the plant of life and the water of life', and asks for his advice. Enki gives instructions how one should act, and this leads on to a description of the ritual, which in turn is followed by the incantation itself with the intention that the demon should become powerless and fail. Here is an example, somewhat abbreviated:

The evil *udug*, which makes the solitary ways difficult to pass over,
which goes forth in secret, covers up the ways,
the evil spirit, which is loose on the steppe,
the robber, who cannot be forced back . . .
they have struck down the wayfaring man as in a storm,
immersed him in gall.
That man goes around 'on the other side of life'.

Asariluḫi saw it, went in to his father Enki in the house and
   addressed him:
'My father! The evil *udug* . . .' (the account is repeated).
'What I shall do in this case I know not.
What can calm him (the sick man)?'
Enki answered his son Asariluḫi:
'My son! What do you not know? . . .
Go, my son Asariluḫi:
Pour water in a jar,
put in it a branch of tamarisk and . . .
and sprinkle it on this man,
set out a censer and a torch.
Then may the demon of fate that is in the man's body go out . . .
May the evil *udug*, the evil *ala* go out,
may the evil spirit of death, the evil spirit go out . . .
may (every kind of illness) go out.
All great gods have conjured you. Go out'![89]

In this way the action and the formula together activate the
divine power which can subjugate the demon. It is interesting that
in general the rites are purification rites in form. The man who is
tormented by demons is regarded as unclean and as contaminated,
and must be purified, usually with water. Often an image of the
sick man is also used in the ritual. It was intended that the
demons should leave the sick man and enter the image; then the
image was destroyed, and the demon thus rendered harmless.

SACRAL KINGSHIP

There can be no doubt that the Sumerian institution of kingship
in historical times had a religious basis and religious functions.
On the other hand, opinion is divided how this institution came
into existence. Jacobsen thinks that both myths and epics reflect
a time when 'primitive democracy' prevailed.[90] The power of
decision in the city-state was exercised by the general assembly of
the people, while an *ensi* functioned as foreman and organizer. On
particularly critical occasions a special leader could be chosen,
who was called *en* ('lord') if it was a question of administrative or
religious and magical affairs, *lugal* ('great man' =king) if it was a
matter of warfare. These positions in the course of time became

permanent. It appears, however, that the position was much less simple than this.[91] There are examples of an *en* with purely secular authority or concerned with military affairs which we would expect to be handled by the *lugal*. It is, however, clear that both *en* and *lugal* have power over a larger area which includes several cities, while the authority of the *ensi* is limited to one city. *Ensi* is the normal title for the sacral leader of a Sumerian city-state.[92] It is in fact asserted in the royal hymns that the king unites in his office the positions of *en* and *lugal*.[93]

We shall confine our treatment in what follows to conditions attested in historical times.

The basic fact is that the king is thought of as having received his position from the god or gods of the state. The 'Sumerian king-list' reports that kingship 'came down from heaven'. A number of royal inscriptions maintain that it is Inanna or Ningirsu or Baba that has given the respective king his position.[94] We are often told that the king was chosen by the gods and received the royal insignia from them:

> The wise god, the lord, who determines the destinies,
> has spoken faithfully to him, An to Urninurta,
> in the land of Sumer he has made him the highest . . .
> a royal throne on an eternally fixed foundation,
> the highest shepherd's crook which gathers all the *me*s in the
>   land of Sumer,
> a righteous sceptre which keeps watch over the numerous men
>   has he given Urninurta.[95]

In a number of cases, when it is said that the god searched out the king 'from the multitude', it has been thought that these were usurpers who had no right of inheritance to the throne.[96] They were therefore specially anxious to insist on their divine election.

But the texts go further and describe the king as son of the god or goddess: 'son of Enki', 'son of Su'en', 'the one begotten of the great mountain (=Enlil)', 'him whom Ninlil bore', 'the child that Ninsuna has begotten'.[97] This idea is sometimes expressed in very concrete form. It is said of Eannatum that 'Inanna took him in her arms, uttered his name and let him sit in the lap of Ninḫursag, Ninḫursag let him suck her holy breast'.[98] The goddess Ninsuna says of Shulgi:

Shulgi, whom I bore to my brother,
the seed of Lugalbanda are you.
In my holy lap I have reared you,
in my holy fold I have determined your destiny.[99]

The king Gudea says in his prayer to the goddess Gatumdug:

I have no mother; you are my mother.
I have no father; you are my father.
My father's seed you received in your womb,
you bore me in the sanctuary.

How is this to be understood? Some have wanted to take the sonship as a relationship of adoption, which expresses the special
divine protection which the king enjoys. But the very common
epithet 'son in the flesh to [the god] *x*', and the texts just quoted,
are an argument against this. On the other hand, it is difficult to
believe that the Sumerians understood these expressions in a
completely literal sense. Perhaps a solution can be found in a
description of the coronation of King Shulgi, where it is said that
Enlil in the temple 'gave him, who is shepherd over all lands, the
sceptre of authority' and that the king, dressed in 'the royal vest-
ments which cannot be cut into pieces, proudly lifted up his head
to heaven', but also that a priestess as representative of the goddess
gave birth to the royal child.[100] The coronation was clearly treated
as a symbolic new birth. This interpretation receives support from
the observation that one and the same king can be son of An, Enlil,
and Nanna; this signifies that he was crowned in Nippur, Uruk,
and Ur, and then proclaimed as the son of the god of the city.[101]

From here to the idea that the king is divine it is not a large step.
In fact a large number of Sumerian kings wrote their names with
the determinative for god, i.e. they put before their names the
sign which is elsewhere used to distinguish a divine name. There
are also several examples of a king quite simply being called 'the
god of the land', 'the god of mankind', 'the sun-god of Sumer', and
similar titles.[102] But this does not mean that they were actually
worshipped as gods. It has been assumed, probably correctly, that
it was the king's functioning as the male partner in the sacred
marriage that gave him the right to call himself divine. In any case
the great power of the king meant that he appeared to his subjects
to be like the gods. Through his call and election by the gods,

through his constant contact with them as the highest custodian of the cult, and through the sacred marriage, he was so different from other men that he seemed to belong as well to the realm of the gods.[103]

From what has been said it is only to be expected that the king should have exceptional attributes. All the wisdom that exists on writing tablets has been given him by the goddess Nisaba, and he possesses unusual wisdom in counsel.[104] For this reason he can also ensure that justice and order rule in the land. Shulgi declares: 'the right I love, the evil I despise, hostile words I hate'.[105] Ishmedagan says.

> Utu has placed the right, the fixed word in my mouth;
> to pronounce justice, to make a decision, to lead the people
>   aright,
> to let justice go before everything,
> to give right leadership to the good, to destroy the wicked ...
> so that the powerful cannot do what they want ...
> to destroy wickedness and violence, but to let justice grow,
> this has Utu, son of Ningal, placed in my lot.[106]

It is primarily wisdom in judgement that is the subject here, but of course the power to maintain law and order also comes in. Several kings declare in inscriptions that they have put an end to social injustices or general lawlessness in the land and ordered everything in the best way. They regard themselves accordingly as representatives of good order against all destructive forces. This is often given a religious motivation. It is said of Urukagina that when he mounted the throne complete chaos reigned in the land. But 'when Ningirsu gave the kingship of Lagash to Urukagina, he enjoined upon him the (divine) decrees of former days'. He freed the land of drought, theft, and murder, released prisoners and 'made a convenant with Ningirsu that a man of power must not commit an injustice against an orphan or widow'.[107] It is striking that we already meet here a concern for the widows and orphans; this subsequently became a royal virtue in all the Ancient Near East. Another interesting detail is the idea of a covenant with the god, which is also typical for the religion of Israel (the similarity is, however, only superficial; in Israel it is Yahweh who offers the people an advantageous agreement, here it is the king who promises the god that he will carry out his will).

As one would expect from this, it is the king who proclaims the laws. The oldest 'law-book' we have is the law of Urnammu from *c.* 2050 B.C. It begins with a prologue which tells how the national god of Ur, the moon-god Nanna, has chosen Urnammu to reign in the land as his representative. In the power of Nanna the king has conquered a hostile prince and then set about social and juridical reforms, taken action against theft and against false weights and measures, protected the weak against the powerful, and so on. Then the laws themselves follow.[108] Another law-code is that of Lipitishtar about 200 years later. This too begins with a general prologue, after which the laws themselves follow. It concludes with a blessing on those who leave in peace the stone on which the laws have been engraved and a curse on any who damage it.[109]

The external aspect of the king's responsibility for order is emphasized when he is described as the one who defeats the enemies of the land and asserts his power also among foreign nations. It is said of Lipitishtar that he acquired wisdom to pronounce judgement in all foreign lands too, and can decide between truth and falsehood in the heart.[110] Iddindagan is a hero in battle, and subdues the rebellious land; 'This has Dagan fixed for you from birth as your destiny.'[111]

It is the king again who has the responsibility for the building and upkeep of the temple, and for the maintenance of the cult. We have already spoken of Gudea's activity as a temple-builder. Inscriptions and royal hymns give clear evidence of the king's care for different sanctuaries. There is a connection between this care and the prosperity of the king:

> For the temple of Ekur you are the man,
> may your food-offering not cease in the house of Enlil!
> May the brick walls of Ekur speak well of you to Enlil and Ninlil
> at the good word of An and Enlil may high strength be granted
>   you, Iddindagan![112]

But the effects of the correct worship of the gods by the king extend further than his own person; the prosperity of the people and of the land depend on it, fertility and fruitfulness are the consequences of it. In a long hymn Lipitishtar represents himself as 'the beloved son of Enlil', 'he who by his supplication gives gladness to Ninlil', 'he whose ear Enki has opened', 'the beloved consort of Inanna', and then it says:

> The one who carries the highest shepherd's crook, the life of the
> land of Sumer am I,
> the farmer who stores his heap of grain am I,
> the shepherd who increases fat and milk in the house of the fold
> am I,
> the one who lets fish and birds grow in the marsh am I,
> the one who constantly gives the watercourses running water in
> abundance am I,
> the one who increases abundant produce for the great mountain
> am I,
> the one to whom Enlil gave highest strength am I,
> Lipitishtar, the youth who shyly worships him am I,
> the one who constantly serves the gods am I,
> the one who incessantly mourns for Ekur am I,
> the king who holds a kid to his breast as an offering am I,
> the one who in humility moves his hand to his mouth (in prayer)
> am I,
> the king who comes forward in prayer am I,
> the one who speaks pleasing words to Enlil am I,
> the one who through his supplication delights Ninlil am I,
> the one who continually stands ready to serve Nusku am I . . .[113]

It is clear that the author sees a link in the king between sacrifice and prayers on the one hand and the prosperity of the land on the other. We should not in this context forget what has already been said about the king's role in the sacred marriage and the results that were expected from it.

The king is therefore a sort of mediator of the blessings of the gods to his people. He is 'like a father and a mother' to his people, he is a protecting wall, 'the protection of Sumer, its sweet shade', as a self-proclamation of Ishmedagan says.[114] A hymn is addressed to Iddindagan:

> Your praise is in the mouth of all,
> your kingdom is good for men,
> since your shepherding has been good for our hearts,
> men will increase in number under your rule,
> men will spread further under your rule,

all hostile lands will lie in peace as on a meadow.
Men will pass their days in abundance,
the look of the black-headed men will be directed to you,
Iddindagan, as it was to your father.[115]

Here the functions of the king are subsumed under the idea of shepherding or pastorate. 'Shepherd' is in fact a very common royal epithet. Several themes are united in it: the leadership of the king, his duty to protect his subjects, and his responsibility for their maintenance. But we must always remember that this is done at the bidding of the gods, and largely through the king's cultic and sacral activity. It is therefore not surprising if he is to a greater or less extent exalted to the divine sphere, and is sometimes quite explicitly called 'god'.

GOD AND MAN
RELIGION AND MORALITY

As we have already seen, the Sumerians took the view that man had been created by the gods with the express purpose of serving them and providing them with food, drink, and lodging. The sacrifices in the many temples were therefore man's first duty, and the responsibility for these being carried out in correct form rested on the king as the representative of his subjects before the gods. It was he too who had to ensure that the temple was kept in order. The purpose of the cult could in turn be described as twofold. Partly it was for that service of the gods, which was intended to make them in some way better equipped to carry out their duties to the benefit of mankind. Sacrifice and hymns were intended to increase the strength or divine potency of the gods. On the other hand, dramatized cultic actions like the *hieros gamos* were intended more directly to strengthen the powers of nature and to keep the processes of life going through the working of analogy.

Men's attitude to the gods seems to have fluctuated to a certain extent between two different types. On the one hand we have the close, almost sentimental, relationship to gods of the Dumuzi type, on the other the respectful attitude to most other gods, which sometimes almost goes as far as literal fear of their 'terrible' divine gaze.

Men were dependent on the gods. The 'destiny' (*nam-tar*) which the gods determined for man could not generally be altered by him. It was part of man's lot that he was mortal. Only the gods had eternal life.

The will of the gods was regarded in general as mysterious and unsearchable. But there were, nevertheless, certain ways of discovering what it was. There is evidence for oracle priests already in the early Sumerian period.[116] There are no systematic omen-texts known in Sumerian, but we do know of a case where a high-priest was chosen with the help of observations of the entrails of a sacrificial animal.[117] Gudea practises observation of entrails when he is going to build his temple. We heard of oracles given with the help of reeds and of prayer. They are called Enki's oracles, because it is he who rules over the water.

In Gudea's case a revelation given in a dream was also important. There were special priests who had the task of interpreting dreams. One of the myths about Dumuzi tells how he was filled with foreboding by a dream:

> My dream, O my sister, my dream,
> This is the heart of my dream!
> Rushes rise up all about me, rushes sprout all about me,
> One reed standing all alone bows its head for me,
> Of the reeds standing in pairs, one is removed for me,
> In the wooded grove, tall trees rise fearsomely all about me,
> Over my holy hearth, water is poured,
> Of my holy churn—its stand is removed,
> The holy cup hanging from a peg, from the peg has fallen . . .[118]

Then the dream is interpreted as referring to Dumuzi's impending death.

The course of the world was governed by the divinely ruled interplay of the *me*-powers, each of which determined the nature of an event or of an occupation. There are signs to suggest that there was an idea of a universal and cosmic order which was then to be realized in the activities of men. The laws of the state are meant to correspond to and express the divine ordering of the world.

We acquire some picture of the ethical ideals of the Sumerians in texts which treat of the king's responsibility for law and justice. Honesty in dealing, care for the rights of the weak, truth and justice are virtues that appear in this context. Several different gods appear as upholders of justice, but in time the sun-god Utu comes to be predominant in this role. In a royal hymn from Isin, for example, it is said that Utu put righteousness in the king's mouth so that he should promote good and destroy evil,

> so that brother should speak truth to brother, fall down before his father,
> not speak against his older sister, show respect to his mother,
> so that the weak should not be left at the mercy of the powerful,
> so that the powerful should not do according to their will,
> so that the one should not take the other in pledge.[119]

Another deity who watches over right is the goddess Nanshe, who is praised in a hymn as the one

> who knows the orphan, who knows the widow,
> knows the oppression of man over man, is the orphan's mother,
> Nanshe, who cares for the widow,
> who seeks out justice for the poorest.[120]

Another section of the same hymn describes how the goddess judges men on New Year's Day. She passes her judgement on men

> who walking in transgressions reach out with high hand . . .
> who transgress the established norms, violate contracts,
> who look with favour on the places of evil . . .
> who substitute a small weight for a large weight,
> who substitute a small measure for a large measure,
> who having eaten (something not belonging to him) does not say 'I have eaten it' . . .

The goddess is in fact called she who 'searches the heart of the people'.

We are given the impression that the primary concern is for social virtues, and that what matters to the Sumerian is to regulate the common life of men. There is no reference here to individual duties, and still less to personal sin. In general such a concept as that of sin is late and rare in Sumerian. When national disasters are sometimes spoken of as divine punishment, it seems to be a matter of cultic offences or omissions, primarily of course on the part of the king (cf. for example the Curse on Agade). An expression such as 'never has a sinless child been born to its mother'[121] stands quite on its own in Sumerian literature. It is significant that we

have a large number of hymns which praise the gods, and prayers
which ask for health, fertility, riches, or victory, but not a single
confession of sin or prayer for forgiveness. The Sumerian incantations contain not the slightest suggestion that illness or misfortune
are the consequence of sin—they are entirely the work of the
demons.

For this reason it is inappropriate to call the poem on Man and
his god 'the Sumerian Job'.[122] There is no question of a 'suffering
righteous man' in this poem. It intends to convey the thought that
one should hold fast to one's personal tutelary deity, and insis-
tently call upon him until he intervenes and helps. The man who is
here presented as an example has been assailed by illness and
suffering, and turns with tears and prayers to 'his god'. He
describes how he has been deserted and put to scorn by his fellow
men, how everything that he undertakes goes wrong.

> Tears, lament, anguish and depression are lodged within me,
> Suffering overwhelms me like one chosen for nothing but tears,
> Evil fate holds me in its hand, carries off my breath of life,
> Malignant sickness bathes my body . . .

So he prays:

> My god, you who are my father who begot me, lift up my face,
> Like an innocent cow, in pity . . . the groan,
> How long will you neglect me, leave me unprotected?
> Like an ox . . .
> How long will you leave me unguided?
> They say—valiant sages—a word righteous and straightforward:
> 'never has a sinless child been born to its mother,
> . . . a sinless youth has not existed from of old.'

It is difficult to decide whether we really have here an example of a
confession of sins. A few lines later there is found a hint that the
man has done something harmful to the god, that his 'sin has now
been revealed' and that he wishes to confess it, but the word 'confess' is according to the editor of the text a pure guess, and it is in
any case not said that the suffering is a punishment. Perhaps it is
rather an appeal to the god's sympathy when he sees man's weak-
ness and imperfection. In any case what follows is not forgiveness,
but an answer to prayer and restoration:

His lamentation and wailing soothed the heart of his god,
The righteous words, the pure words uttered by him, his god
  accepted,
and the sickness-demon left him, the evil fate was avoided
and the suffering changed to joy.

It is partly submissiveness to the decision of the gods, partly a
faithful adherence to the personal tutelary deity which is here
emphasized. If a man earnestly entreats 'his god', he is also heard.
This picture is not altered if we take note also of the rich proverbial
literature which has come to light in this last decade. It is striking
how little the religious element appears in these proverbs. In so
far as it is not a case simply of experience of life, a statement of
what the life of men is like, it is quite general advice, based on
empirical observation. There is hardly once here an instance of
advice being based on a general divine order, and if gods are
mentioned at all it is only in passing. The Sumerian wisdom
literature has no deep religious motivation.

DEATH AND AFTERLIFE

Our knowledge of the ideas of the Sumerians about death and the
dead is very imperfect, and it is primarily through conclusions
drawn indirectly from the content of myths and epic that we can
get an idea of how the existence of the dead was pictured. We know
that the land of the dead was called *kur-nu-gi-a*, i.e. 'the land without return', and the myths emphasize that it is only under extremely exceptional circumstances that anyone can escape from it.
But apart from this it seems that the views held about the land of
the dead were not completely clear nor homogeneous.

If we keep to the written evidence there are five texts which
specially need to be taken into consideration.[123]

The first text deals with the death of King Urnammu.[124] Here
we find first a description of the king lying on his bier in his
palace, mourned by his family and people. Then the scene changes,
and Urnammu is in the underworld, where he presents gifts to its
'seven gods' and sacrifices animals to the important dead; the gods
receive the gifts in their respective palaces. So Urnammu comes to
the place allotted to him, acquires certain of the dead as servants,
and Gilgamesh explains the rules of life in the underworld. The

next section describes how 'after seven days, yea ten days' Ur-nammu hears the weeping and lamentation of those left behind, and responds to this by himself uttering a bitter lament. The end of the text is unfortunately destroyed, so that it is not clear what the purpose of the whole is.

The next text is an elegy or funeral song which S. N. Kramer found on a tablet in the Pushkin Museum in Moscow.[125] From this it appears that it was thought that the sun went through the underworld at night, and gave light to its inhabitants, and that the moon passed its 'days of rest' (when it was completely invisible) there. It is also said that the sun-god Utu passed judgement on the dead, and also that the moon 'determined their destiny', but it is unfortunately not clear what was understood by these expressions. The song concludes with a prayer for the dead.

Our third text is the poem about Gilgamesh, Enkidu, and the underworld.[126] The land of the dead is here called euphemistically 'the great dwelling', and it is told that Gilgamesh dropped two mysterious tools (apparently), so that they fell down into the underworld; there was, therefore, some sort of opening which led down to it. When Gilgamesh's servant Enkidu went down to the underworld—unfortunately we do not hear how—to get them back, he was held fast by 'the cry of the underworld' and could not return. Finally, Gilgamesh called up Enkidu's spirit and questioned him on what things are like in the underworld. This part is badly damaged in the Sumerian version of the text (we will come back again later to the Akkadian version).

The fourth text is a myth about the birth of the moon-god, which tells how Enlil is banished to the underworld together with her consort Ninlil. There we find the idea that there was a 'man-devouring' river, which had to be crossed, and that there was a ferryman there to ferry the dead across.[127]

Finally, the myth of Inanna's descent into the underworld is of interest. This tells of a place called the 'lapis lazuli mountain' with well-locked and carefully guarded gates. It seems also that the laws of the underworld demand that its inhabitants should go naked.[128]

It is clear that it is not possible to derive any unitary conception of the underworld from this disparate material. There is a particular problem about the report of the sun-god's judgement in the underworld, because it is clearly assumed that the judgement can be favourable, and that the dead can therefore in certain circumstances—what they are we do not know—count upon a tolerable future. This is noteworthy in view of the fact that the later Akkadian religion does not seem to have had any such picture (cf. however p. 123).

Still more open to discussion are a number of questions which have been raised by archaeological discoveries. There are royal tombs in Ur from about 2500 B.C., in which a large number of people were buried at the same time.[129] It looks as if kings and queens were followed in death by servants of both sexes, together with all sorts of personal possessions. But the literary texts we possess have no knowledge of such a custom, apart from one possible exception. The poem on the death of Gilgamesh tells how Gilgamesh offers gifts and sacrifices to the deities of the underworld for all who 'lay together with him' in his 'purified palace' in Uruk: wife, son, concubine, musicians, valet, and household attendants. It is possible that this refers to sacrifice for those who were buried together with the dead king. But even if this is the case we do not know what meaning was attached to this custom. (The same poem has later on some very obscure remarks about life after death; these have not yet been interpreted with any certainty.[130])

Still more mysterious are the facts which form the basis of Moortgat's Tammuz theory. He has noticed that in one of the royal tombs in Ur the body has been removed, although there are no signs that the grave has been robbed; this tomb is decorated with numerous Dumuzi symbols. He draws the conclusion that some sort of ritual must be involved. The king has celebrated the sacred marriage, and then has been identified with Dumuzi, and the removal of his body from the tomb signifies his release from death and the underworld. In other words, the Sumerians had some sort of belief in a resurrection connected with the Dumuzi myth, and symbolized by the ritual removal of the body from the tomb. Moortgat's theory has been subjected to powerful criticism, and as things stand at the moment cannot be maintained.

2
Babylonian and Assyrian Religion

INTRODUCTION

We find Semitic tribes already in the country at the dawn of Mesopotamian history. But it is not until about 2350 B.C. that they appear as a power to reckon with in the form of the kingdom of Sargon and Naramsin in Agade (Akkad). This empire lasted for two centuries, but was followed by a Sumerian renaissance, at least in politics and religion. Semitic infiltration, however, continued, and in the eighteenth century the Semites made themselves felt again in earnest. A kingdom came to prominence in Mari, on the upper Euphrates, under the leadership of West Semitic (Amorite) bedouin chiefs, and on the upper Tigris an Assyrian kingdom developed, which for a time was of importance, especially because of its trading colonies in the area of Asia Minor. With Hammurabi's Amorite dynasty in Babylon, however, the Babylonian empire took the lead. In the north the Hurrians came to the fore for a time, and this is true to a certain extent even in religion and culture, while the Cassites, who invaded Babylon in the sixteenth century, very soon adopted Mesopotamian beliefs and customs. The Assyrians gradually recovered from a low position, and from the fourteenth century we can follow Assyria's road to power in what was thought of in theory as a world-empire. In the ninth and eighth centuries the Assyrian empire had a period as a great power, although now the Aramaeans in the north-west and far in the south a group of peoples probably distantly related to them, the Chaldaeans, began to make themselves felt. It was this latter group which with Babylon as its base and with the help of the Medes finally succeeded in destroying Assyria (612) and so founded the neo-Babylonian empire. In culture and religion, however, the Chaldaeans built upon the old native traditions. But their empire was short-lived; in 539 Babylon was captured by Cyrus, king of Persia, and the land became a part of the Persian empire. Its culture and religion still lived on for a time—we have detailed

ritual texts from the Seleucid period (third century B.C.) but
gradually the three thousand year old Mesopotamian culture, and
with it its religion, died out.

It is obvious that in such circumstances it is extremely difficult
to draw a clear line between Sumerian and Assyrio-Babylonian
(Semitic, or Akkadian: the latter term is used with special reference
to language) elements in the religion. In the course of the centuries
a constant process of interchange took place between the two
religious traditions, which initially were quite different, and the
result was a unity in which the original components are almost
impossible to distinguish. It must suffice to make some general
observations.

1. When Sumerian ceased to be the official language with the
development of the old Babylonian empire, a large number of
Sumerian religious texts continued to be transmitted, often provided with an interlinear Akkadian translation (i.e. one line of
Sumerian text, then one of translation). There were even new
poems composed in Sumerian, although the language was no
longer spoken. Clearly Sumerian functioned as a sort of sacred
or ritual language, rather like Latin in the Roman Catholic
Church.

In the Cassite period a sort of canonization of Babylonian
literature took place, so that certain (Sumerian) poems and certain
sorts of literature were rejected and fell into oblivion, while others
continued to be transmitted in a standardized and generally
accepted form. It is considered that this process was complete by
about 1300 B.C. Among the texts rejected were most of the mythical
and epic texts, the hymns which sing of the king as divine, and
most of the Dumuzi texts. On the other hand, new forms of
literature appeared, such as certain forms of psalms and intercessory incantations.

We already see, therefore, in the transmission of the texts
both continuity in religious development, and innovations within
Babylonian-Assyrian religion.

2. The attempt has sometimes been made to give Sumerian
religion a predominantly chthonic character, i.e. it is supposed to
have been specially interested in the earth and its forces. In contrast to this, Semitic religion is supposed to have been more
interested in the powers of heaven, the sun, moon, stars, etc. In

accordance with this view Kramer, for instance, maintains that Inanna, Utu, Nanna, and even Enki are originally Semitic deities which entered the Sumerian pantheon at a very early stage.[1] Against this it must be said that the deities mentioned are already found in the earliest Sumerian documents, so that any really clear evidence for such an assumption is lacking. On the other hand, it can be shown that, for instance, the character of the sun-god alters in the course of time under Semitic influence.

It is a question whether the difference between the chthonic and the astral and celestial element is not found already in the Sumerian period, this depending on the circumstances of nature, so that the southern agricultural culture laid emphasis on the chthonic elements, while the northern pastoral culture was more interested in celestial phenomena.

It is clear that it is only in exceptional cases that it can be demonstrated that a Sumerian deity is of foreign origin, especially if we agree with Kramer that the systematization of the Sumerian pantheon, which largely goes back to about 2500 B.C., is a product of the activity of the Sumerian priests, and includes a bringing together of local deities into a common Sumerian pantheon.

3. As far as the deities are concerned, they continued in large measure to be worshipped under new, Akkadian names. It is often very difficult to discover any real differences in their character between Sumerian and the Akkadian texts. Bottéro asserts that the Akkadian gods are to a lesser extent than the Sumerian gods forces of nature, less linked with natural phenomena, and are universal and cosmic powers, at the same time acquiring a more ethical and moral character.[2] We have already seen that a large part of this development must have taken place already in the Sumerian period. On the other hand, it must of course be pointed out that a number of new deities appear, such as the national gods Marduk and Assur, and the West Semitic gods Dagan and Adad. We shall return to this question when we deal with details of the individual deities.

4. In cosmogony there are certain striking differences between the Sumerian ideas and the ideas that appear in the Babylonian Creation Epic. It appears that we have here the result of a conscious rethinking by the Babylonians, although largely on the basis of ancient material taken over. It is not completely ruled out that

the theme of battle in the creation myth is the result of West Semitic influence.

5. The style of religious poetry has in certain respects altered in the course of the transition from Sumerian to Akkadian. So, for example, the litany-like enumerative style which is dominant in the Sumerian hymnic literature is in large measure replaced by a style which is close to that of the Old Testament psalms, and corresponds more to our own taste. In myths and epics, in so far as they continued to be transmitted, quite extensive rewriting was carried out in the direction of the style of Semitic poetry. Certain alterations in content are still more striking: the psalms of lament and the prayers now emphasize man's sin and intercede for the forgiveness of the gods.[3]

6. It should also be noted that there is a basic difference between Babylonian and Assyrian religion. The Babylonians in the south depended for their livelihood on the supply of water from the rivers, and this also set its mark on their religion and gave it a more calm and static character. The Assyrians in the north depended on the rain, and their religion came to lay more emphasis on atmospheric phenomena, and acquired a more dynamic character. In the course of time a measure of interchange between the two took place.[4]

THE GODS

The Akkadian word for god, *ilu*, is common Semitic. It has not been possible to explain the word etymologically with certainty— both 'mighty' and 'first' are possible—but it can be established that it is used in the different Semitic languages sometimes as a name for the highest god, sometimes as a term for 'god' in general. It is written in Akkadian cuneiform (as is also the corresponding word in Sumerian) with the sign (originally a star) which was also used to signify 'heaven', and Anu, the god of heaven.

As this would suggest, there is no doubt that the gods, although they are represented and conceived of in human form and with human properties, generally have a special connection with heaven and with the celestial bodies. This feature is perhaps more strongly emphasized among the Semites than among the Sumerians.

Connections with the heavens are indicated also by the passage in the Creation Epic (v.2) where the stars are described as the 'images' or symbols (*tamšilu*) of the gods. It is not made clear how the relationship between the gods and the celestial bodies is conceived, but we know from other sources too that planets, stars, and constellations were regarded as each being connected with its own deity. It is not possible, however, to draw from this the conclusion, as was done by the pan-Babylonian school, that Babylonian religion is exclusively an astral religion, and that all the myths reflect events in the heavens. This is only one of many aspects of the Akkadian gods.

Although the gods have human properties, they differ from men in having a much higher degree of perfection.[5] They are 'exalted', 'mighty', 'perfect', they see and know everything, they are unfathomable, and above all immortal:

> When the gods created man,
> they appointed death for man,
> but kept life for themselves. (*The Gilgamesh Epic*)

This at least is how the gods are described in the hymns, and if it sometimes happens in a myth that a god is ignorant of something, or even dies (as in the case of Tammuz), this must be regarded as an exception, which in any case has not affected the piety of the hymns and prayers. Oppenheim in fact thinks that one should not pay too much regard to the myths in this respect; the Akkadian myths which we have are more of the nature of literature than of purely religious texts, and should be studied by a literary critic rather than by an historian of religion.[6] This is an exaggerated claim, but it may contain a grain of truth.

A prominent feature of the gods is the terrifying brightness (*melammu*; the word is Sumerian) which surrounds them. Man's reaction at the sight of this is fear or reverence (*puluḫtu*).

The number of the gods was very large. The extensive list of gods found in the library of Assurbanipal comprises more than 2500 names, and we now know considerably more than 3000 names of gods. But it is obvious that so many deities cannot have had any practical role to play either in the official cult or in popular faith. In fact a large number of these names should be regarded as epithets of the great gods. Others are servants or attendants which priestly speculation thought the gods were in need of. Others again are old local gods, good spirits, and demi-gods. When Hammurabi in the prologue to his code gives a list of about twenty deities, he probably gives round about the number of gods which in practice are important.

First in the Assyrio-Babylonian pantheon comes Anu, whose name is a minimal semitization of the Sumerian An. He is simply the heavens personified, and he is regarded at least in theory as the highest god. In practice he is a rather featureless figure, who retires very much into the background before other more active gods, especially Marduk and Assur. He is above all the god of kingship; it is from him that the office of kingship comes, and he is himself the king of the gods. As a symbol of his might he carries (as does Enlil too) a headdress with horns on it—horns are probably a symbol of strength. He was also called 'the father of the gods'. Strangely enough the demons also derive their origin from him.

For his consort Anu has the goddess Antu, whose name is simply a feminine form of his own, and who has no marked individual character at all. Hammurabi mentions Inanna (Ishtar) instead as the consort of Anu, and a mythological text describes how Anu chooses Ishtar for his wife, exalts her to heaven, and gives her the name Antu. The myth is clearly intended to legitimize Ishtar as the consort of the god of heaven.

Anu's city was Uruk, and here he also had an important part to play in the cult. We have ritual for his temple at Uruk preserved from as late as the Seleucid period.

Enlil (or Ellil) generally keeps his Sumerian name, but also appears with the Akkadian epithet Bêl, 'the lord' (the Akkadian equivalent of the West Semitic Baal). Enlil was 'the king of the lands' (i.e. of the earth), and like his father Anu could be called 'the father of the gods' and 'the king of the gods'. Together with Anu he also confers the office of kingship.

Enlil is the strong and mighty god; one of his epithets is 'the wild ox' (*rîmu*). The hurricane (*abûbu*) is his weapon. His command is irrevocable.

Enlil's attitude to men is ambivalent. It was he who sent the flood upon earth, and hymns describe how his word (the hurricane) causes destruction upon earth. It is also told how once he created a monster Labbu to destroy mankind. But he also watches over order. It is originally he who possesses the tablets of destiny, by

which the destiny of the world is decided. (According to Oppenheim *ṭupšimāti* means not 'tablet of destiny' but 'tablet of office' or
'official tablet', but the symbolic content remains the same: the
one who has this document is ruler and has authority.) Hammurabi invokes Enlil against those who scorn his laws, and prays
the god to send all sorts of punishments upon the king who does
not respect them.

The consort of Enlil was Ninlil; her city was Nippur, where also
her most important temple was situated.

Ea is the Sumerian En-ki. No agreement has been reached on
the origin of the name; usually it is regarded as being really
Sumerian, and as meaning 'house of water', but Kramer has lately
maintained that it is Semitic, and that this shows that Enki is not
a genuine Sumerian god.[7] In any case it is the name Ea that is used
in a Semitic context.

From being the local deity of Eridu, Ea became one of the three
gods who were each given a share of the universe as their dominion
(Anu, Enlil, and Ea), and his sphere of influence was the sweet
water ocean under the earth, *Apsu* (Sumerian *ab-zu*). The Babylonian Creation Epic has him subjugate Apsu, the sweet water, at
an early stage, while Tiamat, the salt water, remains as the enemy
of the gods until she is subdued by Marduk.

Ea is also the god of wisdom, 'the king of wisdom, who creates
understanding', 'the experienced one (*apkallu*) among the gods',
'he who knows everything that has a name'. It is he who gives the
king wisdom. He is also the god of the art of incantation. In his
temple 'the house of Apsu' in Eridu there was a notable tree,
kiškanū, whose branches were used in ritual sprinklings. The water
that was employed to purify the patient in ceremonies of incantation was called 'Ea's water'. The incantation priest was the representative of Ea.

Craftsmen and artists have Ea as their patron, and he is himself
the great artist, 'whose hands have formed mankind'. In the
Creation Epic it is said of him that from the blood of Kingu 'he
created mankind and commanded it to serve the gods', that is, he
is the creator of man.

A Greek author, who cites a Babylonian priest called Berossus,
tells that the god Oannes, who was half man, half fish, taught
mankind the art of building, handicrafts, and all sorts of cultural
skills. There are pictures of Ea with a head of an ibex and a fish's

tail, and at Tell Ḥalaf a picture has been found of a combination of a man and a fish which may very well be Ea. We know also that his priest appeared in a sort of cloak which gave the illusion of the figure of a fish. It is clear from what has been said and from the myths related already about the Sumerian Enki that Ea was the bringer of culture.

Ea's consort is given as Ninki (the feminine parallel form of Enki), Damgalnunna, or Damkina (this last is explained as 'mistress of heaven and earth').

Next after these three cosmic gods comes another group of three, which have a clear connection with celestial bodies: the moon-god Sin, the sun-god Shamash, and the goddess of the morning and evening star, Ishtar.

Sin corresponds to the Sumerian Nanna, and his Akkadian name seems to be of Sumerian origin too (*su-en*). His character as a moon-god appears from a number of symbols. His headdress has four pairs of horns, and is crowned by a crescent moon. The horns are perhaps a stylization of the crescent. In the Creation Epic it is said: 'at the beginning of the month, to shine over the land, you shall shine with horns, to delimit six days'. The new moon is greeted as 'the strong young bull with strong horns'. A combination of symbols which are specially common on boundary stones (*kudurru*) are the crescent moon, the sun's disk, and a star (Sin, Shamash, and Ishtar). The crescent moon could also be taken for a boat; for this reason Sin is sometimes called 'the shining boat of heaven'. The waning moon on the other hand is an old man with a beard, and it is no doubt in this context that we find descriptions of Sin as the wise and unfathomable god, whose 'plans no god knows', and 'who determines the destinies for distant days'. When the moon has an eclipse it is a bad sign. A magic text explains the phenomenon as the result of an attack by 'the seven', the evil demons of the heavens, against Sin, and sacrifices are made to strengthen the god and attempts made to help him in other ways.

Apart from Sin's character as a moon-god it is hard to define his area of activity. In certain circles there is a tendency to exalt Sin to the position of highest god, and to ascribe to him a number of properties which have nothing directly to do with the moon. He is not only the unfathomably wise god, but is also the originator of life, the guardian and leader of mankind, the judge of heaven and earth, the lord of destinies.

> Lord, prince of the gods, who only are high in heaven and on
> earth, . . .
> Mighty young bull with strong horns, perfect limbs,
> with ultramarine coloured beard, full of strength and luxuri-
> ance. . . .
> Merciful, gracious father, who holds all the life of the land in
> your hand!
> Lord, your divinity is like the distant heaven, like the broad sea,
> full of fearfulness . . .
> Strong chieftain, whose deep mind no god penetrates,
> swift runner, whose knees do not tire, who makes a way for his
> brother gods,
> who moves in splendour from the base of heaven to the height
> of heaven, opens the gates of heaven, brings all mankind
> light!
> Father, the source of all things, who sees and protects all
> creatures!
> Lord, who determines the destiny of heaven and earth, whose
> command no one can alter . . .
> In the heavens—who is high? You alone are high.
> On earth—who is high? You alone are high.[8]

Such 'monotheistic' tendencies have sometimes been connected
with the religion of Abraham, for Abraham came according to
Gen. 11.31 from Ur by way of Haran, and these two places are the
most important centres of the cult of the moon-god. But caution is
needed about this suggestion. On the other hand, we know that
Nabonidus, the last king of Babylon, attempted to carry through
certain reforms with the purpose of making Sin the foremost god,
but that his attempts met with strong opposition from the people
and especially from the priests.

His consort has the Sumerian name Nin-gal ('the great lady'),
called in Aramaic and Phoenician Nikkal. Their children are
Shamash and Ishtar.

Shamash is quite simply the common Semitic word for the sun,
which, however, in other places where we have knowledge of
Semitic sun-worship (South Arabia and Ugarit) is a goddess. The
fact that we have here a male deity can probably be ascribed to the
influence of the Sumerian Utu. But the Akkadian Shamash is a
very much more important god than his Sumerian predecessor.

While Utu is only rarely the subject of a hymn,[9] there is an impressive number of hymns to Shamash.

Shamash represents the sun in the first place as the giver of light and of life. The symbol for Shamash is in Babylon the disk of the sun with a four-pointed star inside and rays proceeding from it, in Assyria the disk of the sun with wings. (It is interesting that the latter symbol is also found in Egypt, and, probably under Assyrian influence, in Iranian representations of Ahura Mazda. It is found also among the Hittites.) Shamash is also often represented sitting on a throne like a king, holding in his right hand a staff (or sceptre) and a ring as symbols of straightness and completeness, i.e. justice and righteousness. As sun-god he is thought of as either riding forth on a horse like a hero or crossing the heavens in a boat or chariot.

The properties and functions of Shamash are easily derived from his solar character. He banishes darkness and spreads light over the whole world. He gives life and 'makes the dead to live'. He governs and directs the whole universe. As the conqueror of night and death he is the hero above all others. It is striking that the same image is used of the sun in Psalm 19 in the Bible.

The greatest importance of the sun-god, however, is as the representative of justice, 'the judge of heaven and earth', who sees everything and punishes the guilty. It is Shamash who gives Hammurabi his commission to 'let justice shine in the land', and on the Hammurabi stele he is seen symbolically handing over the law to him. Justice and Righteousness, *Mesharu* and *Kettu*, are the sun-god's attendants, personifications of his most important properties.

But the sun, which sees everything, also pierces through all secrets, and for this reason Shamash is also the god of the art of divination. The seers, *bārū*, have him as their patron god (together with Adad). It is noteworthy that the sun-god plays a comparatively small part in mythology, and is not under any circumstances involved in compromising situations.[10]

The most important cult-centres of the sun-god were Larsa and Sippar. His consort is called Aia, who in her epithets appears specially as the 'beloved' (*narāmtu*) of Shamash and his 'bride' (*kallatu*; cf. the sun which comes forth 'as a bridegroom', in Psalm 19.5).

A couple of typical quotations from different Shamash hymns follow:

Shamash, when you come out of the great mountain . . .
when you come out of the foundations of heaven, where earth
   and heaven meet,
there the great gods appear before you to come to judgement . . .
all nations and men wait for you,
beasts and cattle, all that moves on four feet,
direct their eyes to your great light.[11]

Strong, most powerful, light of the lands,
prince of the gods, righteous judge!
You that lead the people, have charge of the world,
judge that which is above, govern that which is below!
King of heaven and earth, lord of destinies, incorruptible
   judge!
You govern mankind, you rule over the heavenly beings.
Evil and wicked you see through as clearly as the day.[12]

A long hymn to Shamash, which Tallqvist calls 'one of the most
beautiful creations of Babylonian poetry', is especially interesting
for the stress it lays on the ethical properties of the sun-god.[13]

Ishtar, identified with the Sumerian Inanna, is as an astral deity
the planet Venus, the morning and evening star. But this by no
means exhausts her significance, and it is in fact uncertain whether
the astral element is original. Her name is etymologically identical
with the West Semitic Astarte, for whose astral character we have
no definite evidence, and with the South Arabian male deity
'Athtar or Astar, who in Arabia may perhaps be Venus, but in
Ethiopia is the god of heaven in general.

The comparison with the male 'Athtar in South Arabia raises
the problem of the change of sex. In the Ugaritic myths we find
both a female 'Athtart and a male 'Athtar 'Arīẓ. In Mari Ishtar's
name is sometimes preceded by a sign which indicates a male, and
there is a passage in a hymn which speaks of the 'bearded' Ishtar.
It is possible that originally this was a bisexual deity or at least a
deity of indeterminate or varying sex, later made to be either
male or female.

Ishtar appears in several local forms, which to a certain extent
at least may be regarded as having their own individuality, rather
in the same way as do the local madonnas in Roman Catholicism.
There was an Ishtar of Nineveh, an Ishtar of Arbela, and an Ishtar of Bit-kitmuri. Strangely enough we know very little about the

first, although she was one of the most important deities in Assyria and enjoyed high honour beyond the borders of the land, among the Hurrians and the Hittites. It has been suggested, therefore, that her cult in Nineveh was of the 'mystery' type and for this reason was secret. But there is no positive evidence that this was the case.

Two features, which seem irreconcilable, characterize Ishtar. On the one hand, she is the god of love and fertility, on the other, of war. Saggs finds a connecting link between these two aspects in the idea that both when life is cut off in battle and when life is created in the sexual act, there Ishtar is manifest.[14]

As a goddess of war Ishtar was specially popular in Assyria. It was believed that she went at the head of the Assyrian armies and gave them victory. In the Code of Hammurabi she is called 'the mistress of battle and war', and anyone who neglects the Code is threatened with war, defeat, revolution, and shedding of blood through her. Assyrian rulers call her 'the courageous in battle, who does not spare the enemies of Assyria'. On one of Assurbanipal's campaigns she revealed herself to a seer: 'she had a warrior to left and to right, she held a bow in her hand, and had drawn a sharp sword to open battle'. She appeared before Esarhaddon in a theophany and said: 'I am Ishtar of Arbela. Before you, behind you shall I go. Fear not.' Such self-declarations are common with Ishtar, and hymns of self-praise are also especially common. One such, with clear allusion to her astral character, says:

Ishtar, the goddess of the evening am I,
Ishtar, the goddess of the morning am I.[15]

As the evening star she is primarily the goddess of love, as the morning star preponderantly of war.

The love and fertility aspects are primarily a Sumerian inheritance. They are perhaps most emphasized in Inanna's old city of Uruk, 'city of courtesans, harlots and prostitutes' as it has been called on the basis of the temple staff of the goddess. Temple prostitution was in fact an important part of her cult and was thought of as promoting fertility. Epithets such as 'the mistress of love', 'the queen of joy', 'she who loves pleasure and joy', characterize Ishtar in this aspect. In the myth of Ishtar's descent into the underworld we find a description of how all reproduction on the earth ceased when she was away:

Since Ishtar descended to the land of no return,
the bull no longer mounts the cow,
the ass does not couple with the she-ass,
man does not lie with girl in the street.

In the Gilgamesh Epic Ishtar suggests to the hero a sexual union, but he rejects it.

Ishtar is also the deity who in the hymns is the object of the deepest devotion and the most intimate prayers.

You that go before the flock, that love the shepherd,
you that discharge the position of shepherdess in all lands, in all
    the universe,
before you men bow the knee, men seek you.
The oppressed and defeated you lead and secure justice for.[16]

How lovely it is to pray to you! How ready you are to hear!
Your glance is the hearing of prayer, your speech is light.
Be gracious to me, Ishtar, announce to me wealth!
Look faithfully upon me, hear my invocation!
If I follow your footsteps, may my step be firm.
If I hold your leading strings, may I have good courage.
If I bear your yoke, give me relief![17]

Ishtar was therefore a very versatile and very popular goddess. She had numerous temples. In Babylon a special gate was dedicated to her. Her symbol, the eight-pointed star, occurs very often together with the symbols of the sun and the moon. The consequence of Ishtar's great popularity was that a number of less important goddesses came to be more or less identified with her. This went so far that her name could be used as a designation for 'goddess' in general.

A god who was often associated with Shamash and Ishtar was Adad, the god of thunder. The corresponding Sumerian god Ishkur was of secondary importance, while his West Semitic equivalent Hadad was a god of the first importance, and both Hittites and Hurrians counted the god of thunder among their leading gods. Adad is characterized by a certain duality. Thunderstorms can be both beneficial and destructive. The Code of Hammurabi speaks of what should be done if 'Adad inundates' the land, i.e. if violent thunderstorms cause destruction, but he is also described as 'the lord of abundance, the controller of the floodgates of heaven and earth'.[18] Often it is the destructive aspect that is dominant. The Assyrian king Adadnirari I utters the following curse: 'May Adad smite him with a severe inundation. May storms, evil winds, revolution, unrest, thunderstorms, anguish, want, drought, starvation be continuous in his land. May he let loose as it were a flood in his land, may he change it into heaps of rubble and ruins.'

The symbol of Adad is a fork-shaped flash of lightning; the lightning is also his weapon. 'May Adad, my lord, smite him with the lightning of misfortune, may he send hunger in his land, may he slay his army', says Adadnirari of anyone who destroys his memorial. A Sumerian hymn describes Ishkur as the one who rides on the stormy wind or on a great wild beast, which appears in splendour, and by its roar fills the land with terror.[19] Similar ideas are also found in a bilingual hymn which speaks of heaven and earth trembling before the wrath of Adad, and the gods hiding themselves before his 'thunder and noise'.[20]

At a later date Adad was associated for unknown reasons with Shamash as an oracle giver. His consort is Shala, originally the Hurrian goddess Shalash, who has been incorporated into the Babylonian pantheon.

Another storm-god is Ninurta, an originally Sumerian god, who, however, was also worshipped by the Assyrians and Babylonians, and was regarded especially as the god of war and of hunting. It is said that it was he who gave Hammurabi 'the exalted weapon' which gave victory. The hunter theme is most strongly stressed in the middle Assyrian period, when he was specially worshipped in Calaḫ, a city which is now called Nimrud. The Nimrod who was 'a mighty hunter before Yahweh' according to Gen. 10.8f, is none other than Ninurta. His consort was Gula, who was a goddess of healing.

There is an interesting hymn to Ninurta which identifies a series of deities with the different parts of his body: his face is the heaven, his eyes are Enlil and Ninlil, his mouth is 'Ishtar of the stars', his ears Ea and Damkina, etc.[21] We clearly have here a speculation which thought of Ninurta as the embodiment of all divine powers.[22] One can also speak of a pantheistic tendency, since the different parts of the body are identified with the natural phenomena which the deities represent. We are reminded too that

Ningirsu showed himself to Gudea as a man 'whose form was like the heaven, whose form was like the earth'.

A god who was powerful and feared was Nergal, the god of plague and of the underworld. It appears that he was originally a sun-god; there is a text which declares that 'Shamash and Nergal are one'. In that case it must be the burning sun of summer and its consuming heat that are meant. So Nergal is connected with the plague-god Irra, the central character in a myth of Anu punishing cities which rebel against him. Nergal is most important, however, as the lord of the underworld, the land of the dead, with the goddess of death Ereshkigal as his consort (this is her Sumerian name; in Akkadian she is called Allatu).

There is a myth which tells how Nergal became the lord of the underworld.[23] It tells how once Ereshkigal's envoy, when he came to the world of the gods, was greeted with respect by all except Nergal, who for that reason was made to descend to the underworld. In spite of all his precautions he was prevailed upon by Ereshkigal to spend six days with her in her bedroom. On the seventh day he succeeded in obtaining permission to return, but Ereshkigal missed him so much that she asked for him back. Otherwise she would bring to a stop all fertility and all life on earth. Nergal returned, and made himself king of the underworld, and after a further six days in her bedroom he obtained the permission of the gods to remain in the underworld as its ruler. It has been thought that behind this myth lies the reluctance of the Semites to accept a woman in a position of leadership; to their patriarchal cast of mind the ruler of the land of the dead had to be a male divinity. But at the same time we should take note of the fertility aspect of the chthonic goddess Ereshkigal, clearly a Sumerian inheritance.

Nergal was worshipped in the city of Cutha, whose name could in fact be used as a term for the land of the dead. He was also worshipped in many other places. It was necessary to be on good terms with a god who was so mighty and dangerous; his protection too was regarded as being specially effective.

There were also a number of deities who were associated with fire. Among them Gibil and Girru were invoked in incantations as averters of sorcery and witchcraft. Nusku is especially the sacrificial flame which consumes the sacrifice and sends up the smell of incense to the gods. He is praised also as one who drives away demons.

There is a special problem connected with Tammuz (or Ta'ūzu), the Sumerian Dumuzi. Hammurabi does not mention him among the gods whom he invokes as a guarantee for his code, and he does not seem to occur otherwise in official religious documents. But a number of Tammuz texts clearly continued to be transmitted, and were provided with Akkadian translations. In the Assyrian Gilgamesh Epic the hero in his answer to Ishtar's invitations alludes also to the fate of Tammuz:

> For Tammuz, the beloved of your youth
> You determined mourning year after year.

At the end of the Akkadian version of the myth of Ishtar's descent into the underworld there are some apparently disconnected fragments, of which two are connected with the Tammuz cult:

> For Tammuz, the beloved of her youth, pour out pure water;
> anoint with good oil, dress him in a bright red garment!
> Let one play on a flute of lapis lazuli!
> Let courtesans appease his wrath!

This passage clearly refers to the yearly mourning and lament for the death of the god. The next passage is difficult to translate, but may mean:

> On the day on which Tammuz rises up,
> when the flute of lapis lazuli and the ring of cornelian rise up
>   with him,
> when male and female mourners rise up with him,
> may the dead also rise up and inhale the incense.

However obscure these lines are, they must definitely refer to the return of the god to life. But that is the limit of our knowledge. We know that the lamentation for Tammuz was held in midsummer, in the month which bears the name of the god. The lamentation itself took place on the second day of the month; on the ninth, sixteenth, and seventeenth there were processions with torches. On the three last days of the month an image of the god was exposed and buried. These ceremonies are similar to the rites of mourning that we know that the Sabians in Syria in the early Christian period performed, and to the mourning for Adonis in Athens, Byblos, and Alexandria. These took place at the time when the summer drought and heat prevailed and the vegetation withered.

There are bilingual hymns, in copies from a relatively late date, in which Tammuz is clearly connected with different forms of vegetation, for example:

Shepherd, lord, Tammuz, husband of Ishtar!
Prince of the underworld, inhabitant of the shepherds' house.
Tamarisk that has not drunk water from the furrow,
whose head on the steppe has not produced flower!
Sapling that has not been planted by its watercourse,
shoot whose roots have been cut off!
Root that has not drunk water from a runnel!
He goes, he withdraws to the bosom of the earth.
He hastens, satiated with life—his sun went down—to the land
   of the dead . . .
How long shall the fruiting be delayed?
How long shall the appearing of green be hindered?[24]

The last lines clearly speak of the sterility which is caused by the heat of summer. More obscure are a pair of lines in the same text which say:

In his youth he lies in a sinking ship,
in his maturity he has sunk and lies in the harvest.

This seems to allude to some myth unknown to us. But it is in any case clear that Tammuz is connected with corn. It seems, therefore, that the fertility theme came with time to play an increasingly large part, while the shepherd theme lost importance. This corresponds no doubt also to an actual change in the circumstances of food production.

Ever since Frazer's work 'The Dying God', it has been regarded as self-evident that Tammuz was an example of the type of god who embodies in himself the forces of fertility, and whose death and resurrection, celebrated in myth and ritual, reflect the succession of the seasons of the year. It was also taken for granted that a number of local gods, for instance Marduk, had been regarded as manifestations of Tammuz, and like him suffered, died, and rose again in the cult, represented by the sacral king. The presentation given here of the Sumerian Dumuzi and of his Akkadian counterpart has deliberately been very cautious on this point. The attempt has been made to build on what we really know at the present time about Tammuz and his cult. We cannot, as Kramer and others have recently done, simply deny that there is a return of Tammuz to life, but on the other hand it is clear that the dominant features of the Tammuz cult were his death and the lamentation for it. This is also the feature which survived in Christian and Islamic times in these areas. We shall return later to the question of Marduk's death and resurrection. A number of general questions concerning this type of deity must be further discussed in the chapter on West Semitic religion.

There are two gods which owe their dominant position to political developments—the national deities Marduk in Babylon and Assur in Assyria.

Marduk's origin is completely obscure. His name appears to mean 'son of the sun' or 'bull calf of the sun', but he shows no specially solar features. His temple in Babylon is called Esagila, and we know that this was once also the name of a temple in Eridu. Since the Babylonian creation myth, in which the central character is Marduk, has certain points of contact with the cosmogony which was current in Eridu, it seems reasonable to suggest that Marduk belonged originally to that city. He is furthermore regarded as a son of the god of Eridu, Enki or Ea.

But it is as the city god and national god of Babylon that Marduk has won a place in history. He is already mentioned in the Code of Hammurabi, but without any specially privileged position. It is clearly in the centuries after Hammurabi, of which still very little is known, that Marduk obtained his position of prominence. It was probably also in this period that the Babylonian creation myth, the *Enūma elish*, took shape. One of its aims is to show how Marduk became the leading god because, in a critical situation in which the other gods were powerless, he met and conquered Tiamat, the representative of chaos, and then created the world. The epic describes how the gods transfer power to Marduk, and give him 'the tablets of destiny' (see p. 10) as a sign of his supremacy. The final section of the epic lists Marduk's fifty titles, which represent him as the leading god.

As the son of Ea, Marduk seems to have been a god of magic and of incantation from an early date. But in the course of time he acquired other, more important, functions. There was a mono-theistic, or perhaps more accurately henotheistic, tendency here, so that a large number of deities are treated as manifestations of Marduk. He is given the epithet *Bel* ('lord'), and is thus more or less identified with Enlil. Numerous epithets assert his omnipotence, wisdom, and inscrutability, his superiority in war, and his power to heal the sick and 'to make the dead live'. In the ritual for the New Year Festival in Babylon Marduk is identified with a series of astral deities, and the prayer ends with the words: 'My lord is my god, my lord is my ruler, is there any lord apart from him?'

Marduk's consort is called Sarpanitu, 'the shining one', and is sometimes connected with the planet Venus. By a play on words her name was interpreted as *zēr-bānitu*, 'creatress of seed', and is thereby associated with the goddess Aruru, who according to a creation legend created man.

Marduk's son Nabu is also closely connected with him. His home is the neighbouring city of Borsippa. He is worshipped as the god of writing and the patron god of scribes, and in general regarded as a god of wisdom. In the neo-Babylonian period a tendency can be traced to exalt Nabu at the expense of Marduk. His consort was Tashmetu, 'hearing', who simply personifies his function of hearing prayers.

Assur (*Aššur*) is the name not only of the god but also of the capital and of the country, and it is now impossible to decide which is primary. Perhaps originally Assur was a tribal deity who bore the name of the tribe. We find him mentioned already in the oldest Assyrian documents, and throughout the history of Assyria he appears as the leading god of the pantheon, often mentioned even before Anu and Enlil.

It is interesting to see how Assur grows in importance as the position of the city and of the land becomes stronger. The intimate relationship between the god and the king as his priest and representative bound religion and politics together, and identified the purposes of the god with those of the land. As the god grew in importance, he took over more and more of the functions which had belonged to other gods. There is an Assyrian version of the Epic of Creation in which Assur takes the place of Marduk. He plays the part of Anu and Enlil as the bestower of kingship. He takes over the function of the sun-god as judge and guardian of justice. He is the god of war who gives the king the victory in battle. He is the father of the gods, the creator and begetter. He is also praised for his mercy. By associating his name with Anshar, one of the obscure figures from the primeval period of the world's history, an attempt was made to assert that Assur was in fact older and greater than all the other gods.

Dagan is a West Semitic god who had already entered Mesopotamia in the late Sumerian period. Probably he was basically a fertility god, perhaps identical with the corn (Hebrew *dāgān*). Among the Amorites in Mari he plays a pre-eminent role, and we have instances of his taking part in the affairs of the state through his prophets. We shall come back to him again in connection with the deities of the West Semites.

MYTHOLOGY

If the word myth is taken in the sense of cultic myth, that is, a narrative text which has a definite function in a cultic rite, there is in Akkadian literature only one such whose function can be determined with certainty, and this is the Creation Epic. We know that this was both recited and 'enacted' at the New Year's Feast, and this is probably the reason why we have copies of this text from a number of different places.

An intermediate position is held by two cosmogonic texts which appear in rituals for temple building or incantation texts. They tell briefly the origin of the phenomenon with which the ceremony concerned deals (building materials and workers in one case, in the other a worm which causes tooth-ache) and thereby create the conditions for the cultic or magic act.

The Gilgamesh Epic can without hesitation be described as a literary creation. There is nothing to suggest that it had a cultic function. The myth of Ishtar's descent into the underworld is a new version of the Sumerian myth of the same subject, and it *may* have had some function within the Tammuz-Ishtar cult. The disconnected fragments which conclude one recension of it (see p. 64 above) may perhaps point to this, as does also the fact that it has been preserved in several copies.

Four other mythological texts (Anzu, Etana, Adapa, Nergal and Ereshkigal) may be literary creations on the basis of motifs whose cultic functions (if they had any) have been forgotten or have left no trace in writing.[25] A further difficulty is that in several cases the text of the myth is not preserved as a whole.

Among the shorter cosmogonic texts perhaps the most interest-

ing is the so-called Chaldaean cosmogony.[26] It is a bilingual text
from the sixth century B.C., which appears to go back to older
sources. By way of introduction it tells of the time when there was
no temple, no reeds, no brick, no house, no city, and no men, and
when 'all the lands were sea'. Then Eridu arose in Apsu (the
ocean), with its temple and the god Marduk, and Babylon, the
holy city. Then Marduk made a form of reeds and created mud—
clearly the earth is formed of this—and to 'let the gods dwell in a
dwelling place that they take delight in, he created men; (the
goddess) Aruru created with him the seed of man'. Then cattle
and other beasts, gardens and forests, cities and temples are
created.

This cosmogony clearly presupposes the circumstances of the
lower course of the Euphrates and the Tigris; Marduk makes the
foundation for a dwelling place from reeds and mud, as we can
picture the inhabitants of these regions often doing. The account
shows how everything that did not exist at the beginning was
gradually created. It is a recurrent theme that man is created to
serve the gods; it is found also in the account of the creation of
man which appears in the Atraḥasis myth, of which more will be
said later.

The most important cosmogonic text, however, is the Epic of
Creation,[27] often called from its first words *enūma eliš*, 'when on
high'. It is a compilation, created to show the superiority of
Marduk over the other gods. It certainly had its original setting in
the Babylonian *akītu* festival, although it was also known elsewhere,
and is found too in an Assyrian version with Assur as the central
character.

The epic begins typically with a statement that in the beginning,
when there was neither heaven above nor earth beneath, when
there were no temples or gods and 'the destinies had not been
determined', there was only Apsu, the sweet water ocean, and
Tiamat, the salt water ocean (a third figure Mummu has only a
subsidiary function). These two commingled their waters with one
another, and so the gods Laḥmu and Laḥamu were born, then
Anshar and Kishar, and finally Anu and the other gods—among
them Ea is mentioned specially. It is clear that this introduction
reflects the natural circumstances in the delta area, where sweet and
salt water meet, even if one does not necessarily have to go so far
as Jacobsen and identify Laḥmu and Laḥamu with the silt which is

deposited to form new land. The special mention of Ea indicates some connection with his city Eridu.

Now, however, disunity appears between the younger generation of gods and their first parents, which ends with Ea vanquishing Apsu (and Mummu) and erecting his temple 'upon him', i.e. over the sweet water (this is clearly a reference to his sanctuary in Eridu). By this he has manifested himself as lord over the sweet water, and for all future time will have it under his control. Ea's son Marduk is now born 'in Apsu', and his qualities are praised in enthusiastic language.

In the next scene it is Tiamat who takes the offensive to avenge Apsu. She brings forth eleven enormous monsters, and sets the god Kingu at the head of their ranks, and fixes upon his breast 'the tablets of destiny', a symbol which gives his word absolute authority. The gods hesitate in the face of the attack. Neither Anu nor Ea dares to meet the enemy, and a message goes to Marduk. He undertakes the task on condition that he receives the position of leadership within the assembly of the gods, and unlimited authority. So the gods gather together for a feast, and determine his destiny: he is to be the leading god, his command is to have absolute authority, his word shall both destroy and create. So he is acclaimed with the cry 'Marduk is king'. We have every reason to think that this scene was in some form represented visibly in the cult.

Marduk arms himself now for the battle, and goes to meet Tiamat. When she opens her mouth to swallow him, he sends a terrible wind straight into her open mouth, so that she cannot close it, shoots an arrow into her belly and slays her. He takes her followers captive, and fastens Kingu's tablets of destiny on to his own breast. He cuts the body of Tiamat into two halves; one he lifts up, and places the firmament of heaven as a protection against 'her water'; the lower half is clearly the ocean here below. The battle-scenes were pictured on a copper door in the *akītu*-house of Assur; here (as in the corresponding temple in Babylon) the action of the myth was portrayed in a cultic drama. It would seem as if Marduk (or Assur) has here inherited functions from the wind god Enlil or from the hero god Ninurta.

In the epic there now follows a description of how Marduk arranges the constellations of heaven, and after a gap in the text there follows a section about the creation of man. Marduk declares before Ea his intention of creating mankind of blood to serve the gods. It is decided that Kingu shall be put to death as the vicarious representative of the rebellious gods. From his blood Ea creates mankind. Then a temple of Marduk is built in Babylon called Esagila, and Marduk installs himself there. The rest of the epic is devoted to a list with explanations of the fifty names of Marduk. We can see, therefore, that, although it is the wise Ea who is entrusted with the creation of mankind, the epic as a whole is directed towards the exaltation of Marduk. We might expect conclusions to be drawn from the fact that man has within himself the blood of the rebellious Kingu, but we have no evidence of this. Instead it is the idea of a substitute which is important in the Babylonian epic.

Although it is not strictly a myth, the Gilgamesh Epic[28] is one of the most interesting pieces to be found in Akkadian narrative literature. It is of especial interest for the study of literary history that we can see how the Akkadian epic has been put together on the basis of a number of shorter Sumerian texts.

The Akkadian epic consists of eleven tablets together with a supplement. The content of the epic is in brief as follows. Gilgamesh, who is two-thirds god, one-third man, is king in Uruk. His rule is strict. To divert his attention from his subjects, and to give him a worthy rival, a goddess creates a wild man Enkidu. He lives at first among the beasts on the steppe and is an intimate friend of them, but his sexual appetite is awakened through a prostitute, and he becomes completely human, so that the beasts will no longer have anything to do with him. 'Now you are like a god', they say to him. So he comes to Uruk and meets Gilgamesh. After an exciting duel the two heroes are reconciled and gradually become good friends.

Now a series of thrilling adventures begins. First, Gilgamesh, in spite of discouragement from Enkidu, decides to travel to the 'cedar forest' (Lebanon?) to slay Ḫuwawa (Humbaba), a monster whom Enlil has placed as guardian over the forest. He assures himself of the help of the sun-god and goes off accompanied by Enkidu. At this point the fourth tablet is preserved in a very incomplete state, but on the next tablet we hear how the two friends penetrate into the cedar forest, cut down cedars, and slay the monster. On the sixth tablet Ishtar offers her love to Gilgamesh, but is rejected with an allusion to the fate which the previous lovers of the goddess have suffered. To be revenged Ishtar sends the bull of heaven to earth. It causes great damage, but is finally slain by Gilgamesh and Enkidu. The wrath of the gods has, however, been excited by this, and as vengeance for the deaths of Ḫuwawa and of the bull of heaven they cause Enkidu to die. Gilgamesh performs the lament for the dead, and begins to fear that he will also share the fate of his friend. He goes off, therefore, to seek for life, and to find the only man who has obtained everlasting life, Utanapishtim, the hero of the flood. After great difficulties and many adventures he comes finally to the place by 'the source of the rivers' (probably not 'mouth') where Utanapishtim dwells. He now tells the story of the flood (to which we will return) and of how he acquired everlasting life. He also discloses the secret of a plant of life, which 'makes the old young', and Gilgamesh fetches it from the bottom of the sea. He goes off happily on his way home, but while during a rest he is bathing in a pool a snake steals the plant away, and Gilgamesh must therefore return to Uruk with his errand unaccomplished. The twelfth tablet, the supplement, describes finally how Gilgamesh calls forth the spirit of Enkidu, and receives a description of the miserable conditions in the land of the dead.

The Gilgamesh Epic contains various themes of interest to the history of religion. The main theme, man's vain striving to be able to live for ever, is found also in the Adapa myth (see p. 75 below), and it appears in an altered form in the background of the paradise myth of the Bible. Other themes from the Gilgamesh Epic are also found there. The sexual element in man's change from a natural state to a cultural life is found both in the story of Enkidu and in the story of the fall. We also find the role of the serpent as the 'villain of the piece' in both places (one of the ideas in the background here is that the serpent through shedding its skin renews its life).

Nevertheless, the Gilgamesh Epic is not a strictly religious text. The gods are treated in a surprisingly disrespectful manner: Gilgamesh rejects Ishtar in extremely censorious language, the flood story tells of the gods crouching down by the city wall in terror at the rampaging of the flood, and the gods gather like flies to inhale the odour of Utanapishtim's sacrifice. As the epic now is it must be treated in the first place as a literary creation. Precisely this feature is of special interest, because we know Sumerian antecedents to large parts of the epic in the form of independent episodes[29] which have nothing in common except the central character:

1. 'Gilgamesh and the land of the living', which tells of how Gilgamesh and Enkidu with fifty men set out for the cedar forest to slay Ḫuwawa, and succeeded. But this story agrees only in broad outline with the fourth and fifth tablets of the Gilgamesh Epic.

2. 'Gilgamesh and the bull of heaven', which in large measure corresponds to the sixth tablet: Inanna offers her love and her gifts, and after a gap in the text there is a description of how the bull of heaven comes down and rampages upon earth. The end of the story is lost.

3. 'Gilgamesh and the *ḫuluppu*-tree'. This tells how Gilgamesh helps Inanna to fell a tree which was guarded by a snake, a wind-demon, and an eagle, to make of it a chair and a couch. Gilgamesh makes from the root and the branches two objects which he accidentally lets fall into the underworld. When Enkidu tries to fetch them back, he makes a mistake in his instructions and has to remain below. Finally, the spirit of Enkidu reports to Gilgamesh of the situation in the land of the dead. The greater part of this story has been omitted, and only the last scene has been employed by the author of the Gilgamesh Epic.

4. 'The death of Gilgamesh', a very fragmentary text which tells of Gilgamesh in the underworld. Certain phrases recur in the story in the Epic of Gilgamesh about Gilgamesh's desire for eternal life, but apart from this the story is not made use of.

5. 'Gilgamesh and Agga', a story of the struggle of two kings, is also not used.

6. Finally, the flood story has been inserted from another source.

The technique of composition is interesting. The material which could be fitted into the total conception, i.e. the unattainability of everlasting life, has been made use of, the rest has been left out, and when necessary material which originally had no connection with Gilgamesh has been inserted. It is a case of conscious literary creation on the basis of old material.

The flood story is told in two contexts in Akkadian literature, in the Atraḫasis myth, and as we have seen in the Gilgamesh Epic. The former, which has only recently become known in its entirety, was also known by its introductory words *enūma ilū awīlum*, 'when the gods were (like) men . . .' It begins by telling how the gods at the beginning of time had to work so hard that they finally decided to create man to take over the work. On instructions from Ea the mother-goddess Mama (or Mami) created a first man out of clay mixed with blood from a god who was sacrificed (at least in some versions, cf. the Creation Epic). However, the men disturb the gods with their noise and din. In his wrath Enlil wishes to destroy them, and first sends a plague, then a drought, then seven years' famine upon the earth, but by appealing to Ea his devotee Atraḫasis ('the extremely wise') succeeds in saving them. Finally, Enlil sends the flood, but Ea again gives warning to Atraḫasis, who saves himself in the ship 'Preserver of Life'. We know that the whole text at least in the Assyrian period was used as an incantation text at childbirth—and a section about fertile and infertile women seems to be connected with this—but it is uncertain if this was its original function. It seems rather to be an account of the history of mankind from its original creation to the flood and the delivery of Atraḫasis.[30]

The flood story of the Gilgamesh Epic is very reminiscent of the biblical account. It describes how the gods once decided to send an inundation upon the earth. The reason is not given. Ea, however—again without motivation—warns Utanapishtim in Shuruppak, and he builds himself a ship, and in due time takes on board his possessions, his family, and all sorts of animals. Then the catastrophe comes. A cloud comes up, 'in its midst Adad thunders', and the rain falls. The gods themselves are seized with panic, 'they crouch down like dogs', Ishtar cries out like a pregnant woman and repents that she took part in the decision. The gods lament with her. On the seventh day the storm dies down, and gradually the ship sticks on mount Nisir (in Urartu, which is the same as the biblical Ararat). After some days Utanapishtim sends out a dove, which returns, then a swallow, which returns, and finally a raven, which stays away because the waters have gone down. Utanapishtim now leaves the ship and makes a sacrifice. With some humour we are told that the gods recognized the pleasant smell and gathered like flies around him as he made the sacrifice—the gods therefore have need of sacrifice! The end of the story is that Utanapishtim acquires eternal life like the gods, and is allowed to live at the source of the rivers.

The similarity to the biblical account is obvious: the place where the ship stops, the number of birds that are sent out, and the sacrifice after the flood are the same. But the biblical account has a motivation (the sin of man, the righteousness of Noah) which is here lacking (cf. Atraḥasis), the duration of the flood and the species of the birds are not identical, and above all the reactions of the gods are quite different.

The problem of eternal life also dominates the myth of Adapa.[31] Adapa is one of the seven sages (*apkallu*) of the primeval period, of whom we know little but who were invoked in certain magic rites.[32] He was regarded as a son of Ea, and dwelt at Eridu. On a fishing trip he is caught by surprise by the south wind, and breaks its wings. He is summoned to Anu's heaven to be held responsible for this. Ea advises him not to eat or drink anything that is offered to him. Adapa appears before Anu and acknowledges frankly what he has done. When Anu offers him 'the bread of life' and 'the water of life', Adapa refuses to take any for himself. In this way he fails to secure immortality. He returns to earth, and what happens subsequently is not clear; the end of the story is lost, but certain indications suggest that Anu gives Adapa instead great wisdom and the power to combat illness and demons. There is a fragment of the text which suggests that a summary of the Adapa myth was employed as an introduction to incantations to give them more force.

The myth of Etana[33] is unfortunately only preserved in an incomplete form, but it is clear that the basic theme is the question of the continuation of the royal family. Etana is king of Kish. He has no children, and therefore seeks for 'the plant of birth' to get offspring. The sun-god advises him to search for an eagle which is lying wounded in a pit. Here the narrator inserts a story of the eagle and the serpent, whose friendship came to an end when the eagle took the young of the serpent and the serpent duped the eagle so that it was caught in the pit. Etana now releases the eagle, which rapidly recovers and in gratitude carries up its rescuer to heaven, where clearly the 'plant of birth' is to be found. At this point our text ends, and we do not hear if the undertaking exceeded the strength of the eagle, or if Etana really secured the plant and the offspring he wanted. Another tradition does in fact mention a son of Etana as king.

The myth of the storm bird Anzu[34] (or Zu, as it was earlier read[35]) of which fragments have also been found in Sumerian, tells how Anzu, a son of Anu in the form of a bird,[36] stole the Tablets of Destiny and threatened the very existence of the gods. A god, who in different versions is Ninurta or Lugalbanda or Ningirsu, intervenes and defeats Anzu and restores order. We clearly have here a variant of one of the motifs in the Creation Epic, and the main purpose of the account is to glorify the god who is the victor. At the same time there appears to be a certain feeling of uncertainty towards the permanence of the world order—it appears to have been quite easy for a rebellious god to seize the symbols of authority. Security, the order of the cosmos, rested on the strength of the victorious god.

The Epic of the plague-god Irra (Erra)[37] is a very loosely arranged composition, primarily concerned with the restoration of prosperity after war and pestilence. Irra is urged on by 'the seven' (the demons) to activity. His vizier Ishum seeks to hold him back, but he wishes to fight because men have neglected his cult, and he finally succeeds in inducing Marduk to abdicate from his dominion over the world. Marduk has to purify his insignia by fire, and so leaves his throne and descends into the underworld. Irra as his representative misuses his power, and causes chaos and civil war by means of pestilence. Finally, however, Ishum succeeds in calming him, and he acknowledges his guilt. The text concludes with blessings and a promise of prosperity and fortune. Inserted into the composition is a lament upon Babylon which is reminiscent of the Sumerian laments for the destruction of cities. In a final strophe the narrator mentions that all this was revealed to him in a dream.

The function of this myth is not clear. Is the point the protection which the presence of the god of the city brings? Or is it the necessity of the royal power to maintain order that is emphasized? Is there a remote connection with the myth at Ras Shamra of Baal's descent into the underworld and of the substitute king 'Athtar 'Ariẓ? Is there a ritual background, such as the symbolic descent of the king into the underworld? All these are questions which cannot be answered with certainty on the basis of the material which we now have. As the poem now appears it gives the impression of being a consolatory or propaganda composition with a promise of better times for Babylon in a dark period.

THE CULT

THE TEMPLE

It appears that the position of the temples in the early Babylonian period underwent social and economic alteration, their position of power being curtailed to the advantage of the power of the king.[38] On the other hand, their religious significance did not alter, and it is striking that even at a much later date the temples still very often have Sumerian names which express something of their symbolic significance, for example *E-temen-an-ki*, 'the temple of the foundation of heaven and earth', *E-kur*, 'the temple of the mountain (of 'Enlil)' '*E-sag-ila*, 'the temple with a high "head" '. One room in the temple of Enlil is called *Dur-an-ki*, 'the bond of heaven and earth', and so on. We have seen that the first purpose of the temple was to be a dwelling place for the god. In the temple the god was present on earth, for the good of the city and kingdom. His presence was symbolized by the image of the god, which stood in a separate room, corresponding to the Holy of Holies in the Israelite temple. The presence of the god in this image seems to have been thought of in a very concrete form. When the image was carried in procession in the city, or to a nearby city, it was the god himself who was there, or who went on a visit to another god in his sanctuary. And if an image of a god was carried away by a conqueror, this signified that the god had abandoned his city in wrath.

The temple was the place where the god held court, and where men waited on him. The image of the god was dressed and was served with food. This was the duty of the temple staff, and the public in general had no right of access to the temple. At least in a number of cases one could see the image of the god in a niche through a series of doorways. It was only at the great festivals that the people took part and the deity, i.e. his image, appeared before the multitude. The task of the temple was therefore primarily the official cult on behalf of the city and people. To what extent the temple was at the service of the individual is not clear in detail. We know that oaths and ordeals were administered through the temple, while divination and incantations were looked after by specialists, who sometimes, but not always, were connected with temples.

We do not know exactly how the presence of the god in the

image was understood. In the myths we are shown the gods on the cosmic level. Men were conscious that the images were the work of men's hands, but they were consecrated through special nocturnal rituals as instruments for the presence of the deity. They were given 'life', their mouth 'was opened' (*pet pî*) and washed (*mes pî*), so that they could see and eat, and acquired a distinctively holy quality.

Among the larger structures of the temple was included, as we have seen, a temple tower, *ziqqurrat*, which rose to the sky in stages. Its significance and symbolism have been the subjects of much discussion, but no really clear picture has been formed as a result. We know that in connection with the temple tower there is talk of a 'high temple' at the top and a 'low temple', and it has been thought that the god in normal instances was regarded as dwelling in the upper temple, and on certain occasions coming down to the lower. Others think that the 'high temple' was a resting place on the god's way from heaven to the temple on earth. In both cases the tower is a kind of staircase or ladder for him (cf. Gen. 11.3–5; 28.12). There are, however, signs which point towards an actual cult having been practised in the upper temple, and which suggest that the whole tower was regarded as a giant altar (it has been pointed out that Ezek. 43.13–17 describes an altar as a *ziqqurrat* in miniature). Other theories treat the tower as an image of the cosmic mountain where a dying and rising god 'lay buried'. But this view is at the moment quite unproven. The most probable view is that the tower in some way signified a connection between the world of the gods and our world.[39]

We have mentioned that in the temple of Enki in Eridu there was 'planted upon Apsu' a holy tree, *kiškanū*, which was the central point of various rites. A holy grove in the temple is also mentioned. Widengren assumes that every temple had a holy grove or garden with a 'tree of life' under the supervision of the king. He functioned as a 'master-gardener', who watered the tree of life, and so had power over life.[40] Strangely enough the term 'the tree of life' does not occur in any Akkadian text. Sidney Smith has asserted that a yearly renewal of the tree of life is mentioned in an Assyrian letter.[41] In fact no tree is mentioned, but only certain cult objects in the *akītu* house of Nabu and Tashmetu, which clearly underwent renewal. On the other hand, pictorial representations are found of the king carrying out certain rites with a stylized tree, which in modern literature on the subject is often described as the tree of life. It is probably a case of rites of fertility, but unfortunately no texts are known which describe in more detail the content of these pictures.

Rituals have been preserved for the restoration of temples. It appears that first in a nocturnal ceremony it was necessary as it were to destroy all that was old, to reduce it to chaos, and the expression of this included a lament for the destruction of the temple. Before the foundation stone was laid, a new ceremony including a recitation of a cosmogonic text enacted the creation by the gods of the material from which the new temple was to be built. It appears that similar rites of renewal were performed if the temple became impure for any reason, for example, if a dog had entered it. (Annual rites of purification in the temple seem to have had a different pattern.) In this connection attention should be drawn to the following psalm of lament:

> Into Eulmaš, thy sanctuary, the foe entered,
> Thy holy chamber he defiled,
> In thy holy place he set his foot,
> Thy far-famed dwelling he destroyed . . .
> How long, O my lady, has the mighty foe plundered thy sanctuary!
> In thy city, Erech, lamentation is raised . . .[42]

This text has been compared, not without reason, with Psalms 74 and 79 in the psalter. In both cases we may be dealing with a rite of purification of the sort that has been mentioned.

THE TEMPLE STAFF

The services of the temple required a large number of specialists. We know many different classes of priests, and in certain cases also have rituals preserved which give us valuable glimpses of their work.

In theory the king was the head of the cult, and he had, as we shall see in another connection, priestly titles and functions. In practice of course he had to delegate his functions to his subordinates.

The priesthood then was a collection of specialists, whose task was to mediate the contact between men and gods. They did not, however, form an organized hierarchy.[43] Different groups of

specialists formed guilds or colleges which often traced their origin
to some mythical forefather. There is evidence of fathers handing
on their priestly knowledge to their sons, but we do not know if
hereditary priesthood was the rule. In other cases it is clearly
knowledge and skill that are the decisive point. In the case of the
kalū priests we have, furthermore, evidence that their wisdom was
treated as secret, and could not be imparted to the uninitiated.

Our knowledge of the highest priestly offices is unfortunately
incomplete. *Enu* (Sumerian *en*) and *šangu* (Sumerian *sanga*) are
titles which originally applied to the priest-king or the king, but
are in later times also borne by other high priestly dignitaries. The
former according to Oppenheim 'may have related the temple and
its community to the deity in ways which differed from sanctuary
to sanctuary', the latter he thinks held the highest administrative
position inside the temple, while according to others he had over-
sight over sacrifices. In any case the kings of Assyria regularly
call themselves *šangū* of Assur. Another high priest is the *maḫḫu*
(Sumerian *maḫ*, 'high') whose function, however, cannot be more
exactly determined.

We often find the expression *ērib bīti* as a general description for
'priest'; it means literally 'he who may enter into the temple'. The
first place among them is held by the *šešgallu-* (*urigallu-*) priest,
whose name indicates that he acted as some sort of 'watchman' or
'supervisor'. Marduk's *šešgallu* in Babylon even had authority in
the ritual to take away from the king his insignia and to restore
them again.

Two classes of priests have as their task incantations and ceremonies of purification against the harmful activity of demons and
magicians: the *āšipu* seems primarily to have been at the service
of the individual, and to have carried out his rites in the home; the
mašmašu has, furthermore, a function in the official cult, with rites
such as purification of the temple. The task of the *kalū*-priest is to
appease the wrath of the gods with song and music.

There were, furthermore, singers, *nāru* and *zammeru* (feminine
as well as masculine), craftsmen (*mārē ummāni*) and 'swordbearers'
(*nāš paṭri*), as well as others.

Different sorts of divination were looked after by *bārū* ('observers'), *šā'ilu* ('askers'), and at least in certain areas *muḫḫū* or
maḫḫū (ecstatic 'prophets').

In certain cultic acts, especially in the Ishtar cult, castrated priests are found, *kurgarū* and *assinnu*. The cultic staff of Ishtar also included female prostitutes with various titles, the exact significance of which is not clear: *qadištu* (Hebrew *qᵉdēšā*, temple prostitute), *nadītu* ('infertile'), *kulmašitu*, *ḫarimtu* ('consecrated'), *šamḫatu* ('prostitute'), *ištarītu* ('one belonging to Ishtar'), and others.

The priests certainly had special priestly robes. Ritual nakedness had fallen into disuse. Linen robes of various colours were used. In ceremonies of expiation purple-coloured clothes were worn. Pictures show priests with a head-covering rather like a fez. Pictures are found from the neo-Assyrian period which indicate that in certain ceremonies priests wore animal masks.

CULTIC ACTIONS

As we have indicated already the object of the cult was in the first place to give the gods their due provision and to ensure their well-being. This appears also from the usual name for it, *dullu*, 'service', 'work'.

Generally the gods were 'served' with two meals a day, a main one in the morning and a smaller one in the evening. Each meal consisted of two sections, or courses, a 'larger' main dish, and a 'smaller' one. All sorts of food and drink were set out: meat, fowl, fish, fruit, oil, milk, wine, honey, etc. Apart from this incense was burnt, because the gods were thought to take special pleasure in the smell. Drinks were poured out before the images of the gods. It is not said how the god is thought of as availing himself of the food, but we know that a curtain was drawn before the table of the god while he 'ate'—just as the king could not be seen by the multitude when he sat at table. There is evidence that the dishes from the table of the god were sent on to the king to be eaten by him, but it is possible that this is only true of certain occasions; it is inconceivable that the king should have consumed everything that was offered in sacrifice. In any case the idea is clearly that in this way the king comes to share in the blessing of the god. The priests had their share of the sacrificial offerings, but there is no clear evidence that they ate any of the food left over from the table of the god.

It is usually assumed that the blood from the animal sacrifices was poured out before the image of the god and that the sacrifice with blood was therefore called *niqû*, literally 'outpouring'. On the other hand, Oppenheim asserts that blood had no cultic or magical significance in Akkadian religion. In any case there is no single instance attested of the word *damu*, 'blood', occurring in such a context. There is also a clear difference over against Israel in that the burning of the sacrifice as a means of transferring it to the divine world does not occur. If fire is sometimes praised as necessary for sacrifice, this refers to the burning of incense which accompanied every sacrifice.

Certain animals or articles of food were forbidden in the cult of certain deities; so, for example, birds were not allowed in sacrifices to chthonic deities, and sheep were forbidden for other gods. It is clear that ancient ideas of taboo are involved here.

We find a quite different idea in certain rites of expiation and incantation: an animal is a replacement or substitute (*pūḫu*, *dinānu*) for a man. It is the sacrificial animal that the anger of the gods (or of the demons) falls upon. One incantation ritual says: 'put the pig in his (the sick man's) place, flesh for his flesh, blood for his blood, may they (the demons) accept it!' An incantation rite against 'the evil demons' (*utukkē lemnūti*) says: 'The lamb is a representative (*dinānu*) of the man; for his life shall he give the lamb: the head of the lamb shall he give for his head, the neck of the lamb shall he give for his neck, the breast of the lamb for his breast.'

The same idea is expressed in a treaty between prince Mati'el of Arpad and the king of Assyria. A ram is offered, and it is explained that its head is the head of Mati'el, its thigh is the thigh of Mati'el, his sons and his people; if they transgress the terms of the convenant, their fate will be that of the sacrificial beast.

Sacrificial meals were regularly set out for the deities every day. But there were special days which required extra sacrifices and special ceremonies. Every day was sacred to a particular god. Special lists, the so-called hemerologies, enumerate these, and mark the lucky and dangerous ('evil') days. The seventh, fourteenth, nineteenth, twenty-first, and twenty-eighth of each month are especially unlucky. This has been thought to be an early stage in the development of the seven-day week and the institution of the sabbath, but it should be noted that while men abstained from certain activities on these days, the cause was not the same as in the case of the Israelite sabbath: these days were evil and danger-ous, while the sabbath had a positive value. Special feast days in each month were, for instance, the day of the new moon (the first) and the day of the full moon (the fifteenth), which was later called *šapattu*. There is perhaps some connection here with the Israelite *šabbāth*, the sabbath; it is interesting that the phrase 'new moons and sabbaths' is found in the oldest parts of the Old Testament.

Apart from this every sanctuary had its special feast days, as appears from the different festival calendars. Perhaps the most important feast, in any case that which has attracted most interest from scholars, is the *akītu* festival,[44] which at least in Babylon and probably also in Assyria was a New Year Feast. There were also other *akītu* festivals, but we are not so well-informed about these. Since it appears that the course of the Babylonian and of the Assyrian feasts were quite different, we shall treat each of them separately now.

The Babylonian *akītu* festival was celebrated on the first eleven days of the month Nisan at the vernal equinox. From the second to the fifth day of the month we have preserved a quite detailed ritual from the Seleucid period,[45] but it is unfortunately mostly concerned with the preparatory ceremonies. On the second of Nisan we hear primarily of the prayer of the *šešhgallu* priest (the word was earlier read *urigallu*) to Marduk, in which he speaks of the god's victory over his enemies, and prays for his mercy towards the city, the people, and the temple. On the third of Nisan two images of wood, gold, and precious stones were made, which were then to be used in a ceremony on the sixth. On the fourth of Nisan the *šešhgallu* greeted the rise of a certain constellation early in the morning with a special incantation; in the evening the Epic of Creation was to be recited.

On the fifth day the temple of Marduk was purified. A sheep was killed and its body carried around the temple, clearly to take upon itself all that was evil and unclean; then it was thrown into the river, and took with itself all the uncleanness. We are reminded of the scapegoat on the Israelite Day of Atonement (Lev. 16). Somewhat later the king went in to the statue of Marduk, where the *šešhgallu*-priest took from him his royal insignia and laid them down before Marduk. The priest struck the king's face, and pulled his ears. The king had to bow the knee before Marduk and to make a declaration that he had not neglected certain sacred duties (a 'negative confession'):

I have not sinned, O lord of the lands, I have not been negligent
  in respect of your divinity;
I have not destroyed Babylon, I have not let it be subverted;
I have not . . . Esagila, I have not forgotten its rites,
I have not struck a subordinate on the cheek,
I have not humiliated them,
I have taken care of Babylon,
I have not broken down its walls.

After this there is a gap in the text, and then the *šešhgallu*-priest
is speaking:

Fear not . . .
. . . which Bel . . .
Bel will hear your prayer . . .
he will uphold your kingship,
he will make your dominion strong . . .
Bel will bless you for ever,
he will destroy your enemies,
he will smite down your opponents.

After this 'absolution' the king received back his position and was
given his insignia again. The priest had to smite his cheek once
more, and it was regarded as of significance for the future whether
this brought tears to his eyes or not. The point of this whole
ceremony is clearly to hold the king responsible to Marduk once a
year and to renew his kingship. It has been assumed that the king
was thought of as suffering vicariously on behalf of the sins of the
people, and so atoning for them, but this is not expressed at least
in the texts of the ritual. After this in the evening there followed
a ceremony with a bull and a pyre which was ignited. Here
unfortunately the text is broken, and the continuation has been
lost. For a reconstruction of the ritual of the remaining days we
have to rely on allusions in various texts which are not directly
connected with the *akītu* festival. We know that Nabu (i.e. his
statue) arrived on the fifth of Nisan from the neighbouring city
of Borsippa to take part in the festival, and stayed in Babylon
until the twelfth. It also appears that in some way he took part
in a ceremony on the sixth of Nisan, when the images made on
the second were destroyed. We know further that on the eighth
and eleventh of Nisan Marduk is on the 'throne of destiny' (*parak*

šīmāti); we may assume that we have here a ceremony for 'the determining of destiny', and we may be reminded of the scenes of the determining of destinies in the Creation Epic.

Several texts refer to the king 'taking Marduk's hand'; this is an expression for his leading the statue of the god out in procession. It goes to the *akītu*-house outside the city (*ina ṣēri*, 'in the field') where special ceremonies took place. We know that the procession went there on the tenth of Nisan, and returned to Esagila on the eleventh. What happened in the *akītu*-house has long been the subject of all sorts of conjectures. Three recently found allusions show that Marduk's triumph over Tiamat was celebrated,[46] clearly through some sort of cultic drama. This theory is supported by the fact that the *akītu*-house erected by Sennacherib in Assur contained pictorial representations of the creation struggle.[47] It seems to have been the case that Sennacherib was represented in the role of the god Assur as the victor over Tiamat. We may draw the conclusion that at least in Assur the king 'played' the god in the 'sham fight' of the cultic drama.

There is, furthermore, a fragmentary text, a sort of festival calendar, where in connection with the *akītu* festival in Nisan it is said that Marduk 'hastened to the wedding' from the *akītu*-house. This seems to indicate that a *hieros gamos* ceremony was a part of the feast, and that this was celebrated in the main temple Esagila. It seems a reasonable suggestion in view of the Sumerian heritage that the second determination of the destinies took place in connection with this. We have more explicit evidence about the sacred marriage of Nabu and Tashmetu, from which we learn that they stayed in the bedchamber from the fifth to the tenth day of the month. So long a time seems to be excluded in the case of Marduk. Here it must be a matter of a single night only.

We come finally to a very controversial question, that of Marduk's supposed cultic death and resurrection in the *akītu* festival. The feast is sometimes called 'Marduk's *tabê*' (i.e. resurrection), and it has been supposed that this is an indication that the 'Tammuz theme' of the death and resurrection of the god had been transferred to Marduk and was expressed in the rites of the feast. However, the verb *tebû* means simply 'rise', 'stand up', 'start', and the reference could as well be to the beginning of a procession (cf. the verb *qûm*, 'stand up', of Yahweh in the Song of the Ark, Num. 10.35).

Further support for the theory of a death and resurrection of Marduk has been found in a strange text which seems to form a commentary on, or symbolic exposition of, certain cultic ceremonies which were apparently connected with the *akītu* festival, and which have Marduk and his consort as the principal characters.[48]

The character of the text appears from the following excerpts:

... [it is Bel who is] shut up [in the mountain] ... his lord's messenger: 'who brings him out?' ... [...] goes; he goes to 'the mountain' ... Nabu who comes from Borsippa; [he comes] for the safety of his captive father [...] who runs through the streets, seeks Bel: 'Where is he held captive?' [...] who spreads out her hands; she prays to Sin and Shamash: 'Bring Bel back to life' (or 'keep Bel alive') ... those who stand at the gate of Esagila are his guards, who are placed to guard him [...] after the gods had shut him in; [...] they have carried him down from there ... After Bel went to the 'mountain' the city is in confusion on account of him; they fight in it ...

The *mašmašhu* priests who go before him and recite an incantation, they are his people who mourn for him. The *mahhu* priest who goes before the mistress of Babylon is a messenger who weeps at her breast: 'They have taken him to the "mountain"'. She cries: 'my brother, my brother' ... *Enūma eliš*, which is recited before Bel in Nisan, it concerns him who is in captivity; he makes prayers to them, calls upon them. [Father Shamash?], he says: 'It is good for Assur, he did it, what then is his sin?' [...] who looks to heaven, prays to Sin and Shamash: 'Let me live'. [He] who looks towards the earth ... he comes out of the 'mountain' [... who] does not go out with Bel to the *akītu* house, bears a prisoner's [...]; he sits with him ... [...] before which a pig is slaughtered on the eighth of Nisan [...] the mistress of the house asks: 'Who is the transgressor?' ... The foot-race that was performed in Nisan before Bel and all the cities: when Assur sent Ninurta to take Anzu captive the god said [...] before Assur: 'Anzu is taken.' Anu said: 'Go, report it before all the gods.' He reports it and [they rejoice] over it ... The cart that goes to the *akītu* house and comes: its lord is not upon it, without its lord it sways along ... He entered in to the temple and bolted the door. They made holes in the door and are fighting inside.

Here the text itself comes to an end, and there follows a curse on those who do not make its content known to the ignorant. (This is striking, because such texts usually conclude with an injunction not to impart their content to the uninitiated.)

Since Zimmern drew attention to this text in 1918, it has been taken for granted that it tells of how Marduk was held captive in the underworld ('the mountain'), while his consort and the city seek for him, after which he is in the end freed and returns to life. This interpretation has, however, now met with strong opposition in an article by von Soden, published in 1955. He observes there that the text is written in the Assyrian dialect and cannot therefore be from Babylon. Further he interprets *ḫursānu* not as 'mountain' (which it certainly may mean) but as 'place of ordeal' and observes that all the passages that could allude to the death of Marduk *can* also be interpreted differently, while there is no mention of a final triumph. He would therefore understand the text as an Assyrian propaganda work directed against the introduction of the cult of Marduk in Assyria, and makes it allude to a process of ordeal, in which Marduk is the accused.

The objection can of course be made that it is a somewhat unexpected form for a propaganda text to take, and that it would hardly have been chosen if there were not some cultic realities for it to allude to. And when von Soden also argues from what is possible, or conceivable, or not in question with a Babylonian god, his reasoning is somewhat *a priori*. Probably the last word has still not been said about this text, which even if it does not deal with the death and resurrection of Marduk, clearly speaks of his humiliation in forms which *may* reflect cultic actions.

There are also two other similar commentary texts, which interpret cultic actions in obscure language. One tells of how Kingu is burnt up by fire, and how the hostile deities, Anzu and Ashakku, are defeated, and it appears that the king performs actions which represent what Marduk did in the myth.[49] The other mentions that a bull which 'is thrown live into bitumen (?)' is Kingu, and that a dove which is divided into two halves is Tiamat, which was indeed cloven by Marduk. It is also said that a cart which goes without a seat bears the body of Enmesharra and is drawn by horses which represent Anzu, while the cart is driven by the king, who 'is' Ninurta.[50] It would appear that elements from the myth of Ninurta have been taken up here and united with the myth of creation. In any case it is clear that the king plays the part of the god in the cultic drama, whose purpose is to actualize the myth and renew its results.

For Assyria we have evidence for the *akītu* festival in a number of different cities and at different times of the year. Our information is best about the festival at Assur. It was celebrated in the month of Nisan, but seems to have lasted at least twenty days. It appears from the previously mentioned pictures in the *akītu* house that the work of creation was one of the basic motifs of the festival. On the other hand, in contrast to the Babylonian festival, one of the main themes was a banquet, *tākultu*, to which all the gods were formally invited by name; it concluded in a prayer for a long and successful reign for the king.[51] The position of the king was different here from that in Babylon; he took the lead the whole time, and a humiliation such as that found in Babylon is inconceivable in Assyria. There is a ritual which was described by its first editor as a coronation ritual,[52] but which is perhaps better taken as a ritual for the renewal of kingship in the *akītu* festival.[53] Here a procession is first described in which the king takes part, while a priest cries 'Assur is king! Assur is king!' (cf. 'Marduk is king' in the Creation Epic). Then follow sacrifices which the king offers, and a coronation ceremony, in which the priest of the god Assur gives the king the crown and sceptre, and utters a prayer of blessing. Then the officials appear before him and lay down their offices, whereupon they are restored to office by the king (in Babylon it is the king himself who has to undergo this!).

Finally, from Uruk we have a number of ritual texts for the two *akītu* festivals of Anu, one in Nisan, the other in Tishrit (September–October). Here a whole series of different ceremonies are described in detail, without any real information being given about their content. There is an interesting description of the great procession with details of the hymns and incantations to be performed at the different stages of the journey: 'the king sets out', 'King of heaven and earth', 'Great Anu, may heaven and earth bless you', 'Anu, my king, to your gracious heart', etc.[54]

It is in any case clear that the *akītu* festival is a feast of joy and triumph, which is connected with the beginning of a new period of time (the year, the season of the year) and the renewal of the forces of nature in connection with this. The ancient *hieros gamos* rite has been united with it, since it too had as its purpose the renewal of the forces of life and creation of a 'kingdom of god'.

INCANTATIONS

The sacrificial cult and the festivals were public occasions. The king was responsible for them on behalf of the people. The individual took part only indirectly in these forms of cult. On the other hand, there were other forms of cultic activity which directly concerned the individual. Among these were incantations and the art of divination.

It was believed that the life of men was constantly threatened by evil powers or demons which caused sickness and suffering. In the normal way man was protected by his god, but if he incurred the wrath of the god the demons had free play. He could also be attacked by witchcraft, i.e. magic arts practised by wizards.

A belief in demons played a very important part, therefore, in the life of ancient Mesopotamia. Not even the gods were thought of as free from the attacks of the demons: there is a text which speaks of how 'the seven evil' demons attacked Sin, so that the moon was darkened. Different groups were distinguished among the demons, which themselves were countless in number; men spoke, for instance, of 'the seven' or of 'the evil spirits' (*utukkē lemnūti*)—in fact a number of them were credited with real individuality, for example Lamashtu, a female demon which attacked women in childbirth, Namtaru, the demon of the plague, Pazuzu, the south-west wind which causes malaria, Rābiṣu, 'the lier in wait', Lilitu, who disturbs rest at night and who appears also in the Bible (Isa. 34.14). More general descriptions are *alū* and *gallu*, monsters without faces, who tear in pieces those whom they get into their power. The spirits of the dead, *eṭimmu*, can also cause all sorts of mischief.

The seven evil spirits are vividly described in an incantation text:

> Seven they are, seven they are,
> in the caves of the underworld, seven they are,
> sitting down in heaven, seven they are;
> in a cave in the depths of the underworld they have grown up,
> they are neither male nor female,

destructive whirlwinds they are,
they have not taken to themselves wives and they have not
    begotten children.
They are not acquainted with compassion and mercy,
they do not hearken to prayer and invocation,
grown up horses on the mountain they are,
hostile to Ea they are,
mighty among the gods they are.
They cause disasters on the roads, on the roads of the land they
    lie and crouch,
evil they are, evil they are,
seven they are, seven they are, seven times seven they are.

Amulets are employed against the demons as a means of protection. If in spite of everything one comes into their power, one must
have recourse to a ceremony of incantation (*šiptu*=incantation).
A specialist (*āšipu* or *mašmašu*, incantation priest, exorcist) was
called in, and he found out which demon or demons were troubling
the man concerned, and carried out the ceremonies which he
decided were required in each particular case.[55]
    A number of collections of prescriptions and rituals for such
occasions are preserved to us which are in effect handbooks in the
art of incantation. The two best known are called *Šurpu* and
Maqlū.[56] Both these words mean 'fire' or 'burning', and show the
important part that fire played in these rituals. In the former case
fire served as a means to remove sin and uncleanness, in the latter
it served to set at nought the magic powers of the wizards. Another
important collection is called simply *Utukkē lemnūti*, 'the evil
spirits';[57] it contains incantations against certain specified types
of demons. But there are also many other texts. A catalogue of
them gives rubrics such as, for example, 'headaches', 'toothaches',
'to loose a curse', 'snake-bite', 'rites for town, house, field, orchard,
and river', etc.
    As regards the methods of incantation, it is interesting to note
how practical measures, different sorts of magic and prayer to the
gods are mixed up together. An incantation against toothache, for
instance, contains a mythical introduction concerning the worm
which causes the pain, but also a command to pull out the tooth
and finally a prayer that Ea may 'smite' the worm. It is clear that
the Babylonians themselves made no distinction between 'religion'

and 'magic', such as the historians of religion of our own day have made at their desks, and that they did not even draw a clear line between rational (medicinal) and irrational (magical or religious) measures.

Sympathetic magic plays an important part. In instructions concerning a man who has been attacked by a *gallu*-demon and therefore has been assailed by 'silence, an evil curse, a spell, a headache' and has been abandoned by 'his god and his goddess' he is treated thus:

> Take him to the pure ablution-house,
> loose his spell, loose his spell,
> that the activating evil of his body,
> whether the curse of his father,
>   or the curse of his mother,
>   or the curse of his elder brother,
>   or the curse of the murder of a man he does not know,
> By the conjuration of Ea
> Let the curse be peeled off like this onion,
> Let it be wrenched apart like this date,
> Let it be untwined like this wick.

For each of the three objects which is destroyed in the ritual there follows a special incantation, for example:

> Like this onion which he peels and throws into the fire,
> which the fire consumes entirely . . .
> whose roots will not take hold in the soil,
> whose shoots will not sprout,
> that will not be used for the meal of a god or a king,
> so may oath, curse . . . sickness,
> weariness, guilt, sin, wickedness, transgression,
> the sickness that is in my body, my flesh or my limbs,
> be peeled off like this onion;
> may the fire consume it entirely today;
> may the curse be taken away that I may see the light.[58]

The reference to 'the pure ablution-house' indicates that this ceremony was carried out in a special sanctuary. Otherwise the rites of incantation could take place in the home, in the sick-room, or in any other place in case of need.

In other ceremonies the thought of substitution which has

already been mentioned plays a leading part. A text from Assur
gives the following instructions for a man 'wanted by the goddess
of death': at sunset a kid is to be placed in his bed. In the morning
the sick man shall carry the kid to a house where there is a tamarisk.
The priest shall make them both lie on the ground and touch the
throat of the sick man with a wooden dagger and cut the throat of
the kid with a bronze dagger. Then he is to dress the kid like a man
and put the turban of the sick man on it and treat it like a dead
man. The sick man is to give the priest his clothes and go away,
the kid is to be lamented and buried. In this way, therefore, the
goddess of death has received a kid as substitute for the man, the
kid has, as it were, taken the place of the sick man and died in his
place.[59]

In other cases again the attempt was made to catch the demons
in an object and then get rid of it. For example, a clay image was
made of the demon in question and it was placed by the head of the
sick man for a time; then it was removed, beaten, and buried.
Clearly the idea was that the demon goes into the image and so
shares its fate when it is destroyed.[60] In another case instructions
are given for a man who cannot open his mouth that a goat is to be
placed by his head and then together with a staff, a cup, and a
bough, is carried out into the country, where the goat is put to
death, skinned, and cooked, after which the bough is dressed in the
skin and the forelegs are tied together, and so on. 'That man will
live. The god who is on him will depart, whereupon he will open
his mouth and eat food and drink water'.[61] The demon of the
sickness is thus rendered harmless by the destruction of the goat.

We see an interesting aspect of the technique of incantation in
the so-called *bīt-rimki* series, which deals with certain rites of
incantation which the king had to go through in 'the ablution-
house' to ward off certain disasters. The ritual shows Ea sending
his priest as a messenger to the sun-god with a request to judge
between the king and the demons. This presentation of man's
cause before the judgement-seat of Shamash, which also occurs in
other incantations, is described as 'being at the place of the Sun-
god' (*Ki-ᵈUtu-kam*); this is an allusion to the fact that the lawsuit
ritual was performed before the sun at sunrise.[62] The idea, therefore, is that the sun-god in his capacity as judge of the world
secures justice for man over against the demonic powers.

It should be mentioned that it was not only evil powers that affected men. There were also good ones, protecting spirits, such as *šēdu* and *lamassu*, which were well-disposed towards men and protected them from all sorts of disasters. Images of such protecting spirits were often placed at the gates of palaces and houses; they had the bodies of bulls and the faces of men. At a later period they were sometimes called *kuribu* (cf. the cherubim of the Bible).

DIVINATION

Divination[63] presupposes the idea that the gods have determined the destinies of men and that through various occurrences or signs they let them know their will and their purposes. As a rule such information is intended as a warning, so that a man should be able to avoid a disaster which threatens. It is therefore not a question of an inflexible destiny, but of disasters which can be avoided or averted (through special rites of purification, *namburbē*) or of a choice between two possibilities, of which one is fortunate, the other unfortunate.

Divination is already attested in the Sumerian period: Gudea has inquiries made in various ways into the most propitious day to begin the building of the temple, and we also hear of how he learnt the will of the gods through dreams. But strangely enough it is only in the Babylonian and Assyrian period that we have systematic presentations of divinatory methods, whole series of tablets which explain the significance of different signs. They generally consist of long lists, where the sign is described in a conditional clause, and the interpretation is given in the following main clause, for example: 'If a man treads on a lizard and kills it, he will prevail over his adversary.' By and large the methods can be divided into two categories: in one the man himself brings about the sign which is thought of as communicating the will of the god, in the other he observes events and occurrences which take place without intentional action on his part, and interprets them as a message from the gods.

Such interpretations naturally need specialists. There were, as we have seen, two classes of priests which were responsible for divination, *šā'ilu* ('asker') and *bārū* ('observer').[64] We know that the former was concerned among other things with the interpretation of dreams, but apart from this we cannot delimit the functions of the two types. The technique of oracles was under the protection of Shamash and Adad, and in several cases we have prayers for use before recourse to an oracle, in which these gods are invoked for a reliable and fortunate answer.

In the case of technical oracles, i.e. such that in some way the sign is first brought about and then interpreted, this can to a certain extent be regarded as a way to ask the advice of the deity. A question is formulated, and the sign is made to give the answer. The custom of casting lots and throwing dice is one such method. These occurred in ancient Mesopotamia too, but do not appear to have had any cultic status.[65] In Ezek. 21.21 it is said that the king of Babylon employed arrows for casting lots, but although this is a very widespread technique, it has not up till now been found mentioned in Babylonian sources.

Another technical method of obtaining oracles is lecanomancy, or cup divination. This is done by letting drops of oil fall into a cup with water in it, and then observing the shapes which are formed. The principle is the same as in the reading of tea-leaves of a more modern period.

Extispicy, i.e. the observation of the entrails of the sacrificial beast, had an important place among methods of divination.[66] It was of two types, one which concentrated on the liver, one which took into consideration all the entrails. The former, which is represented, for instance, by a number of models of the liver in clay with explanations inscribed on them, is a widespread phenomenon, and occurs also, as is well known, among the Etruscans, while the latter type seems to have evolved in Mesopotamia. Before divination was begun prayer was made to Shamash and Adad to 'write' their message upon the entrails of the sacrificial animal.

As regards the other main type of divination, the observation of uncaused events, augury or observation of birds is of special interest, because this is widespread also in Asia Minor (the Etruscans may in fact have come from here), Syria, and Palestine, and appears to be a substratum phenomenon, i.e. it existed in the land before the Sumerians and Akkadians arrived there.[67] However, the omen literature deals with a large number of other observations, for example the animals one meets and how they behave, malformed young of animals, etc. This has developed into a whole science, which claims to depend upon experience. If a certain observation was once followed by a particular event, it was expected that the same consequence would always follow when the same phenomenon was encountered again. In a number of cases a general conclusion is not given, but an historical event is recounted which has occurred after a certain omen. It is clearly thought that history repeats itself, so that one can learn from what has happened in the past. In other cases we clearly also have further speculations arising from specific observations. A certain regularity in life is always presupposed, so that the same phenomenon always has the same consequences.

Among these omens can also be counted observations of celestial and meteorological phenomena, such as haloes around the sun and moon, eclipses, etc. In course of time observations of the heavenly bodies are developed to an astrological system.[68] The planets are each connected with a god, and their course in heaven is assigned significance for events on earth. The starry sky is sometimes called 'the book of heaven' (*šiṭir šamê*), i.e. a writing which reveals the intentions of the gods. In the Creation Epic it is said that the earth is a copy of heaven, so that what happens up there has its corresponding event on earth. We do not know for certain when and where the theory arose that a man's life depends on the position of the stars at the moment of birth, which led to the establishment of the horoscope, but there is much to suggest that it was precisely in Babylonia, where the oldest known horoscopes come from 410 B.C., while examples from Egypt and Greece do not go back further in time than the first century B.C.

Apart from this we meet from time to time in the texts seers of an ecstatic type, *maḫḫû*.[69] Most of the examples come from the border territories to the west (Mari, Asia Minor, and at a late date Assyria, possibly under Aramaean influence). They have in general a low social status and are often associated with witchcraft. An exception is the prophetesses of Ishtar, who pronounced the will of the goddess either in the third person, or in the first person as if the goddess was speaking through them. In a number of cases the *maḫḫû* seem to have received their revelations in the form of dreams.

Of special interest are the *maḫḫû* oracles which have been found at Mari.[70] Here we have examples of such 'prophets' who spontaneously received messages from a deity and then passed them on to the ruler. So we are told, for instance, in a letter about a man who in a dream felt himself translated to the temple of Dagan, and there received the following message from the god: 'Go! I am

sending you to Zimrilim (the king); you shall say to him: Send
your messengers to me and make a full report to me. Then I shall
make the princes of the Benjaminites flounder in a basket of fish,
and set them before you.' In another case the writer of the letter
reports that a *maḥḥû* came with the message: 'The god has sent
me; send quickly a message to the king to make a sacrifice for the
dead to the spirit of Yahdunlim.' The formal similarity to the
prophets of the Old Testament should be noted, a similarity which
is perhaps even more striking in the following text:

> In oracles has Adad, lord of Kallassu, spoken thus: 'Am I not
> Adad, lord of Kallassu, who have brought him (the king) up on my
> knee and set him upon the throne of his father's line? After I
> set him upon his father's throne, I have also given him a dwell-
> ing. Now, as I have set him upon the throne, so I can take
> Niḫlatu out of his hand. If he does not fulfil the provision (of
> sacrificial animals), I am lord over the throne, the district and
> the city, and I can take from him what I have given him. But
> if he fulfils my desire, I shall give him thrones upon thrones,
> houses upon houses, districts upon districts, cities upon cities,
> and I shall give him the land from the west to the east.

It is interesting that the god here takes the initiative through the
prophet in the same manner as in the Old Testament, and that the
god appears as one who appoints and deposes kings according to
their obedience or disobedience.

From a purely technical point of view we can note that dreams
and direct revelations appear to alternate. In one case a man
dreams that together with another he goes into the temple of
Dagan and falls down before him, that the god then speaks directly
to him, and that thereafter he makes a sacrifice. This presupposes,
therefore, that the word of revelation is received in the course of a
cultic action.

A number of oracular answers are preserved, especially from
Assyria. These utter words of encouragement to the king and
promise him divine assistance. It does not appear from the text
whether these have been communicated on the basis of the
observation of sacrificial animals or through direct revelation given
in ecstasy, but in many cases we do know which priest or priestess
has mediated the oracle. Most of them are characterized by the
introductory words 'Fear not' [*lā tapallaḥ*]. Two examples follow:

Fear not, Esarhaddon! I, the god Bel, speak to you. The beams
of your heart I strengthen, like your mother, who caused you to
exist. Sixty great gods are standing together with me and
protect you. The god Sin is at your right, the god Shamash at
your left; sixty great gods stand round about you, ranged for
battle. Do not trust men! Turn your eyes to me, look at me! I am
Ishtar of Arbela; I have turned Assur's favour unto you. When
you were small I sustained you. Fear not, praise me!

Fear not, O Assurbanipal! Now, as I have spoken, it will come
to pass: I shall grant (it) to you. Over the people of the four
languages (and) over the armament of the princes you will
exercise sovereignty . . . (The kings) of the countries confer
together (saying), 'Come, (let us rise) against Assurbanipal . . .
The fate of our fathers and our grandfathers (the Assyrians) have
fixed; [Let not his might] cause divisions among us!' [Nin]lil
answered saying: '[The kings] of the lands [I shall over]throw,
place under the yoke, bind their feet in [strong fetters]. For the
second time I proclaim to you that as with the land of Elam and
the Cimmerians [I shall proceed]. I shall arise, break the thorns,
open up widely my way through the briers. With blood shall I
turn the land into a rain shower, (fill it with) lamentation and
wailing. . . . Fear not, my son, whom I have raised.[71]

It should be mentioned in this connection that there are also oracles
which kings have received directly in dreams. In form they differ
hardly at all from the oracles which we have given.

There are some texts in the form of prophecies, whose function
has still not been established with certainty. These are a series of
pronouncements on the appearance of certain kings whose names
are not given, and their good or bad reigns. Here are a few examples:

[A prince will arise] and rule for eighteen years. The land will
rest secure, fare well, (and its) people will [enjoy] prosperity.
The gods will ordain good things for the land, favourable winds
[will blow]. The . . . and the furrow will yield abundant crops.
Sakkan (the god of beasts) and Nisaba (the god of grain) will . . .
in the land. There will be rain and floods. The people will enjoy
themselves. But that prince will be put to the sword in a revolution.

A prince will arise and rule for thirteen years. There will be an Elamite attack on Akkad and the booty of Akkad will be carried off. The shrines of the great gods will be destroyed. Akkad will suffer a defeat. There will be confusion, disturbance and disorder in the land. The nobility will lose prestige. Another man who is unknown will arise, seize the throne as king, and put his grandees to the sword . . .

. . . At the conquest of Babylon the builder of that palace will lament. That prince will suffer misfortune. He will not be happy. During his reign battle and strife will not cease. In that reign brother will eat brother (and) people will sell their children. All the lands will fall into anarchy. Husband will abandon wife and wife will leave husband. Mother will bar the door to daughter. The property of Babylon will enter Subartu and Assyria. The king of Babylon will send out the possessions of his palace, his property, to the prince of Aššur in Assyria.[72]

Are we dealing here with real events, which for some reason have been presented in the form of prophecies? If so, it is impossible to identify them with the help of the vague allusions. The idea behind these texts is perhaps that history repeats itself, and that one can therefore derive instruction for the future from what has happened in the past. Perhaps the intention of the authors is to criticize rulers and their manner of ruling in veiled language. In certain cases there seems to be a connection between the king's manner of ruling and his fate. The last example quoted is interesting for its description of the disintegration of community and family, which is somewhat reminiscent of Mic. 7.6.

We have an interesting further development of the literary form of the omen in an old Babylonian text, which has been described by its editor Kraus as 'a moral code in the form of an omen'.[73] In the part corresponding to the omen text's description of the sign found (expressed in a conditional clause), there is given a certain ethical action, in the apodosis the consequences of the action are given. Here we are of course dealing with a purely literary imitation.

Another text influenced by the form of the omen literature is one which Böhl called 'the Babylonian "mirror of princes"'.[74] A couple of excerpts will show its nature:

If a king does not heed justice, his people will be thrown into
chaos, and his land will be devastated . . .

If he does not heed his nobles, his life will be cut short. . . .

If he heeds the message of Ea, the great gods will lead him
by oracles in the ways of righteousness.

KINGSHIP

It appears that the reign of Hammurabi marks a change in the
way kingship is viewed, in that the usage of writing the king's name
with a determinative for 'god' then disappeared. On the other
hand, the king remained a person with sacral duties and functions,
and in most respects his special position in respect of religion
remained. A factor that is often neglected is that certain differences in the understanding of kingship existed as between Assyria
and Babylonia, so that the Assyrian king had a stronger and more
stable position than the Babylonian king.

Kingship was undoubtedly regarded as a divine institution. The
Etana myth tells of the time when sceptre, tiara, and staff were
deposited in heaven before Anu, and no king ruled mankind. Then
'kingship came down from heaven' and, it is implied, the people
received its divine leadership.[75] This means no doubt that it is the
office and not its holder that was of divine origin.

In spite of this, and in spite of the fact that the absence of the
determinative for 'god' with the name of the king indicates that the
king did not officially claim to be divine, it is not difficult to find
examples of his being treated as a sacred person, who in many
respects is different from ordinary men. It is often said, especially
of the Assyrian kings, that the supernatural (divine) radiance
(*melammû*) which surrounds them strikes fear into their enemies.[76]
There are many examples of kings and gods being pictured in the
same clothes, and it is not difficult to see an extensive similarity
between the epithets which are applied to the king and those
which are applied to various deities.[77] Other royal epithets emphasize a claim to world dominion, for example, *šar kiššati*, 'king of
the universe', *šar kibrātim arba'im*, 'king over the four points of the
compass'. In conformity with this the king is sometimes said to
reign 'from the Upper Sea (the Mediterranean) to the Lower
(the Persian Gulf)'.

It is often stated that the king is chosen by the gods for his office. Hammurabi says that Shamash fixed his shining look upon him, Shalmaneser was 'chosen (selected) with a shining look'. Esarhaddon has the gods direct their eyes upon him with joy and choose him as king. In other cases it is said that the king was chosen for his office already before he was born. Assurbanipal says that Assur and Sin 'from "far off days" named his name for dominion', Nabonidus assures us that Sin and Ningal, while he was still in his mother's womb, determined that he should be king. It has been claimed that these and similar phrases reflect a 'ritual of election', in which the king was first 'looked upon with favour by the gods', after which 'his name was named' and finally 'his destiny was fixed'.[78] But it seems more probable that these expressions are synonymous and describe divine election in different aspects. It can also be said that the king is 'sent' by the gods.[79]

In a number of special instances this idea has received mythological expression. The following legend is told in the first person of Sargon, the founder of the old Akkadian kingdom:

> Sargon, the mighty king, king of Agade am I. My mother was a changeling, my father I knew not. The brother(s) of my father loved the hills . . . My changeling mother conceived me, in secret she bore me. She set me in a basket of rushes, with bitumen she sealed my lid. She cast me into the river, which rose not (over) me. The river bore me up and carried me to Akki, the drawer of water. Akki the drawer of water lifted me out as he dipped his e[w]er. Akki, the drawer of water, [took me] as his son (and) reared me. Akki, the drawer of water, appointed me as his gardener. While I was a gardener, Ishtar granted me (her) love, and for four and [. . .] years I exercised kingship.[80]

It is strange that this legendary motif came to be applied to so many people. We know it from the Bible in connection with Moses, and from the story of Rome with Romulus and Remus; Herodotus tells it of the Persian king Cyrus. It is clearly intended to assert the divine protection which its hero is given. Here it is also connected with the idea of Ishtar's love and election of the new king.

A similar tendency underlies the following words, which Assurnasirpal directs towards Ishtar:

I was born amid mountains which no one knew,
I did not recognize thy might and did not pray to thee.
The Assyrians did not know of thy godhead and did not pray to
    thee.
But thou, O Ishtar, fearsome mistress of the gods,
Thou didst single me out with the glance of thine eyes; thou
    didst desire to see me rule.
Thou didst take me from among the mountains, thou didst call
    me to be a shepherd of men,
Thou didst grant me the sceptre of justice.[81]

Sargon was not of royal birth, and could for this reason have
needed to provide himself with legitimation. But Assurnasirpal
was the son of a king. Clearly, therefore, divine election was
regarded as more important than royal birth.

Even when the Persian king Cyrus had captured Babylon, he
justified his claim to dominion in the following manner: Marduk
'looked over all lands, and when he saw them, he sought a righteous
king after his heart, who could hold his hand (i.e. celebrate his
akitu festival). He named his name "Cyrus of Anshan" and determined his name for kingship over all.'[82]

The expressions which make the king son of a god or goddess go
yet further. We have already seen how Gudea declared that he
had neither father nor mother other than the goddess of the city.
Similar phrases are found, for example, in the case of Assurbanipal,
who says: 'I knew not father and mother; in the ... of my goddesses
I grew up.' The same king says to Adad: 'I am thy servant, ...
offspring of my god Assur and my goddess Aššuritu.' Another
time he addresses Ninlil: 'I am thy servant Assurbanipal whom
thy hands have formed without father and mother—whom thou,
queen, hast caused to reach maturity.'[83] Hammurabi declares that
he is son now of Sin, another time of Dagan, another time of
Marduk. This variation indicates clearly that sonship was not
understood physically but in some way symbolically. When it is
said that a deity has formed the king in his mother's womb (which
is quite common) the idea must be that he came into existence
with divine help, but this does not have to have been thought of
as a physical conception. In other cases one can compare the
personal names which describe a man as son of a deity; the idea is
here that he stands under the special protection of the deity. The

same is true of a passage such as the following, a dialogue between the god Nabu and King Assurbanipal: the god says:

> You are little, Assurbanipal, you whom I have entrusted to the Queen of Nineveh (Ishtar),
> You are a child, Assurbanipal, you who sit upon the knees of the goddess Queen of Nineveh;
> her four nipples are placed near your mouth; you suck two of them, you hide your face in the other two.[84]

There are even instances where the king is said to be the image of the god (for example, of Marduk or Shamash). It is also said: 'the shadow of the god is the man, and men are the shadow of the man. The man, he is the king, who is as it were an image of the god.'[85]

From one point of view, therefore, the king is a representative of the world of the gods over against his subjects. The Akkadian equivalent of the Sumerian royal title *ensi*, that is *iššakku*, perhaps gives expression to this idea; it is usually translated 'governor' or the like,[86] although the meaning is not completely certain. In any case the king is placed by this title in a specific relation to the national god: he is 'the *iššakku* of Assur'.

But the same idea appears in many other ways. When the king at the head of his armies fights against the enemies of the land (and this is true especially of the Assyrian king) he does this under divine commission and with divine strength. The victor lays upon the conquered people 'the yoke of his god', he punishes savagely those who have 'slandered the name of his god'.[87] It is the divine radiance of the king that inspires terror in the enemy. In the report of Esarhaddon's struggle for the throne Ishtar is said to have broken the bows of the enemy soldiers. Assurbanipal in his campaign against the Arabs received the help of 'the wild cow' Ninlil, 'who tosses the enemies on her powerful horns'. Esarhaddon says that the enemies 'trusted in their own strength', while he himself 'trusted in his lord Assur' and therefore was victorious. Typical expressions of these ideas are the epic poem *šar tamḫarim* ('the king of the battle'), which tells of Sargon's achievements, and what used to be called the Cuthean legend of his son Naramsin.[88] These show how the king through his exceptional endowments turns desperate situations into victory.

Tasks of a more peaceful nature are alluded to by the very

common royal epithet 'shepherd' (*rē'ū*).[89] The title goes back to the Sumerian period—in which it was perhaps associated with Dumuzi as shepherd—and was employed throughout the period with which we are dealing. Hammurabi called himself 'the shepherd named by Enlil', Assurnasirpal II says that he was appointed by Ishtar as 'shepherd of men', and in a dialogue from the neo-Babylonian period the king is called 'the shepherd, the sun (god) of the people'. As the shepherd had to care for his flock and protect it, so it was the duty of the king to care for and to defend his subjects. Hammurabi says:

> 'I am . . . the one . . . who assigns the pastures and watering places for Lagash and Girsu . . . I am . . . the founder of dwelling places for them . . . the shelter of the land, who gathered the scattered people of Isin . . . I . . . did not neglect the black-headed people whose shepherdship Marduk had entrusted to me, I sought peaceful regions for them.

In a letter to an Assyrian king a quotation is made from a song: 'All the people trust in thee, O shepherd, with the propitious utterance of thy mouth.'

It was the duty of the royal shepherd to make justice and righteousness prevail in the land. The texts speak of *mēšaru* and *kettu*, righteousness and justice (or truth), and by this mean both the cosmic laws which are of divine origin and the laws which are instituted by men. Hammurabi speaks of himself as 'the king of righteousness (*mēšaru*) to whom Shamash has entrusted justice (the law: *kettu*)'. He is called by Anu and Bel 'to promote the well-being of men, to create justice in the land, to destroy the evil and ill-willed, so that the strong should not oppress the weak'. Similar utterances are attested in respect of many kings. Special emphasis is placed on the duty of the ruler to care for the rights of the widow and the fatherless. So his sceptre also can be said to be 'a sceptre of righteousness'. When the king is sometimes called 'the (sun) god of his land', 'the (sun) god of all mankind', and the like, this may in fact be in connection with his justice, since the sun-god is among other things the guardian of justice. But Hammurabi can also say: 'I am the sun (god) of Babylon, who makes light shine upon the land of Sumer and of Akkad.'

As the chosen servant of the gods the king should also maintain harmony between society and nature. [90] He is 'he who maintains the life of his country', it is said. A letter-writer says flatteringly: 'We were dead dogs, but our lord the king gave us life by placing the herb of life under our noses.' By this he clearly means that the king in a symbolic sense has the herb of life or immortality which Gilgamesh sought for, and this means that he has the life of his subjects in his hands. (If there is any direct connection between this and the idea of a 'tree of life', it cannot be attested from the text.) But he can only do this by ensuring that society gives the gods the service and worship which is due to them. His faithful service ensures prosperity and well-being in the land. So Assurbanipal says:

> Since Assur, Sin, Shamash [and several others] have allowed me to take my place in gladness upon my father's throne, Adad let loose his showers, Ea opened his fountains, the corn grew five ells high in the straw, the spike became five sixths of an ell long, the harvest was good, the yield was rich, the pastures were continuously abundant, the orchard gave rich fruit, the cattle gave birth successfully—in my kingdom the abundance has been overflowing, in my years the plenty has been heaped up. [91]

That is, Assurbanipal, who became king 'at the order of the great gods, whom he invoked, and whose honour he upheld', functioned as a channel for the blessing of fertility which the gods, clearly for his sake, gave the land.

It is usual in this connection also to quote a letter from an official to Esarhaddon, which says:

> Shamash and Adad have through their veracious oracles appointed my lord to kingship over the lands. Good ruling, right days, right years, rich rain, full rivers, good prices. The gods are benevolent, the fear of the gods is great, the temples are rich. . . . Old men dance, young men sing, girls enjoy themselves, men take wives, who give birth . . . the birth goes successfully. . . . You release those who for many years have been prisoners. Those who for a long time have been ill live. The hungry are full, the thin become fat, the naked have clothes. [92]

Dhorme, who first called attention to this text, remarked: 'One could not ask for a more complete messianism.' [93] Frankfort makes the objection that the letter must be understood in the light of the peculiar circumstances under which it was written: one must allow for an excess of adulation.[94] But it remains true that the material difference in comparison with the proclamation of Assurbanipal is not all that large. On the other hand, Frankfort is completely correct in observing that the prosperity of the land is dependent upon the king's good conduct towards the gods and that he must pray to the gods for this kind of blessing.[95] He quotes a prayer of Sargon of Assyria:

> O Ea, lord of wisdom, creator of all things, to Sargon, king of the universe, king of Assyria, viceroy of Babylon, king of Sumer and Akkad, builder of thine abode—open thy fountains; let his springs send forth the waters of plenty and abundance; give water in abundance to his fields. Quick understanding and an open mind decree for him; prosper his work; let him attain unto his desire.

In other words in the last resort the king's power to maintain the harmony of nature is a gift of the gods, and is dependent on the extent to which he can obtain their favour by serving them.

This brings us to the second aspect of the functions of the king: he represents the people to the gods. He does this primarily by being the high priest of his land, and as such ultimately responsible for the temple building and the temple service.

We have seen how the Sumerian king had to look after the building of new temples and the restoration of the old. This responsibility also fell fully upon the Assyrian and Babylonian kings. It was necessary to maintain the temples in good condition, for if a temple fell into disrepair, the gods could leave it, with disastrous consequences for the city and the country. Consequently the kings made a point of building and restoring temples, and numerous inscriptions bear witness to this. The last king of Babylon, Nabonidus, was outstanding in this respect.

The kings, especially the Assyrian kings, can apply to themselves priestly titles. 'The priest of Assur' is a common royal title; the king often speaks of himself as 'he whose priesthood is pleasant before your godhead' or 'the highest priest whose priesthood is pleasant before the great gods'. Nominally the king is leader of the oracle priests, and he can himself, for example, receive dream oracles through sleeping a night in the temple (incubation). As we have seen, the gods sometimes address the king directly in oracles.

We cannot determine in detail which priestly services the king in practice carried out. We know in any case that the Assyrian king had certain specified ritual functions, both in regularly recurring ritual acts, and in others occasioned by special circumstances. The Babylonian king had to 'take the king's hand' in the *akītu*-feast to lead him (i.e. his statue) in procession; if the king was not present to do this, the feast could not be celebrated. Probably also the king in connection with the New Year Festival played the part of the god in certain parts of the cult drama. So the Assyrian king, for instance, appears in the role of Assur in the creation myth.

In this aspect the king was responsible to the gods for his performance of his office. We have seen that the Babylonian king—at least at a late period—had to do penance before Marduk in the New Year Festival, and asseverate that he has not sinned and has not neglected the temple service. The inscriptions which tell of temple building and temple restorations are in fact to be regarded as reports to the god. In such reports accounts could then also be inserted of military campaigns and other achievements. A good example of how the king made a report in this way to the gods is a letter from Sargon II of Assyria to the god Assur, in which the king reports a great military campaign.[96] It begins:

> To Assur, father of the gods, the great lord, who dwells in his great temple Eḫursaggal-kurkurra, may it be very well!
> To the gods of Fates and the goddesses who dwell in their great temple Eḫursaggal-kurkurra, may it be very very well! . . .
> To the city and its people may it be well! To the palace situated in its midst may it be well!
> It is very very well with Sargon, the pure priest, the slave who reverences your great god-head; and (likewise with) his camp.

The responsibility of the king was exceptionally serious when unfavourable omens threatened disaster for him and for his people. It was then possible to choose a 'substitute king' (*šar pūḫi*), who for a hundred days exercised royal power, and then apparently was slain. It is said of one of them in a letter that he 'has taken upon himself all the omens of heaven and earth', i.e. he took upon himself the responsibility which rested upon the king and the disasters which threatened him. [97] In one case we know that such a substitute king seized the throne, when the proper king died during the critical period.

All this shows how it was thought that the prosperity of the land depended on the person of the king. But there is perhaps not sufficient reason in this last case to assume a survival of the 'primitive' custom of killing the king when his powers failed and he could therefore no longer bear the responsibility for the well-being of his subjects (in any case the 'primitive' character of this custom rests on a questionable theory).

It may be possible to connect this custom with a statement in the Greek author Athenaeus, according to which the Babylonian priest Berossus told of a festival celebrated in Babylon, Sakaia (Sacaea), at which a criminal for a time played the part of the king, and then was killed. [98] It was for a long time assumed that this 'feast of Sacaea' was identical with the Babylonian New Year Festival (i.e. the *akitu*), but so far as we know no such ceremony had a place in this festival. Other Greek authors seem in fact to treat Sacaea as a Persian festival, but in the Iranian sphere too we have no contemporary evidence for such a feast. It is possible that some confusion is involved.

GOD AND MAN
RELIGION AND MORALITY

It is of course extremely difficult to obtain some idea of the inner nature of a long-dead religion. In respect of Babylonian and Assyrian religion the difficulty is increased by the fact that the documents which we have predominantly refer to what we may call the state religion, the official practice of religion. We must, nevertheless, allow that, for example, the rich psalm literature, even if it is rooted in the official cult of the temple, must to some degree have been the expression of genuine religious conviction. There are, however, other sources too. Literary works of different kinds often give in passing information about attitudes to life and about religious ideas. Letters often touch on the subject of religion and cult from the point of view of the individual. And theophoric personal names as a rule give expression to religiously based desires and hopes which were connected with the new-born child. In this way they give indirect evidence of what men thought they had received or expected from the gods.

A large number of mythological texts, as we have seen, are intended to show that man derived his origin from a divine act of creation. But this was true of the prototype, so to speak, of man as a class. Personal names show that every new-born child was thought of as a creation or a gift from a divinity: Ilu-bānī, 'god is the creator', Marduk-apla-iddina (Merodach-baladan), 'Marduk has given a son', Aššur-aḫa-iddina (Esarhaddon), 'Assur has given a brother', Aššur-bāni-apla (Assurbanipal), 'Assur creates a son', Nidin-Ištar, 'gift of Ishtar', etc.

Life is, therefore, a gift of the gods, and prayers for long life and for a successful life are very common, for example, 'May the gods give him a life of many days, years of prosperity and fertility', or, 'May Bel and Belit determine for him a destiny of life', or 'Sin has the life of the whole land in his hand'.[99]

We have seen how the idea of life as a gift of the gods was expressed in such symbols as the plant of life, which Gilgamesh sought, or the water of life and the bread of life, which Adapa was offered in heaven. But the 'plant of life' is mentioned also elsewhere as a symbol of something very attractive. Life-giving water also occurs often in pictorial representations, and men often pray that the gods shall 'pour out life like water'.

But if the gods have given man life, they can also take it away from him. Everlasting life is, as we have seen, reserved for the gods. Health and sickness also lie in the hands of the gods, and numerous prayers bear witness to how men expected relief for all sorts of suffering from the gods. It is probably this that lies behind the very common divine epithet *muballiṭ mītē*, 'who makes the dead live'—the idea of a resurrection from the dead is not known in Babylonian religion, but, on the other hand, illness can be treated as a potential death, and often in the psalms of lamentation a sick man speaks of himself as if he were already in the hands of death.

We have already met several times the idea of the fixing of destinies: at the New Year Festival a good destiny was determined for the coming year, a deity determines a good destiny for the king, etc. There is also an idea that every man has his destiny, which has been determined by the gods. The Akkadian word for 'destiny', *šimtu*, literally means 'that which is set', 'determined'. In most cases it looks as if this refers to a fixed length of life, for it is said of one who dies a premature death that 'he was snatched away on a day which was not that of his destiny'. But there are other instances which point to the *šimtu* being a predetermined share of fortune and misfortune, which determines the direction and configuration of the whole of life.[100] Assurnasirpal II speaks of his victories and conquests as his share of the destiny which the gods have pronounced for him, and which therefore had to come to realization. Sometimes the *šimtu* assumes the significance of nature or character, so, for example, in the Akkadian version of the old Ninurta myth, in which the god gives every precious stone its *šimtu*, i.e. its nature and properties. We can understand, therefore, how 'Destiny' becomes a summary of all that forms man and his life, even if the accent falls most often upon the length of life and upon death. Unfortunately we do not know how the logical contradiction was solved between a destiny determined beforehand, and a death at a time that was not fixed. But such inconsistencies are a natural result of a belief in destiny. It is possible that 'destiny' in the phrase that we are dealing with means rather that which is 'normally' assigned to a man. In any case it should be realized that it is never a question of an absolute force of destiny of an impersonal nature, but that the destiny of man is always understood as sent by the gods.

A study of personal names witnesses to a very positive attitude to the gods. 'Sin/Shamash/Adad is his strength', 'Sin/Shamash is my light', they say. The name can also express a wish or perhaps simply a conviction of being loved by a particular god. Naram-Sin means 'the beloved of Sin'; other names mean 'the god *x* loves' or 'is benevolent', or again 'I trust in Sin/Shamash/Marduk'.[101]

The idea of a personal tutelary deity for each man, which we found already in the Sumerian period, is fully alive also among the Babylonians and Assyrians. In incantations and prayers to heal the sick or to purify sinners 'the patient' is often called 'the man, the son/child of his god'. The intention is clearly to invoke the aid and protection of the man's own god. 'May the man, son of his god, be pure, may he be radiant, may he be splendid', it is said. The demon which causes sickness is addressed: 'Come not near, trouble not the body of the man, the child of his god.' It does in fact appear that it is when his tutelary deity for any reason turns away from a man that the demons have free play, and can inflict suffering upon him. 'A man's god is a shepherd who seeks for food for him.'[102]

We obtain an idea of attitudes to the gods through the prayers which are directed to them. As a rule it is prayers of kings which have been preserved, and they pray most often for long life, a successful reign, and victory over enemies. But here and there other aspects also appear. So, for example, Nebuchadnezzar II prays at his accession to Marduk:

> Everlasting lord, master of all that exists, grant to the king, whom you love, and whose name you name, all that is pleasant to you. Keep him on the right way. I am the prince, your favourite, a creation of your hand: you have created me and entrusted to me the dominion over all peoples. O lord, let me according to your grace, which you pour over them all, love your exalted might, and create in my heart fear of your divinity.

The same king prays to Shamash for 'a righteous sceptre, a good shepherding, a reliable shepherd's staff, which brings men well-being'. Nabonidus, the last king of Babylon, prays to Sin for those who serve in the temple: 'Set in their heart fear for thy high godhead, so that they may not sin against thy high godhead and their foundation may be as firm as the heaven.' For himself and for his son he prays: 'Free me from sin against your high godhead, and grant me a life of long days. My eldest son, Bel-shar-uṣur (the Belshazzar of Daniel 5), who proceeded from my heart, set in his heart fear for your high godhead. May he not commit sin, may he be satisfied with the fullness of life.'[103]

A side of Assyrian and Babylonian piety which is less often expressed can be detected in the following excerpt from an Assyrian processional psalm:

> Verily it is good to be ever going behind Ištar,
> It is good to go behind her, the mistress of Eanna.
> Before I regularly went behind Ištar,
> But used to go from house to house like a beggar,
> And used to lie on doorsteps like a dog,
> There were thorns in my feet and prickles in my clothing.[104]

Here, therefore, it is the experience of the positive psychological effects of the cult that is expressed. One almost has a feeling of being in the presence of 'conversion to Ishtar'.

It may be observed in this connection that, in the introductory invocation of the psalms of lament, the god to whom the speaker is turning upon this occasion is represented as the greatest, most exalted, the incomparable and only one. This has been interpreted as flattery and ingratiation. But we come nearer to the truth if we say that precisely this god at that moment so fills the thoughts and interests of the man praying that he is in effect the only one for him.[105]

Here we have already touched upon another side of the conception of the gods and of man's relationship to the gods. Man was created once to serve the gods, or perhaps rather to wait upon them. The god is the lord (*bēlu*), man is servant, slave (*ardu*). *Aradka*, 'your servant (or slave)' is in many religious texts a natural periphrasis for 'I'. Man's fear (*puluḫtu*) corresponds to the dazzling brilliance of the god (*melammu*—an originally Sumerian word). 'To fear the gods' is the expression for the correct attitude to them. Kings boast of being *pāliḫ ilāni rabûti*, 'fearful of the great gods'. But, just as in the Old Testament, the expression comes to mean to show reverence and respect, even to worship or pray in general. One can even say, 'The day on which the gods were feared was the joy of my heart',[106] or, 'With all my heart I love the fear of their divinity; I fear their dominion.'[107] One who 'does not fear the gods' is an infamous criminal.

'Service' to the gods was in the creation narrative primarily cultic service: sacrifice, prayers, festivals. When 'the Babylonian Job' laments over his misfortune and his suffering, he says:

(It was) like one who did not offer a libation to a god,
And at meal-time did not invoke a goddess,
Who did not bow his face and did not know reverence,
In whose mouth prayer and supplication ceased,
For whom the holiday had been eliminated, the *eššešu* festival
    had been curtailed,
Who became negligent, despised their images,
Who did not teach his people religion and reverence.[108]

The duties seem to have been primarily of a cultic and ritual nature. Similar ideas appear in the following excerpt from a collection of advice of a wisdom nature:

Every day worship your god.
Sacrifice and benediction are the proper accompaniment of
   incense.
Present your free-will offering to your god,
for this is proper towards the gods.
Prayer, supplication, and prostration
Offer him daily, and you will get your reward.
Then you will have full communion with your god.
In your wisdom study the tablet,
Reverence begets favour,
Sacrifice prolongs life,
And prayer atones for guilt.
He who fears the gods is not slighted by [. . .].
He who fears the Anunnaki extends (his days).[109]

We notice that fear of the gods is the basic idea which is expressed in cultic service, in sacrifice, prayer, etc. Everything turns
out in the end to be to the advantage of mankind, since this earns
them the favour of the gods and long life. It almost looks as if the
basic motive of this is to obtain one's own advantage. But it is
possible that this point of view has been given special emphasis
in this text, which has much in common with the Egyptian and
biblical wisdom texts, in which it is again the good consequences
of good deeds that is emphasized. But the point of view is not
unknown in other texts, as, for example, when Tiglath-pileser I
says of an ancestor that 'his life and his sacrifices pleased the great
gods, so that he attained a great age', or when Assurnasirpal
dedicates an altar 'so that my life may be long and my days many'.[110]
It is clear, therefore, that success and long life were regarded as
the reward of the gods to one who scrupulously fulfilled his duties
to them.
   But every man also had his duties to his fellow men, and these
duties also had some religious character. We have seen that one
of the reasons why the gods gave power to the king is that he is to
see that 'justice and righteousness' reign in the land, and that both
these concepts include order and justice in social life. The
Akkadian words *mēšaru* and *kettu* mean literally 'straightness,
rightness', and 'firmness, truth', but they have come to signify the
basic virtues upon which the communal life of man rests. An
attempt has been made to show that *kettu* literally refers to 'the sum

of cosmic and immutable truths', which is then deposited in concrete enactments, while *mēšaru* is the process (or perhaps better the principle of the process) through which the laws are put into practice and made to function.[111] On the other hand, there are also examples which suggest that *mēšaru* also had a cosmic side to it: the correct order of nature, which is expressed in the regular changes of the seasons, etc.[112] It is, however, doubtful whether the thought was carried to its conclusion and the correct behaviour of man regarded as an adaptation to the laws of the universe and of nature.

If we ask for more detail about the content of the ethical demand, we have some guidance from the 'mirror of sins' which is found in the second tablet of the incantation series *Shurpu*.[113] Here the attempt is made to discover what sin a man afflicted by suffering has committed, in order to banish the evil with the correct rites. We have here a large collection of actions which were regarded as causing the wrath of the gods, and so also indirectly an idea of what was regarded as well-pleasing and good.

> Has he alienated son and father,
> has he alienated father from son,
> has he alienated daughter from mother . . .
> has he alienated brother from brother,
> has he alienated friend from friend,
> has he alienated comrade from comrade?

It is important in other words to respect the given forms of the community, especially the family, and it is a sin to cause dissension between friends.

> Has he not freed the captive, has he not loosed the bound?
> Has he not let prisoners see the light of day?

We know that it is part of a king's duties to set free innocent prisoners, but here it seems to be a more general rule.

> Is it an unconscious sin against a god, a conscious transgression
>   against a goddess?
> Has he offended a god, despised a goddess?
> Is his sin against his (tutelary) god, is his offence against his
>   (tutelary) goddess?

Here a purely religious aspect is presented; the reference may be especially to cultic transgressions and omissions.

> Is it an offence against an ancestor, hostility to an elder brother?
> Has he despised father (and) mother, treated with contempt an
>   elder sister?

Here it is clearly not only a question of the rights of ancestors but also of older brothers and sisters.

> Has he said 'yes' instead of 'no'?
> Has he said 'no' instead of 'yes'?
> Has he said anything impure in disobedience?

The ideal is clearly true and candid utterance, just as in Jesus' Sermon on the Mount. The next question concerns slander and insulting language. Then the text continues about honesty in trade:

> Has he used false scales?
> Has he accepted 'impure' money, refused to accept 'pure' money?
> Has he kept a legitimate heir from his inheritance, or given rights
>   of inheritance to a wrongful heir?
> Has he set up a false boundary stone, not set up a correct
>   boundary stone?
> Has he moved a boundary line, a boundary path or a boundary
>   stone?

Respect for property boundaries seems to have been great in all the ancient Near East; Egyptian and Israelite precepts lay a similar degree of emphasis on this matter. The boundary stone, *kudurru*, was under the protection of the gods.

> Has he entered his neighbour's house?
> Has he approached his neighbour's wife?
> Has he shed his neighbour's blood?
> Has he carried off his neighbour's clothing?

The life and property of one's fellow man (and this includes his wife) are thus protected by religiously motivated custom. The next question is about neglect to help a poor man 'in his nakedness'; this is noteworthy because it is not a case of a transgression of a prohibition, but of failure to help. After two questions which again concern the unity and harmony of the family, it is said: 'Has he given himself airs in relation to a subordinate'? This again concerns larger social units. A question about intention and purpose is left until last:

> Was his mouth true, but was his heart false?
> Did his mouth say 'yes' but his heart 'no'?

After some general phrases comes a summary:

> Has he followed the ways of evil?
> Has he transgressed the limits of righteousness?
> Has he done what is unbecoming?

Some (added?) lines then speak of magic and the arts of sorcery, and the breaking of taboo rules.

It will be agreed that the list is very comprehensive. It shows that no difference was made in principle between cultic, social, and moral transgressions—all could serve equally as the cause of the wrath of the gods.

We find some more positive rules for life in the wisdom text already quoted:

> Do not return evil to the man who disputes with you,
> requite with kindness your evil-doer,
> maintain justice to your enemy, . . .
> Let not your heart be induced to do evil . . .
> Give food to eat, beer to drink,
> The one begging for alms honour, clothe;
> In this a man's god takes pleasure,
> it is pleasing to Shamash, who will repay him with favour.
> Be helpful, do good.[114]

The text in fact comes very near the ideas of the Sermon on the Mount. Unfortunately we know nothing more precise about its origin and purpose. It is a text of the same genre as the Book of Proverbs in the Bible, and it is in any case older than 700 B.C.

'Law comes from the gods, justice descends from heaven, duties are imposed through divine commands; sin is the transgression of the law, the violation of justice, forgetfulness of the command' (Dhorme).[115] Among the words for sin should be noted the common Semitic *ḫiṭu* (Hebrew *ḥēṭ'*, etc.), which literally means 'mistake' or 'false step', *annu* or *arnu* with the basic meaning of 'rebellion', and *qillatu*, which can also mean a 'curse'. The

aspect of rebellion seems to be prominent: sin is rebellion against
the gods. Sometimes the idea is met that sin is man's self-
sufficiency, wishing to live 'on one's own account' (*ina ramānišu*),
without troubling about the gods. But it can also be said that sin is
that which awakens the wrath of the gods, and it is implied that
they punish man by means of sickness or misfortune. It is not
hard to find evidence for this idea. One psalm of lamentation and
penitence says:

> In vexation of heart the lord has looked upon me,
> my god has visited me in the wrath of his heart,
> in anger the goddess gave me pain.[116]

In an incantation the priest describes the unfortunate man in this
way:

> Sickness, headache, curse and sleeplessness
> have they poured continuously over him, poverty and sighing,
> . . . resistance, terror and fright,
> have been sent to him, and have removed his lament.[117]

And when the sick man himself speaks, he confesses: 'Many are
my sins, in numerous ways have I offended.'

If a man has fallen into such a situation, there is only one way
out: to turn to the offended deity with prayer for forgiveness.
'Prayer looses the guilt of sin', it is said in a text which we have
already quoted, and Babylonian religious literature is rich in
psalms of prayer and penitence. It is not difficult to find examples
both of a deep sense of sinfulness and of confidence in the deity's
mercy. So it is said, for instance, in a prayer 'to every god':

> My offence is great, O lord, serious my deed,
> O god, numerous are my sins,
> great is my burden of sin, O goddess,
> great is my guilt, O deity, known and unknown.
> Great is my guilt, O goddess, known and unknown.[118]

In a prayer to Marduk it is said:

> Who has not erred, who has not offended?
> The way of god—who knows it?
> . . . Against thee have I, thy servant, committed sins,
> God's limits I have transgressed.

What I have done since my childhood witting or unwitting,
  forget it!
Let your heart not be troubled! Forgive my sin! Pardon my
  misdeed.[119]

It is especially in the lamentations to Ishtar that a strong com-
mitment appears, for example:

To thee, O goddess, I give heed, to thee is my mind directed,
thee, yea thee I call upon: loose my curse!
Loose my guilt, my offence, my wrong-doing and my sin;
pardon my evil deed, receive my invocation!
undo my shackles, bring me deliverance,
lead my steps aright, so that like a hero I may travel the way in
  light with the living!
. . .
let my genuflection be pleasing to you, hear my prayer;
look faithfully upon me, receive my invocation.
How long, mistress, will you be wroth with averted face?
How long, mistress, will you be provoked, bitter in mind?
Turn your head, which you averted! Direct your mind to
  friendly speech![120]

One can hardly avoid noticing the almost biblical language of
this psalm. In fact it is clear that biblical and Babylonian psalm
composition share in the same poetic tradition, a point that appears
perhaps most clearly in the psalms of lamentation.

This can be seen both in the form of the psalms and in their
poetic imagery.[121] Both Babylonian and Israelite lamentations
contain as a rule the following elements: invocation of the god,
description of the suffering, prayer for help, possibly also confession of sins, and prayer for pardon together with promise of thank-
offering. In the description of the suffering similarities will be
noticed in such points as that the man praying says that he has been
attacked by enemies, assailed by wild beasts or demons, or that
he says that he is sinking in water or mire (an image for death and
the land of the dead).

A special problem is set by the very common reference to unknown sins: 'The sin that I have committed I know not'. The idea
is clearly that one can transgress a divine prohibition or break a
taboo without knowing it, but in spite of that incur the anger and

punishment of the gods. Then advice must be taken on which sin it is that has been committed, and pardon sought for it. It is striking how rarely concrete sins are mentioned in the psalms of lamentation. Instead we meet general phrases: 'My transgressions are innumerable', 'seven times seven sins have I committed'. This may of course depend on the need for these psalms to be usable for several different occasions and people, so that they are formulas to fit different eventualities. It is also possible that there was a desire to insure oneself and not to forget any sin in one's confession. No man is without sin, and it is easy to break a commandment without knowing it. But if it is 'prayer which looses guilt', it is important to allow for all possible sins in one's prayer and confession.

Although no formulated dogmatic pattern has been found, the Babylonians and Assyrians looked for a divine retribution. It was regarded as obvious that sin is punished and obedience rewarded.

The idea of retribution is extended also to the nation and to history. In the Weidner Chronicle we are told of a series of rulers who transgress and therefore lose power and are overthrown. The fall of a dynasty is interpreted as Marduk's punishment for cultic offences. He who does not respect Marduk and his cult is punished for it. The judgement is anachronistic, but no less characteristic. Several examples show how war and national disasters are treated as punishment of the gods, and how kings are the tool of the gods for deliverance.[122]

As far as the individual is concerned, however, there is also evidence that difficulties were felt in applying this rule to the realities of life. Just as in Israel we have texts which deal with the problem of the suffering of the righteous man, especially the so-called Babylonian Job, or, as it is called after its first words, *Ludlul bēl nimēqi* ('I will praise the lord of wisdom').[123]

Strictly the poem is not a poem about a problem but a psalm of thanksgiving, which looks back over suffering that has been surmounted. But the description of it occupies so much space that the poem is already noteworthy just for this reason. The writer describes how he was assailed by severe suffering: 'I look about me: evil upon evil! My affliction increases, right I cannot find. I implored the god, but he did not turn his countenance'. No necromancer could find the cause of his suffering. Whence come the evil things everywhere? he asks. It is as if he had completely neglected the worship of the gods. And yet:

I myself was thinking only of prayer and supplication:
Supplication was my concern, sacrifice my rule;
The day of the worship of the gods was my delight,
The day of my goddess's procession was my profit and wealth.
Veneration of the king was my joy . . .
I taught my land to observe the divine ordinances,
To honour the name of the goddess I instructed my people.
The king's majesty I equated to that of a god.

Obviously the scale of values of the gods is different from that of men. 'Who can understand the counsel of the gods in the midst of heaven? The plan of a god is deep waters, who can comprehend it?' The life of man is short and transient:

He who was living yesterday has died today:
Instantly he is made gloomy, suddenly he is crushed.
One moment he sings a happy song,
And in an instant he will moan like a mourner.
Like day and night their mood changes.
When they are hungry they resemble corpses,
When they are sated they rival their god;
In good luck they speak of ascending to heaven,
When they are afflicted they grumble about going down to the
    underworld.

Then follows a long description of illness and suffering in a very florid style, and it is asserted once again that no oracle-priest could find the cause, and that no god helped or had mercy.

Then comes the turning point: in three dreams the sufferer receives promises of pardon, cleansing, and restoration. Then Marduk intervenes; he causes the wind to carry away the man's transgressions, sends the storm and drives away the demons that have been plaguing him. 'From distress he saved me, out of the (underworld) river Hubur he drew me. Marduk seized my hand, and lifted high my head.' So he 'who had gone down into the grave' could again go into Marduk's temple to present his thanksgiving. We are told how he enters in through the twelve gates of the temple, and presents his sacrifice of thanksgiving. The poem concludes with a eulogy of Marduk and his consort, who alone can 'revive in the grave' and 'deliver from destruction', and therefore are worthy of praise.

The question is what the purpose of this poem was. It is usually asserted that it is not cultic (so most recently Oppenheim), but in view of the emphasis that is laid upon the description of the thank-offering in the temple of Marduk, it is perhaps legitimate to question this. On the other hand, we can hardly (with, for example, Engnell) assert that it is a royal psalm of thanksgiving after the suffering of the king in the New Year Festival, both because in a couple of passages the king is clearly another person than the 'I' of the poem, and because the lament for the suffering of the innocent does not fit the thought-pattern of the New Year Festival. In any case we must not lose sight of the fact that the climax of the poem is the sacrifice of thanksgiving in the temple of Marduk and the glorification of the saving might of the god.

In the so-called Babylonian theodicy[124] or 'Babylonian Ecclesiastes' the same problem is taken up. It is written in an artificial form such that the name of the author is given acrostically in the first words of the strophes, and it consists of a dialogue between a sceptic and a religious man. The sceptic time and again takes up the theme of the success of the wicked and the misfortune of the righteous, while his friend represents the traditional point of view: he who suffers must have transgressed the commandments of the gods (strophe 8), he who thinks that he has been unjustly treated does the gods an injustice, for we men can in the end not understand their plans (strophe 24). No real conclusion is reached: the last strophes seem to suggest that the discontented man has misused the gift of speech which the gods have given man, and that therefore he must turn to Ninurta and Ishtar in humble prayer for help.

A third poem is the 'pessimistic dialogue'[125] between a master and his slave. If it is taken in full seriousness, it is deeply pessimistic, but there is much to suggest that it is intended to be humorous. The master gives command after command, and the slave answers expressing his readiness to serve with proverbial phrases which show that the idea of the master is not a good one. Then the master changes his mind and is ready to do the opposite, and the slave has at once a new phrase of concurrence ready. The purpose according to Oppenheim was to show that one cannot rely on proverbial wisdom.[126] In any case the dialogue is not representative of a religious attitude.

BELIEF IN AN AFTERLIFE

The Assyrian and Babylonian texts are relatively silent as regards the position of mankind after death. It is known that life or 'the breath of life' is a gift of the gods, who also have the power to take it back. Death is the fate which awaits all mankind. The myths attempt to explain, as they do in so many other countries, how it comes about that man must die; according to the Adapa myth it is a blunder, according to the myth upon which the Gilgamesh Epic builds a mischance, which makes man fail to secure everlasting life, which belongs by right to the gods alone. There is an element of resignation to be found in these myths.

It is in keeping with this that the concepts of life after death have a completely negative and pessimistic quality. Man without the god-given breath of life is a weak and powerless being of shadows, an *eṭimmu* or ghost, which can perhaps trouble and torment the living as a demon, and must then be driven away with incantations, but the life of such a creature is not pleasant.

There is also a concept of a land of the dead, which as in Sumerian can be called 'the land without return' (*erṣet lā târi*). Of this the Akkadian version of the myth of Ishtar's descent into the underworld says:

The house which no one who steps into it leaves,
the way on which no one returns,
the house whose inhabitant is deprived of light.

And it is said of the dead who dwell there:

Dust is their food and clay their nourishment,
they see no light, where they dwell in darkness.

Almost exactly the same phrases recur in a passage in the Epic of Gilgamesh, in which the dying Enkidu sees what is awaiting him. The passage goes on to say:

In the house of dust, where I went in,
I saw rulers—whose crowns were laid aside,
I saw princes who bore crowns
and governed lands long since,
these doubles of Anu and Enlil served roast joints,
they served meat and poured out cold water from the bottles.

He also sees priests of different ranks, and sees the mistress of the land of the dead, Ereshkigal, who when he comes lifts up her face and asks: 'Who has brought this one hither?' One cannot help thinking of the description in Isaiah 14 of how the shades in the land of the dead are disturbed by the king of Babylon on his descent.

We have a somewhat more detailed description of the state of the dead at the end of the twelfth tablet of the Gilgamesh Epic, where the hero has called up the spirit of Enkidu and questions him what it is like in the land of the dead. 'I do not want to tell', says Enkidu, 'for if I do so, you will sit down and weep.' In the continuation a large part of the text has unfortunately been lost, but we can see references to worms which destroy the body, and to dust. After this the text clearly talks of the different fate of different people among the dead: some have a relatively tolerable existence, for we can make out such phrases as 'he eats bread', 'he drinks water', 'his heart rejoices'. At the end it is said that he who dies a sudden death 'lies upon a sofa and drinks pure water', and that he who was killed in battle, 'his father and his mother lift up his head, and his wife weeps for him'. But 'he whose corpse was cast out upon the steppe . . . his spirit finds no rest in the underworld', and 'he whose spirit has no one to tend it' . . . 'eats crumbs of bread and garbage in the street'. It is clear that the last two examples refer to such as have not received proper burial, and whose grave does not receive correct attention (with gifts or sacrifices at the grave), and that it is such as these that wander about as revenants. But it is clear from the context that the fate of the others, even if it was better and more tolerable, was regarded as far from enviable.

There is a unique text from the eighth century B.C. which tells how an Assyrian crown prince descends to the underworld in a dream,[127] and finds himself surrounded there by terrible demons, which in form are a marvellous mixture of lion, bull, bird, serpent, etc. In their midst Nergal is enthroned as king of the underworld, surrounded by the 600 Anunnaki, the judges of the underworld. He is brought before Nergal, and feels himself pierced by his testing glance. He waits for his sentence, but Ishum makes intercession for him: 'slay him not'. He is allowed to return to life with the promise that he who celebrates the *akītu* festival 'has an orchard of abundance' and 'is a god' who is protected from all sorts of evil.

The text unfortunately leaves us in ignorance what its real purpose is—it is clear that it is not primarily intended to give us information about the land of the dead. Its last word is *namburbē*, which is a term for certain rites of purification and atonement, and it is possible that this gives a hint of its function. There are incantation texts which speak of a judgement in the underworld, and the meaning is clearly that a sick man is really in the land of the dead, and that his fate will be determined by a verdict, which by reason of the incantation is one of acquittal. The texts which speak of this, however, are few in number and obscure, so that it is difficult to build any definite conclusions upon them. It is in any case clear that there is no question of a judgement in the Christian sense, or of a resurrection.

There are, it should be said, certain tablets which have been found in graves in Susa from the sixth and fifth centuries B.C., and which speak of some sort of judgement, which gives the good some advantage over the wicked,[128] but they can hardly represent genuinely Babylonian ideas. Probably we have here Iranian ideas; in any case these documents are an exception, and cannot be made the basis for any conclusions about Babylonian and Assyrian belief about life after death in general.

3
West Semitic Religion

INTRODUCTION
SOURCES

At the beginning of the second millennium B.C. West Semitic tribes appeared in the region of the Upper Euphrates and founded kingdoms there, including one around the city of Mari. These people were called in Akkadian *Amurru*, or in an Anglicized form (based on the Old Testament *'ᵃmōrī*), Amorites. The great king of Babylon, Hammurabi, was of West Semitic (Amorite) origin.

At about the same time related tribes invaded what is now Palestine. It is not inconceivable that the biblical stories of the patriarchs preserve memories of these events. The Bible usually makes a distinction between the Amorites in the hill-country and the Canaanites on the coast and on the plains, but it has recently been claimed from archaeological evidence that it is a question not of two different peoples, but of a special development of Amorite culture in the coastal district, which acquired the name Canaan (Akkadian *kinaḫḫu*) from a shell-fish famous for a dye it produced.

On the northern part of this coast a distinct culture, the Phoenician, developed, so called after the Greek name for the people (they themselves used the word Canaanites). It is a disputed question exactly where we should draw the boundary between Canaanite culture in general and Phoenician in particular, and depends on whether the Ugaritic culture about the middle of the second millennium B.C. should be called early Phoenician or not. The oldest inscriptions with Phoenician alphabet and in a distinctively Phoenician language date from about 1000 B.C.

The Phoenicians were a trading nation with the cities of Tyre, Sidon, and Byblos as their main centres, but with colonies around the whole of the eastern Mediterranean. Their remains are especially numerous on Cyprus. The most important colony, however, was Carthage ('the new city') ,which soon came to have an independent position, and which also displays some distinctive

features in its religion. The people there were called Punic
(Latin *Poeni*), in distinction from the Phoenicians of the mother-
land.

To the east of the territory of the Canaanites and Phoenicians we
find other West Semitic tribes, the Aramaeans, with a language
which is clearly different from the Canaanite dialects. From the
twelfth century they are often mentioned in Assyrian inscriptions,
and about 1000 B.C. there were a number of Aramaean states with
Damascus as a central point, which made up a formidable power.
David conquered them and incorporated them in his kingdom, but
Israel was able to control their territory for only a brief period, and
later in the history of Israel the Aramaeans of Damascus were a
dreaded enemy. The Aramaic language acquired widespread
currency. After the exile it gradually became the language of the
Jews, and it was the common language of government for the
western parts of the Persian empire.

The Aramaean religion survived until the centuries about the
beginning of our era, although often strongly infused with Hellenistic elements. This is true, for instance, of the religion to which the
inscriptions from Palmyra, written in an Aramaic dialect, bear
witness. The Nabataeans to the east of the Dead Sea and the
Jordan also wrote their inscriptions in an Aramaic dialect, but their
religion is predominantly Arabian. It would take too long, and
make this account too heterogeneous, to deal with all these late
and often considerably altered forms of religion. Finally, it should
also be remembered that the Israelites too belong to the West
Semitic group of peoples, although their religion came to develop
in a very distinctive manner.

It is, therefore, a long period of time and a geographically very
widespread area that we must deal with. As we have seen, there
are also significant cultural differences. Furthermore, the sources
are scanty and incomplete, and of very varied nature.

For a long time our primary source for Canaanite religion was
simply the presentation of it in the Old Testament. This, as is well
known, is of a polemical nature, and can therefore not be expected
to give an objectively correct picture of the religion. Furthermore,
it is not an ordered presentation but one consisting of individual
remarks made in passing.

The only supplement to this available was for a long time the
descriptions of West Semitic religion given by classical authors.

The most important is Lucian (died after A.D. 180), a Greek writer from Samosata in Syria, who in his work, *On the Syrian Goddess*, gives a description of the temple and cult of Astarte in the Syrian city of Hierapolis. Although this source is late and often clearly influenced by Hellenistic ideas, it gives some information that is of value. Another important source is the work that Philo of Byblos (Philo Byblius, *c.* 100 B.C.) wrote about Phoenician religion (only preserved in excerpts, especially in Eusebius' *Praeparatio Evangelica*). According to his own account, which there is no reason to doubt, he bases his work upon what a Phoenician priest called Sanchuniaton told him. The discoveries of the last decades have in general confirmed that his facts are reliable, but it should always be remembered that he has a very strong tendency to systematize his material, and that he gives his own euhemeristic interpretation of it in presenting the gods as men who because of their services to mankind have come to receive worship.

Plutarch's work, *Of Isis and Osiris*, also contains a number of interesting facts, and various other Greek writers give information about the Adonis cult. The philosopher Damascius, from *c.* A.D. 500, gives some facts about Phoenician ideas of creation. Allusions in Roman literature (for example, the *Poenulus* of Plautus) are also of value for the Punic religion of Carthage.

In addition to these sources, however, we have to an ever increasing extent the evidence of archaeology too. Discoveries of temples and cultic objects give valuable information, but as long as it is not supplemented by written material its value in deepening our understanding of the religion is of course limited. Large numbers of inscriptions are now known both from the Phoenician–Canaanite and from the Aramaic areas, but because of their nature and content they can give only incidental information about religious matters.

The cuneiform letters from El-Amarna (discovered in 1887–8) —letters from Canaanite tributary kings and neighbouring rulers to the Egyptian Pharaoh—give an exceptionally clear picture of the political situation in Canaan in the first half of the fourteenth century, but naturally contain only sporadic references to religion. These may also to a certain extent be adapted to Egyptian ways of thought.

In these circumstances the discovery in 1929 of the texts from Ras Shamra in northern Syria, the ancient Ugarit, represents a revolution. Here for the first time authentic religious texts, including myths and lists of sacrifices, were found in the Canaanite area. They are written in a previously unknown alphabetic cuneiform script (in which the vowels are not written) in an archaic form of the Canaanite language, and give an extremely good picture of the religious situation at the height of Ugarit's prosperity, *c.* 1440–1360 B.C. Later excavations have supplemented this material with further documentary sources. We shall come back to these texts again later for a more detailed discussion.

It should also be mentioned for the sake of completeness that Egyptian texts too give scattered details about Canaanite religion. For instance, the Semitic elements among the Hyksos—who for a period, *c.* 1730–1580, ruled Egypt—retained their gods, so that they are mentioned in inscriptions, and a number of the 'execration texts', which were employed with magical intent against Canaanite and other enemies, contain a number of personal names which are very often theophoric, i.e. contain a god's name.

It is evident that in such circumstances a complete picture of the religion of the West Semitic peoples is impossible. Even at the one point at which we have fairly detailed texts from the country itself, in the case of Ugarit, there are various facets of religious life for which we lack information. It is in general only the externals that we encounter. If we are to have respect for the various local forms of West Semitic religion and avoid generalizations, we must proceed with great caution. On the other hand, it should be recognized that the material available points to great similarities, and much that is common to the whole area. A measure of Mesopotamian influence can be detected at many points (this should, however, not be exaggerated), but on the other hand West Semitic religion has also influenced Babylonian–Assyrian religion. A certain degree of common Semitic material is an important presupposition for this.

THE CANAANITE GODS

The pantheon is the side of West Semitic religion that we know best. A large number of names of deities is known, but unfortunately many of them, if not indeed most of them, remain mere names, and the functions and mutual relationship of the gods can either not be determined at all, or only very incompletely.

It is often said—especially from a theological viewpoint—that Canaanite religion is a nature religion, and that the gods are completely tied to natural phenomena. As far as the highest god, El, is concerned, this is in any case clearly incorrect, and in a large number of other cases it must be said that even if a divinity has a clear nature aspect, he is by no means identical with the natural phenomenon in question, nor is his character fully explained by a reference to the natural phenomenon. West Semitic religion has a strongly marked interest in fertility, but this is a separate question.

The usual word for 'god' contains the root 'ēl, which is also the name of the highest deity. The etymology of the word is not completely clear. It is difficult to decide between the senses 'strong, powerful' and 'first, foremost'; it would also be conceivable that both senses are combined in some such meaning as 'leader'.[1] In Ugarit 'il is also the general word for 'god', which can also occur in the plural; the same is true of the expanded form 'iln. The position in Phoenician is similar ('l, or 'ln); Aramaic inscriptions have 'elāh, which agrees with the Hebrew 'elō^ah, with its plural 'elōhīm.

Both in Ugaritic and in Phoenician inscriptions the gods are given the epithet qdš, holy, the same word which in Hebrew (qādōš) describes the deity as one exalted above everything human, the completely other, who is both terrible and fascinating. To what extent the same sense holds for the West Semites in general does not appear from the instances we have, but it may be presumed that the difference was not all that great. It may be added that another root with the meaning 'holy', ḥrm (which in Hebrew is used for the so-called 'ban' or 'total destruction', and occurs in Arabic, for instance, in the name of a holy place ḥaram) is not at present attested as a divine epithet, but only as a verb in the sense of 'to hallow', 'to consecrate', and in the name Hermon, which means 'holy mountain'. It is not improbable that the primary sense of the root is not 'divine', but simply 'to hand over to a god'.

We cannot of course decide to what extent a regular pantheon is found among the different West Semitic peoples, but in one case, that of Ugarit, we know that there was a specific term for the concept of 'the assembly of the gods', pḥr 'ilm, sometimes also mpḥrt bn 'il, 'the assembly of the sons of the gods (i.e. of divine beings)', or dr 'il, 'the generation of the god (El)'. Sacrificial tables and similar lists also indicate by their enumerating a series of deities that the concept of a pantheon was known. A similar phrase is also found in an inscription from Byblos from the tenth century B.C.[2]

In the Ugaritic texts El takes first place among the gods. The name is identical with the word for god, but here it is a proper noun: the god before all others, 'God'. He has supreme authority among the gods, where he reigns as king 'at the source of the rivers', which is perhaps the place where the waters of heaven and earth meet, or a place like the biblical Eden, from which four rivers water the whole earth. It is El who has the decisive authority regarding both gods and men. He is 'the father of the sons of the gods', but also 'the father of mankind' (*'ab 'adm*). Another epithet describes him as the father of *šnm*, but it is uncertain whether *šnm* means 'the years' and El is therefore 'the old' or the lord of time itself, or if it is in fact a place-name, or something else again.

One of the most common epithets of El is 'the bull', which is meant to emphasize either his strength or his power to procreate. A pictorial representation on a stele from Ras Shamra shows a god with horn symbols and beard sitting on a throne, and it is probable that it represents El. The beard is perhaps reminiscent of a passage where it is said that 'El is great and wise, and his grey hairs instruct him'.

Another of the standing epithets of El is *ltpn 'il dp'id*, which means roughly 'the benevolent and merciful'. He is also called 'creator of that which is created', and *qny*, which either means 'creator' or 'owner'.

An atmosphere of remote majesty and elevated tranquillity surrounds El in the Ras Shamra texts, and the conclusion has often been drawn that he is a *deus otiosus* or 'inactive god'. This is only partially true. It has also been asserted that El is rather an example of the virtue that the Arabs call *ḥilm*, 'a mixture of goodness, kindliness and wisdom which leads to self-control and patience, but which in the last resort rests upon self-confidence and faith in one's own powers'.[3] El represents omnipotence, but it cannot be denied that in his exalted majesty he is omnipotence at a distance, interfering only on certain decisive occasions. He was in any case the object of regular worship: sacrifices to him are included in the sacrificial lists, and he occurs also elsewhere in cultic texts.

Philo Byblius also mentions a god Elos among the gods of the Phoenicians, and compares him with the Kronos of the Greeks.

Numerous personal names which contain the element '*ēl* could possibly allude to 'god' in general, or to a god whose name happens not to be given, but it is more probable that the reference is to the god El.

The bilingual Karatepe inscription mentions in its Phoenician section an '*l qn 'rṣ*, 'El the creator of the earth' (or possibly 'owner, Lord'); the same epithet is found in a late Punic inscription, and possibly (in the form *Il kunirša*) in a Canaanite myth in Hittite translation. It is interesting that we find a variant of this epithet in Gen. 14.19, 22, where Melchizedek speaks of 'El 'Elyon, creator of heaven and earth' ('*ēl 'elyōn qōnē šāmayim wā'āreṣ*).

Melchizedek was 'priest of El 'Elyon ("God most High")' in Salem', i.e. Jerusalem, and it is clear that he represents Canaanite religion. It is true that the narratives of the patriarchs in their present form treat El 'Elyon as identical with Yahweh the god of Israel, but he is shown to be a genuine Canaanite god by the fact that Philo Byblius mentions 'Elioun, who was called *hypsistos* (the most high)' among the Phoenician gods, and that an Aramaic inscription from *c.* 750 B.C. speaks of an agreement being made 'before El and 'Elyān and before heaven and earth and the depth of the sea and the wells and before day and night' as witnesses. The puzzling thing is that in Philo Elioun is not the same as Elos, and that in the inscription quoted El and 'Elyān appear to be regarded as two different gods. However, Philo's genealogies of the gods are thoroughly confused, and one sometimes has the impression that the same deity appears in several places under different names, while as regards the conjunction of El and 'Elyān, there are at least two examples in the Ugaritic texts of a single god having a name which consists of two elements linked by an 'and'. The question is not, however, completely clear.

It has sometimes been claimed that 'the Canaanite god El 'Elyōn' was a sun-god. There is, however, no real evidence for this assertion, and the more indirect indications which have been adduced cannot be said to be convincing.

Clearly there is a connection with the other epithets containing the element El preserved in the Old Testament and particularly in the patriarchal narratives: '*Ēl shaddai*, traditionally translated 'God almighty', but of uncertain meaning (possibly 'El, the mountain god'), '*Ēl 'Ōlām*, 'El of eternity (or of the course of time?)', '*Ēl Bēt-'ēl*, 'the god of Bethel', or 'El in Bethel'. The first two of these are attested only in the Old Testament, while the case of El-Bethel is rather more complicated. According to Philo Baitylos, i.e. Bethel, is the brother of El, and therefore a separate god. Bethel is mentioned as an independent god also in Assyrian and Babylonian sources, for instance in a treaty between Esarhaddon and a king of Tyre (*c.* 675 B.C.), and from papyrus texts in Aramaic from Elephantine in Egypt it appears that the Jewish colony there worshipped the god Bethel among others. Perhaps it is also the god and not the place Bethel that is referred to in Jer. 48.13, since the parallel part of the verse mentions Chemosh, the god of the Moabites.

In all these cases it may be a question of local forms of one and the same El, and this is to some extent supported by the fact that the Israelites could identify them all with their god Yahweh. It appears that El belonged to the type of god which is usually called 'high gods', omnipotent gods who are determiners of fates, and have a certain tendency to distance and passivity. A large number of high gods are sky-gods, but there is no direct evidence that El was regarded as identical with the sky or with any celestial object.

The god who plays the most prominent part in the Ugaritic texts is Baal. The name itself means 'lord' or 'owner', and it is also clear that the word is sometimes used in an appellative significance. In the Old Testament it always has the definite article, and it can be used in the plural, 'the baals'. It appears also as the first element in a number of names of local deities; the second element is then most often a place name, for example, Baal-Hazor, Baal-Peor, Baal-Sidon, Baal-Lebanon, Baal-Haran (cf. also the Phoenician Ba'alat-Gebal, 'the mistress of Byblos'), occasionally another word, for example, Baal-berith, 'the lord of the covenant' (Judg. 9.4) and Baal-Marqod ('the lord of the dance'). An old theory maintains that every place and every object in nature or the life of man had its *ba'al* or lord, and that from these ideas the idea of a specific god, the Lord above others, Baal with a capital letter, gradually crystallized out. Our material is unfortunately insufficient to determine the exact relationship between the Baal of the Ugaritic texts and the Baal of whom the Old Testament talks, but it is clear that both the Ugaritic texts and the Amarna letters show that in the fifteenth and sixteenth centuries we are already dealing with a proper name. The Baals with accompanying names are probably local forms of this god in his character of tutelary deity of, for instance, a city.

In the Ugaritic texts Baal is often called Al'iyan Ba'al, with an epithet which appears to mean 'the strong, the mighty'. Another epithet is *rkb 'rpt*, 'he who rides on the clouds'; Baal is thus characterized as a storm and rain god (a similar epithet is employed of Yahweh in Ps. 68.4; cf. also Ps. 18.10). Baal's connection with rain and fertility also appears from a passage in one of the Ras Shamra texts, where it is said that when Baal has acquired his temple

> he will give abundance of rain,
> abundance of moisture with snow,
> he will utter his voice in the clouds
> and his flashings and lightnings on the earth.
>   (II AB V, 8ff)

And when the temple is complete and Baal is installed in it, it is said:

> Baal uttered his holy voice,
> Baal repeated the issue of his lips,
> his holy voice made the earth . . .
>   the mountains tremble,
> [. . .] trembled,
> east and west, the high places of the earth shook.
> The enemies of Baal fled to the forests,
> the enemies of Hadad to the innermost parts of the mountain.
>   (II AB VII, 29ff)

In this section Baal and the thunder god Hadad (written *hd*, i.e. Hadd) appear to be identical. There are several other passages in the Ras Shamra texts too where this is the case. In fact the name Hadad (which of course is the same as the Akkadian Adad) occurs mostly in Aramaic inscriptions from Zenjirli. It looks, therefore, as if Baal, 'the lord', is the Canaanites' name for the god who among the Aramaeans and in Mesopotamia is called Hadad (Adad).

Another noteworthy epithet of Baal in the Ugaritic texts is *zbl*, which is usually translated 'prince';[4] once we also find the compound phrase *zbl b'l 'arṣ*, 'the prince, the lord of the earth'. It is probable that Baal-Zebub, 'the lord of the flies', who is mentioned in 2 Kings 1 as the god of the city of Ekron, is a deliberate distortion of Ba'al-Zebul, and that therefore the New Testament name for the devil, Beelzebul, preserves the form which is linguistically more correct (with -l in place of -b).

Another interesting epithet is given to Baal in one of the Keret texts, where he is called *'ly*, i.e. *'ali* or something similar, which clearly means 'the high, exalted'. It is said that a sacrifice was offered

for Baal's rain on the earth
and the rain of the Most High on the fields;
pleasant is Baal's rain on the earth,
and on the field the rain of the Most High. (II K III, 6–8)

This gives new support to Nyberg's attempt to find a god 'Al, whom he believed to be identical with 'Elyon, in a number of (as he claimed) misunderstood passages in Hosea and elsewhere in the Old Testament.[5] But since Hosea's struggle is primarily directed against Baal, and no antagonism to 'Elyon is found elsewhere in the Old Testament, it is more probable that we are dealing with an epithet of Baal. It is especially interesting that one such misunderstood 'Al is found in 1 Sam. 2.10, in a context mentioning thunder; while in Ps. 18.13 'Elyon occurs in a similar context. It is well known that Yahweh has some features of an atmospheric god of the Baal type.

Baal is often described in the texts as the son of Dagan (Dagon), but there are also passages where he appears to regard El as his father.

Baal's dwelling place is the mount Sapān (Saphon), north of Ugarit, the Kasios of the Greeks. This mountain was clearly to the Canaanites what Olympus was to the Greeks; it was not only the dwelling place of Baal but the site of the assembly of the gods. An echo of these ideas is found in Ps. 48.2, where Mount Sion to our surprise is placed 'in the far north'—but the north in Hebrew is *ṣāphōn*, and it is clearly the intention to allude to Saphon, the mountain of the gods.

In a recently published text a description is given of how Baal, who is also called Hadd, sits enthroned upon his mountain, here called both Sapān and 'the mount of victory'. The description of the god that follows has a number of obscure points, but it is at least clear that he is surrounded by seven lightning flashes, that he has dew upon his forehead, that he has two horns, and that his head 'moves in the heaven'. There is also reference to a bull behind him or under (?) him.

More will be said later on about the role played by Baal in the myths. Here it need only be said that he is represented as the vanquisher of the Sea in a battle which in some respects can be compared with the battle with Tiamat of the Babylonian creation myth, but that the consequence is not a creation of the world, but rather that Baal takes dominion over it as king. The most important of the myths, however, is that which tells of Baal's defeat at the hands of his enemy Mot (probably 'death') and his descent into the land of the dead, from which, however, after the intervention of his sister 'Anat he returns to life. It is clear that we have here a vegetation myth. Baal is closely connected with fertility, and Mot is clearly the drought and heat of summer which withers the vegetation. The death of Baal coincides with the withering of the vegetation and his resurrection with the coming of the rainy season and the regeneration of the vegetation. The myth must have been expressed in rites of which the purpose was to keep this cycle of nature in motion.

There are several pictorial representations of Baal. One typical one shows him as a god of lightning and thunder; he has a pointed beard and a helmet with horns, in one hand he carries a club, in the other a spear, clearly as a symbol for lightning. The horns seem to indicate that Baal was regarded as a bull, although this is never stated in the texts. There is, however, a myth which tells of Baal's love for a heifer, and another passage says: 'a bull is born to Baal, a bull calf to him who rides upon the clouds'.

There is a particular problem with *Ba'alshamēm*, 'the Baal of heaven'. Is he a separate god of heaven, or a form of the storm and thunder god as connected with the heavens? Philo Byblius tells us that the first living beings on earth when there was a drought lifted up their hands towards the sun, which they regarded as the only god, the lord of heaven, for they called him Beelsamen, which is the same as the Zeus of the Greeks. This information is rather puzzling. Zeus and Baal-Hadad are certainly comparable in their capacity as storm-gods, and Hadad is often identified in the Hellenistic period with Zeus, but there is no evidence for any connection with the sun for Baal.

Ba'alshamēm is mentioned in Phoenician inscriptions, in Esarhaddon's treaty with the king of Tyre, in Carthage, and in the Roman comedy writer Plautus—and also in a number of Aramaic inscriptions, down to the Hellenistic period, and at Karatepe—but none of them gives any guidance towards forming a view of the character of the god. It is possible that the hieroglyphic Hittite version of the Karatepe inscription will be of assistance, for there Baalshamem is represented by a sign for the Hittite storm and thunder god Tarḫunt.

In Carthage a Ba'al Ḥammōn was worshipped. The name has been interpreted as 'the lord of the altar of incense'. He is known from countless dedications, on his own in the oldest inscriptions, later usually together with the goddess Tinnit, and then always mentioned *after* her. There are a few attestations of his cult in Phoenicia (the Kilamuwa inscription) and in Palmyra. In Latin inscriptions he is called *frugifer*, 'the fruit-bearer', and *deus frugum*, 'the god of the fruits', which points in the direction of a vegetation god. Later he was identified with the Egyptian Ammon in Siva, and this led to Ammon being portrayed with a beard and horn. In Greek he is identified with Kronos, in Latin with Saturn, but also sometimes with Jupiter. The suggestion has been made that he can be identified with El, since the latter is not mentioned on African soil, but it has not been possible to produce firm evidence for this.

As we have seen, Baal is often called in the texts 'the son of Dagan'. But Dagan (Dagon) himself has no part to play in mythology, and his name occurs elsewhere too only rarely. There are, however, a number of theophoric personal names, sacrificial lists, and two votive inscriptions in which it does occur. We know also that he had a temple near that of Baal at Ugarit. There is also a place Beth-Dagon ('the house (i.e. temple) of Dagon'), on the south Palestinian coastline, and 1 Sam. 5.1–2 mentions the worship of Dagon in the Philistine city Ashdod. These facts, however, give little information about the functions of the god, and it has only been possible to conclude from the etymology of the name that he has some connection with corn, which in Hebrew is called *dāgān* (a derivation from Arabic *dağn*, rain, is less probable). It is improbable that his name has any connection with *dāg*, fish, although a god with a fish's tail is portrayed on a coin from Aradus.

Adonis is the Greek name for a deity who, according to Greek writers, was worshipped in Syria and Phoenicia, and was also taken over by the Greeks from the seventh century B.C. at the latest. The name is identical with the Phoenician word 'ādōn, 'lord', but this is not attested as the proper name of any god, only as an epithet. We may, therefore, presume that Adonis is the Greek equivalent of some local form of Baal.

According to the Greek sources Adonis when young was the object of the love both of Aphrodite and of Persephone, the goddess of the land of the dead. When the latter would not let him go, Aphrodite descended to the underworld to release him. The dispute was resolved by Zeus, who decided that he should spend half the year with Aphrodite, and half the year in the underworld with Persephone. Finally Adonis was killed by a boar, bitterly bemoaned by Aphrodite. There is no difficulty in recognizing elements from the mythologies of Tammuz and of Baal in this report, and it must be an accident that it is not possible to attest this connection from inscriptions.

The most important cultic centres of Adonis were Byblos on the coast of Syria and Paphos in Cyprus. In the former place there was, according to Lucian, a temple to Aphrodite (i.e. Astarte), where secret rites were celebrated in honour of Adonis.

> They assert that the legend about Adonis and the wild boar is true, and that the facts occurred in their land, and in memory of this calamity they beat their breasts, and wail every year . . . When they have finished their mourning and wailing, they sacrifice in the first place to Adonis, as to one who has departed this life; after this they allege that he is alive again, and exhibit his effigy to the sky.[6]

The river that debouches at Byblos bears the name of Adonis, and at its source there was a temple of Astarte at Aphaca. At this place there was an image of Adonis being slain by a bear (!) and of the goddess weeping over his death. When the water of the river was coloured red in the spring by certain kinds of earth, this was connected with the blood of Adonis. At the same time the red anemone flowers, and it was told that it got its colour from the blood of the god. The name of the flower in Arabic, 'the wound of na'mān', seems to preserve an epithet of Adonis, na'mān, 'the pleasant'.[7] In Isa. 17.10 of the same word is used in an allusion to the so-called gardens of Adonis, already mentioned in Plato, bowls containing plants which were forced to shoot up very fast, and then withered just as fast—a symbol of the flourishing and death of Adonis.

Eshmun, who is mentioned in various Phoenician inscriptions and belonged especially to Sidon, but also came to be of great importance in Carthage, was probably also a god of fertility. A trilingual inscription from Sardinia identifies him with Asklepios (Aesculapius), which shows that he was regarded as a god of healing.[8] This, however, is probably a secondary trait. It has also been suggested that Eshmun is identical with Adonis; it is in any case certain that (like many other gods) he could be called *'ādōn*, 'the lord'.[9] There is also a story in Damascius that when he was a youth he was pursued in the course of a hunt by the mother of the gods Astronoë (=Astarte?) and in his flight castrated himself. He died, but was resurrected by the life-giving warmth of the goddess and became a god, and was called Eshmun after this warmth (cf. *'ēš*, 'fire'). Apart from the fact that the explanation of the name is artificial and secondary, the account shows such a composite character in other respects that it is hard to draw any definite conclusions on the basis of it alone.

Resheph (so in Hebrew, other forms attested being Rashap, Rashpan/Rashpon)[10] is attested from as early as the Mari and Ras Shamra texts down to the Punic inscriptions from Carthage and Egyptian texts. The word means either 'fire' or 'pestilence'; in Hebrew it refers to the lightning (Ps. 78.48), to arrows as 'flames of the bow' (Ps. 76.3) or to sparks as sons of Resheph, or it is linked with hunger and pestilence as in Deut. 32.24, or with 'plague' as in Hab. 3.5. Resheph is on the one hand the god of plague who spreads death around himself, and the Keret epic says that he had taken away a large part of the family of Keret. When one of the Amarna letters says that Nergal slew the people of the land, including the letter-writer's own son, it is probably Resheph that is the god referred to. Resheph is sometimes called *b'l ḥṣ*, 'the lord of the arrow', which in view of the fact that he is usually identified with Apollo probably alludes to arrows that bring sickness. On the other hand, Resheph is also invoked for healing. An omen text mentions him as 'door-keeper' of the sun-goddess as she sets, which may suggest a role as keeper of the underworld and of the land of the dead, the more so in that it is a question of a sign that presages disaster.[11] On another occasion 'Resheph in his house' is mentioned among eleven deities who assist the sun goddess.[12] The Resheph *ṣprm* (of the birds? of a place?) who is mentioned at Karatepe cannot be regarded with certainty as Phoenician.

Pictures of Resheph are known only from Egypt. They represent him in battle-array with shield, spear, and battle-axe, together with a crown with emblems in the form of a gazelle's head. A similar picture from Beisan in the Jordan valley represents according to the accompanying inscription 'Mekal, the god of Beisan'.[13] The name Mekal, however, is also known from Cyprus, where it stands together with Resheph. Although a trilingual inscription identifies Mekal with Apollo Amyclaeus, we may well conclude that Resheph and Mekal are two gods of similar qualities, but not identical.

Melqart (properly Milk-qart, 'the king of the city') was the god of the city of Tyre, but was worshipped also in the daughter city of Carthage, usually under the name of Baal Melqart. His name occurs for the first time in Esarhaddon's treaty with the king of Tyre. It has been thought that he was originally a sun-god, but it appears that the solar traits are relatively late. He is, however, also connected with the sea and with navigation; on coins he is portrayed as riding upon a sea-horse, and he seems to have been worshipped on rocky promontories; a Cape Melqart (*rš mlqrt*) is known from Sicily. Frazer included Melqart among the dying and rising gods, but his evidence for this is not completely unambiguous. We know that Melqart was identified with Herakles, and there is evidence that the myth that he was burnt on a funeral pyre on mount Oeta was also attributed to Tyre. There is evidence that a feast with the name 'the awakening (*égersis*) of Herakles' was celebrated in January. And a Greek writer also tells us that the Phoenicians sacrificed quails to Herakles, because on this journey in Libya he had been killed by Typhon, but reawakened to life by Iolaos, who held a quail (according to another variant roast quails) under his nose; the god smelt the bird, and returned to life again. It is clearly not easy to reconstruct from these scattered facts a myth of the death of Melqart by fire, celebrated in the cult by the burning of a doll—the evidence for which, however, is capable of other interpretations—and his subsequent resurrection. Elements from Greek mythology have been mixed together with data from Phoenician religion, without there being any certainty that they have anything to do with one another.

On coins an eagle and a lion are the symbols of Melqart. His temple apparently had no image in it, but a perpetual flame burnt upon the altar.

Ḥoron is a Canaanite deity who is known through personal and place names from about 1900 to about 600 B.C. According to the Book of Joshua there are two places called Beth-Horon ('the house, i.e. temple of Horon') in Ephraim. A prince called *Haurān-abum*, 'Horon is the father' is cursed in an Egyptian text of the twelfth dynasty. Egyptian texts mention Ḥoron together with Resheph and the goddess Anath. In Ugarit hẹ is invoked by Keret in a curse, as he is also in a Phoenician incantation from Arslan Tash of the seventh century B.C. He is known as the tutelary deity of the city of Jabneh (Jamnia), and an ostracon found just to the north of Tel Aviv speaks of 'gold for Ḥoron's temple'. It has been conjectured that Horon was a chthonic deity, but there is no firm evidence for this.

We know little more of Chemosh (or perhaps better, to judge by the cuneiform version, Kamosh), the national god of the Moabites than that he is mentioned several times in the Old Testament and in the inscription of King Mesha, usually in a warlike context. A couple of personal names with the name of the god as an element give no real information about him; but a list of gods puts him together with Nergal. Moabite coins show a warlike figure between two torches—this *may* be Chemosh.

Milkom the god of the Ammonites is mentioned several times in the Old Testament (2 Sam. 12.30; 1 Kings 11.5, 7; 2 Kings 23.13; Jer. 49.3; Zeph. 1.5). The name is an expansion of *milk*, king. No further details of him are known.

A difficult text from Ras Shamra tells of how two gods, Shaḥar and Shalim, were born of 'El's two consorts'. The text gives no information about their functions, so that we can only draw conclusions from their names. Shaḥar means 'the dawn', and occurs with mythological colouring also a couple of times in the Old Testament: in Isa. 14.12 we hear of Helal (the moon), son of Shaḥar. We must therefore be dealing with a Ugaritic (male) equivalent of Eos or Aurora. Shalim should then be the god of the evening or twilight, and this is perhaps supported by the fact that the sunset is called in Akkadian *šalām šamši*. The name appears to occur as the second element in Jeru-shalem, the first element meaning 'foundation' or 'stronghold'.

When we turn to the female deities, we find especially three variants of the great mother-goddess and goddess of love, only slightly differentiated from one another, called Athirat, Athtart (Astarte), and 'Anat. All three occur in the Ugaritic texts, but each is also known from elsewhere.

Evidence that the worship of divinity in its feminine aspect had a place of importance in Canaan and Syria is given by the numerous small female statuettes with sexual characteristics emphasized which have been found by archaeologists. But this goddess remains anonymous. We cannot tell whether she was given any of the three names which we know from written sources. But it is clear that the worship of this goddess fits in well with the Canaanite fertility cult, and the number of these figurines attests to the high measure of popularity which she enjoyed. It can be assumed that the three goddesses mentioned represent different developments of the motif of the feminine generative power as something divine and important for the continuation of life and of the community.

Athirat (Ashera) appears to be the consort of El, and the highest goddess in the Ugaritic texts; in lists of sacrifices and other similar lists the two are usually mentioned together. Sometimes she is called *'ilt*, 'the goddess', and this perhaps suggests that she is the female complement of El. Her most common epithet is *rbt 'aṭrt ym*, 'the lady, Ashera of the sea'—other interpretations suggested, for example, 'she who walks on the sea', are extremely uncertain. It is not clear from the texts what her special connection with the sea is. She is also called *qnyt 'ilm* 'the creator, or progenitor, of the gods', and correspondingly 'the sons of Athirat' are the same as 'the gods' (*'ilm*). In the Keret Epic she and 'Anat are described as the divine wet-nurses who give suck to the king's son (III K II, 25–8).

Apart from Ugarit we know Ashera from the Amorites in the period of the first Babylonian dynasty, when she is the consort of the national god Amurru, called 'the daughter-in-law of the king of heaven' and 'the mistress of fruitfulness and sensual pleasure'. An Amorite king is called Abdi-Aširta, i.e. the servant of Ashera, and a 'soothsayer of Aširat' is mentioned in a cuneiform letter from Taanach in Palestine. In the Old Testament mention is often made of the asherah or of asherahs (Hebrew *'ašērā*), and by this is usually meant a cultic object of wood, a pole or something similar,

which clearly represented the goddess upon the cultic site. Sometimes, however, the personal name seems to be intended, as in the
report of Elijah and the prophets of Baal in 1 Kings 18.19, where
she is said like Baal to have 400 prophets in Israel, and in the
mention of the image of Asherah which Manasseh had in the
temple of Jerusalem (2 Kings 21.7; 23.6).

'Athtart ('Ashtart, Astarte) is mentioned in the Ugaritic texts
only in formulaic phrases and in cultic and liturgical texts. She
plays a much larger part in the descriptions of the classical authors,
where she is often identified with Aphrodite. Like the Assyrian
and Babylonian Ishtar she has both a benevolent and a terrifying
aspect: she is a goddess of love and fertility and also of war.

In the Keret Epic we hear that 'Athtart and 'Anat are beautiful.
A connection with the fertility god Baal is suggested by the
epithet *šm bʻl*, 'the name of Baal' (hardly 'the heavens of Baal'),
which also occurs in a Phoenician inscription. Astarte appears as a
war-goddess in a mention in 1 Sam. 31.10, according to which war-
booty is dedicated to her and brought to her temple, and also to a
pronounced degree in the Egyptian sources: there she is called
'mighty on horseback', 'mistress of horses and of chariots', 'the
mistress of battles, goddess of the Asiatics'. In a fragmentary
mythological papyrus from the nineteenth dynasty the story is
told of her being given in marriage to the tyrannical god of the sea,
a motif which is otherwise unknown.

In the Old Testament Astarte is mentioned a number of times
as the goddess of the Sidonians (1 Kings 11.5, 33; 2 Kings 23.13)
and it is probably she who is meant also by 'the queen of heaven'
in Jer. 7.18 and 44.17ff.

According to Philo Byblius Astarte wore the horns of the bull as
a symbol of dominion. There may be a connection between this
statement and the place-name 'Ašterot-qarnaim (Gen. 14.5),
'Astarte of (the two) horns'. A picture from Beth-shean of a
goddess with horns may also be connected with this. The identification is, however, uncertain, as it is also in the case of another
picture from Minet el-Beida, where a goddess is shown flanked
by two goats—a reworking of the old *potnia thērōn* (mistress of the
beasts) motif. In another instance Astarte carries a crown with
decorations like plums, an obvious fertility symbol. There is
evidence that the dove was regarded as her holy bird. The snake
also seems to have been a symbol of the mother-goddess from of

old; snakes and doves are found combined upon a sacrificial offering-stand from Beth-shean.[14]

A special problem is posed by the comparative aspect of the question. The name Astarte is identical with the Akkadian Ishtar, except that there the feminine ending -*t* is lacking. In South Arabia 'Athtar is a male deity, and in fact there is also evidence in the Ugaritic texts for a male 'Athtar, and the Mesha stone has the compound name 'Ashtar-Chemosh. The Ugaritic 'Athtar appears as an abortive replacement for Baal during the time that he is in the underworld; he has the epithet '*ariẓ*, 'the cruel, terrible'.

It is clear that we are dealing with a differentiation of a deity who was originally bisexual or of indeterminate sex. (In Ugarit there are personal names which describe 'Athtar both as 'father' and as 'mother'.[15]) Since Ishtar–Astarte was in any case very early connected with the planet Venus, it has been suggested that we are dealing with the role of the planet as morning and evening star. But it would then be hard to explain why in certain areas only one of these aspects became an object of worship.[16] Another possibility would be that we are dealing with an ancient sky-god—it is by no means unusual for these to be of indeterminate sex—and that the god and goddess represent different developments of this.[17] But the material available to us now is not sufficient for this question to be definitively answered.

'Anat (Anath) is in the Ugaritic texts the most active of the three goddesses. She also had an important role in Egypt through the Hyksos. On an Egyptian stele from Beth-shean she is called 'the queen of heaven, the mistress of the gods'. Apart from this there is relatively poor attestation for her: in a bilingual inscription from Cyprus she is equated with Athene; an 'Anat-Bethel is attested for Tyre by a cuneiform document, and for the Jewish colony at Elephantine, where there is also an 'Anat-Yahu, i.e. an 'Anat connected with Yahweh occurs; finally, we have a Shamgar son of 'Anath in Judg. 5.6 and place-names such as Beth-'Anath (Josh. 19.38; Judg. 1.33) and 'Anathoth (the home town of the prophet Jeremiah).

In Ugarit 'Anat has the epithet *btlt*, virgin (cf. Hebrew *bᵉthūlāh*), a fact which, however, by no means contradicts her fertility aspect; rather it emphasizes, as Eissfeldt stresses, her youthfulness and powers of life and generation. The epithet *rḥm* seems to have a similar significance ('girl'); it is perhaps connected with the Hebrew *reḥem*, womb. She appears as the sister of Baal, but it is not impossible that this word, as in, for example, the Song of Songs, has the meaning of 'beloved' or 'bride'. There is certainly a sexual meaning in the epithet *ybmt l'imm*, 'the *ybmt* of the people', in which the first word seems to have the meaning 'sister-in-law' (Eissfeldt: 'mistress'; Röllig: 'widow?'). We have already seen her as the wet-nurse of the king's child. There are texts, unfortunately very fragmentary, which appear to show her in a sexual function. One text tells of how she sings of her love for Baal, but the text ends abruptly where we should have expected the words of the song.

It is, however, without doubt her warlike functions which predominate. In the Aqhat text she is seized by a desire to possess Aqhat's bow. In the poems of the Baal cycle she laments and buries her dead brother, but then goes on the rampage, and kills Mot, the slayer of Baal. Another scene shows her fighting against enemies and wading through their blood. She is portrayed with helmet, battle-axe, and spear. In Egypt she is sometimes given the symbols of Hathor.

In Carthage the great goddess is called Tinnit (formerly read as Tanit). She has so high a position that she is usually listed first of all the deities, even before Baal Hammon. It appears that Tinnit is the special Carthaginian form of Astarte, but strangely enough there are no personal names compounded with Tinnit, while there are some which contain the name Astarte. The name appears to be of local origin; it has not so far been possible to find an explanation of its meaning.

Tinnit regularly has the epithet *pn b'l*, 'the face of Baal'. The meaning of this is contested. It has been thought that her cultic image may have stood 'before the face of Baal', or that the meaning is 'reflection' or 'manifestation' of Baal, or that the epithet is meant to describe her as the consort of Baal. At present none of these explanations can be regarded as convincing.[18]

So far as we can tell from identifications with Greek and Roman divinities Tinnit appears to have the role especially of mistress of heaven. There are indications that like 'Anat she was regarded as a virgin, but she is also called mother and *nutrix*. Her symbols are the usual ones for a goddess of fertility: the pomegranate, an ear of wheat, a dove, and also a hand in a position of blessing or of protection. There is also a special Tinnit symbol, a triangle with a horizontal arm at its apex, upon which a crescent moon sits—the meaning is not clear, but Tinnit does not in any case seem to have been a moon-goddess.

Symbols for the sun and the moon occur in the recently discovered Canaanite temple at Hazor. But we hear surprisingly little of any sun and moon worship. In Ugarit there is a sun-goddess, 'Shapsh (Shapash) the light of the gods',[19] but she does not have a position of prominence, and in sacrificial and similar lists she does not occur at all. On the coastal plain towards the south there lies a Beth-Shemesh, 'the house, or temple, of the sun', and such a personal name as Samson (*šimšōn*) seems to allude to the sun cult. The Old Testament repudiates completely the worship of the heavenly bodies. There is a reference to horses dedicated to the sun in 2 Kings 23.11.

A moon-god Yariḥ occurs in one Ras Shamra text, where we hear of his marriage to Nikkal (the goddess's name is Sumerian, Ningal). Place-names which may attest the moon-cult are Beth-yeraḥ and Jericho (*yᵉrēḥō*).

MYTHOLOGY

Our knowledge of Canaanite and Phoenician mythology was extremely small until the discovery of the Ras Shamra texts. All we had was a couple of versions of the Phoenician cosmogony, which were to be found in classical authors, one in Philo Byblius and one in the philosopher Damascius.

According to Philo (or his informant) at the beginning of all things there was a dark wind-shaped air, and a dark miry chaos. The wind, however, 'became fond of its own beginning', and as Pothos (desire) it brought forth a being Mot (probably 'mud, mire'; hardly identical with Baal's enemy Mot). From this creature there then arose the rest of creation in the form of an egg, which 'shone forth' together with the sun, the moon, and the stars. At the same time there also arose rational beings which were called Zofesamin or 'observers of the heavens'—we unfortunately do not hear what they were. When the air became light and warm, there arose 'through the heat of the sea and of the land' clouds and rain, thunder and lightning, so that the rational creatures were terrified and began to move as male and female on the land and in the sea.

Philo adds to this a long genealogical table of the gods, and describes their exploits.

Damascius has two versions of the story of creation. According to one, at first there were Chronos, Pothos (desire), and Omichle (darkness); from the two latter there arose Aer (the air), 'the unmixed spiritual', and Aura, 'the model which the spiritual set in motion'. These then gave birth to Otos, which is the spiritual basic material. According to the other version, at the beginning there were Aither (the ether) and Aer (the air) (or according to a variant only the wind), from whom came Ulomus (clearly *'ōlām*, eternity), and Chusor (a god of handicrafts who is also known from Ugarit, as Kothar, and through Philo), then an egg which burst and brought forth heaven and earth.

It is obvious that these reports show clear traces of assimilation to Hellenistic thought patterns. But some names are authentic, and certain basic features may also well be authentically Phoenician. We know the water of chaos also from the *t^ehōm*, the primeval sea, of the Old Testament; the wind corresponds to the *rūaḥ* of god (spirit or wind) in Gen. 1.2. The Babylonian Creation Epic also has both the water of chaos and the storm-wind which defeats Tiamat. The egg, on the other hand, is otherwise unknown in the Semitic thought world, but is attested in certain Egyptian cosmogonies and in the Orphic cosmogony. The picture of the processes of creation as a sequence of births of the gods has parallels in Egypt and in Babylon. It is useless to speculate about details in view of the nature of the sources. The most important point is that the starting point for creation is similar in the Phoenician cosmogony and in the Israelite and Babylonian cosmogonies.

The role of the sea as a chaos element in Babylon and Israel makes it tempting to bring in for comparison also the section of the Baal cycle from Ugarit which tells of Baal's struggle with Yam, i.e. the sea. The previous story is obscure. In any case Yam attacks Baal with the approval of El. He sends his messenger to the terrified assembly of the gods, and El gives his consent to Baal being handed over. Baal, however, seizes his weapons and attacks first the messenger and then Yam himself. He acquires weapons with magic powers from the skilled craftsman Kothar-wa-Ḥasis, and succeeds in defeating his enemies with them. The end of the text is incomplete. Certain expressions seem to suggest that Baal slew or at least wished to slay Yam ('Yam is dead, Baal shall be king'), others again suggest that 'Athtart intervened and declared that Yam should only be held captive; he is defeated and must henceforward keep himself to his own province, while Baal has won the position of king.

It looks as if we have here a struggle for world dominion. In the Old Testament we have references to similar ideas in connection with Yahweh and the sea (or in other versions a sea monster), but there the whole story is connected with creation: the sea being put in its place and not allowed to overstep the fixed limits is an element in Yahweh's ordering of the world. It seems an inevitable conclusion that we are dealing with variants of the same basic motif.

The problem of this Baal myth is its connection with the other episodes which are related in the so-called Baal cycle from Ugarit, which covers eight large clay tablets and a number of fragments. There is a tendency for scholarship to combine all these episodes into a coherent epic cycle, but agreement has not been reached on the sequence of events, partly because certain tablets are damaged and so cannot be read in full. The idea has, however, been put forward that there may be a number of independent myths. It is also possible that the Baal cycle is an epic composition out of originally independent motifs much as in the Gilgamesh Epic. We have already dealt with one of the three main motifs in the Baal cycle, the fight against the Sea (Yam). The two others are the building of Baal's 'house', i.e. temple, and Baal's death and 'resurrection'.

Baal's 'housebuilding' is spoken of in two texts. In one the goddess 'Anat is the central character, and we hear how she fights a mighty battle and wades in the blood of her dead enemies, whereupon Baal sends a message to her that he dislikes war and the shedding of blood. 'I have a word to say to you', he says, which is

> the speech of wood and the whispering of the stone,
> the talk of heaven with the earth,
> (the talk) of the deep with the stars,
> lightning so that the heavens may know,
> thunder so that mankind may know
> and the multitudes of the earth may understand.
>
> (V AB C, 20–5)

(This has been compared with Psalm 19, which speaks of the heavens declaring the glory of God.) When the messengers approach 'Anat, she wonders what is the matter, and says: 'verily I have smitten Yam . . . I have defeated the dragon', etc. and so claims for herself the victory over all Baal's enemies, including Yam, who in other texts is defeated by Baal himself. This indicates that it is not a question of *one* consistent narrative, but of variant traditions. The messengers, however, deliver their message, and 'Anat promises to 'take away war from the earth', but then makes her way hastily to Baal. Here unfortunately a portion of the text is missing, but when it begins again there is a lament for the fact that Baal has not got a house or a palace like the other gods, and 'Anat goes to El to secure a promise that one will be built. The idea is clearly that Baal cannot exercise his royal power if he does not have a palace (temple). The last portion of the text that is preserved tells how a message is sent to the craftsman god Kothar-wa-Ḥasis, who is obviously to build the house.

The second text begins directly with Baal's lament that he does not have a 'house', for which reason he and 'Anat go to the goddess Athirat. In her presence he also laments that he does not receive proper food:

Abominable food was placed on my table,
worthless drink I drank from my cup.
Two sorts of sacrifice does Baal hate,
three sorts he that rides on the clouds,
a sacrifice of shame,
a sacrifice of meanness,
a sacrifice of the profligacy of the maidservants.[20]
(II AB III, 15–21)

It is not completely clear if it is unsuitable sacrifices that are in mind, or ignominious treatment in the 'assembly of the gods'. Athirat goes off, however, accompanied by 'Anat to El, and lays the matter before him, and he decides that a house shall be built for Baal 'as for the other gods'. Athirat adds that Baal will now make himself known in thunder and lightning, and give rain abundantly. Now a message is sent to Kothar-wa-Ḥasis—which indicates that this text does not follow on directly from the preceding one—and he comes and sets at once to work. Cedar-wood is obtained, and for six days 'fire burnt in the temple' (obviously the fire of the smiths), but on the seventh day the fire was extinguished and the house stood ready. Baal inaugurates his house with a great banquet for the gods. After a strange interlude in which Baal 'takes' a large number of cities and villages, Baal declares that he wants a window in his house, something which he had previously refused to let Kothar-wa-Ḥasis make. His command is carried out, and Baal makes the thunder sound, so that the mountains quake and his enemies flee away to the forests and to the hills. Baal proudly declares that now no one can contest his position as king. Finally, he sends a message that he has now built his house, to Mot, 'the darling of El', who is clearly thought of as dwelling in the underworld (the land of the dead). It appears that he also threatens the life of Mot. The name Mot is certainly identical with the Hebrew *māweth* (*môth*), which means 'death'. A couple of lines which tell how Shapsh, the lamp of the gods, i.e. the sun, burns hot without rain for the sake of Mot, indicate that Mot is at the same time the god of the summer heat and drought which make the vegetation wither.

An attempt has sometimes been made to interpret this myth as an indication that Baal is a newcomer in the Ugaritic pantheon, and that it is only at a late date that he acquired a temple and a regular cult. This is very dubious. On the other hand, the basic motif is certainly that Baal as victor and king must have a palace fitting for him, i.e. a temple. We are dealing, therefore, with a temple foundation myth, which may very well have had a place in an annual festival. The scene of the opening of the window may refer to some rain rite. In any case the context gives clear information about Baal's character as a god of thunder, rain, and fertility.

The appearance of Mot at the end of the last-mentioned text leads us on to the last and perhaps the most important theme in the myths of the Baal cycle: the death of the god and his return to life. These events are described on two large tablets, which are not, however, preserved in full, so that various gaps in the text make the understanding of the continuity of the story more difficult.

The text begins very abruptly with a message from Mot to Baal, perhaps as an answer to the message which Baal sent to Mot after the accomplishment of the building of the temple:

When you crushed Lotan, the swift serpent,
and made an end of the coiled serpent,

the tyrant (?) with seven heads,
the heavens drooped and hung loose
like the belt on your clothes;
and I was consumed like blood-red funeral meats and died.
Truly you shall climb down into the mouth of Mot the son of
   god,
into the miry throat of the hero, the beloved of El.
(I* AB I, 1–8)

This section is interesting from many points of view. Lòtan is
clearly identical with the Leviathan of the Bible, the monster
which was defeated by Yahweh at creation, and which in Isa. 27.1
is described in exactly the same words as here. Probably Lotan is
identical with, or a representative of, Yam, the Sea, which Baal
defeated. It is striking that the defeat of Lotan also signifies
the death of Mot, i.e. his exile to the land of the dead. But now
it will be Baal's turn to go down to the underworld, which is
described pictorially as Mot's miry throat (notice the connection
of the land of the dead with mire and water, as in the Old
Testament).

Mot's message also contains a long passage, on the interpretation
of which no consensus has been reached. It looks as if Baal did not
understand its real content; in any case he declares that he is Mot's
servant for ever. A renewed call to Baal to 'descend into the deep
of the earth, and become one of those who go down into the
earth', is followed by a brief description of Baal's intercourse with
a heifer 'in the plain of death' with the birth of a boy (or a bull-
calf?) as the consequence. The meaning is clearly to ensure a
descendant in case Baal's expedition to the underworld should go
wrong.

When the text begins again after a long gap, news is brought of
the death of Baal:

Baal has fallen to the ground,
Al'iyan Baal is dead,
the prince, lord of the earth has perished.
(I* AB VI, 8–10)

When El hears this he descends from his throne, and performs rites
of mourning: rolls himself in the dust, tears his clothes asunder,
gashes his breast, and cries:

Baal is dead. What shall come of the people of the son of Dagan,
what of the multitudes that belong to Baal?
I will go down into the earth (cf. Gen. 37.35).

(I* AB VI, 24–6)

'Anat joins El in the rites of mourning. The sun-goddess carries
Baal's body back, and 'Anat buries him up in the north with rich
funeral offerings.

El and Athirat now make 'Athtar 'the terrible' king in place of
Baal, but he soon has to admit that he cannot fill the place of Baal.
After a time 'Anat is seized with longing for Baal and goes to look
for Mot, attacks him, and kills him.

After a long gap we come in again in the middle of the report
of a dream:

In a dream, O El the gentle,
in a vision, O creator of the creation,
the heavens rained fatness,
the streams flowed with honey.
I know that Al'iyan Baal lives,
that the prince, lord of earth, exists.

(I AB III–IV, 5–9)

El receives the message with gladness. But the dream is not yet a
reality, for we still hear that the furrows are parched and dried up.
But after a further gap in the text we hear that Baal again ascends
his royal throne; and after another gap Baal and Mot fight together
in a great duel, which ends finally with the defeat of Mot.

Various allusions in the text of the myth make it clear that it is
the alternation of the seasons and the death and renewal of vegetation that form the basis in nature of the myth. But we do not have
here a purely symbolic account: various features of the text are
best explained if we assume that the recital of it was accompanied
by rites and actions which made concrete what was reported. We are
clearly dealing with a cultic drama, in which the death and resurrection of the god were presented visually in rites which at the same
time had the purpose of maintaining the course of nature which is
reflected in the myths, and in this way ensuring the fertility of the
land.

A further Baal text has no clear connection with any of the three
motifs that have been mentioned, or with any Baal epic there may

have been. This is a tablet preserved only fragmentarily, which tells of how Baal in the course of a hunt meets 'the virgin 'Anat' and has intercourse with her. It looks as if the result is the birth of a bull-calf; in any case in the final lines the 'good news' (*bsrt* = Heb. *beśōrā*, Greek *euangelion*) is proclaimed that 'a wild ox is born to Baal, a buffalo to him that rides on the clouds'. It is extremely probable that the text has something to do with a *hieros gamos* celebration. A recently published text which refers to 'Anat's praise of Baal's beauty may belong in the same cultic context.

A similar cultic situation is also presupposed by the short text about the birth of 'the gracious gods'. Here we are told how Baal meets two women, and begets first two sons, Shaḥar and Shalim ('dawn' and 'twilight'), and then two more 'gracious and fair' beings, who turn out to have a voracious appetite and are sent out into the desert, where they wander around for a time and meet 'the watchman of the sown land'. The text is interesting because of the way it combines stage-directions—which seem to point to a connection with vine-gathering—with parts which narrate the myth. It reflects, therefore, a cultic drama. The description of the great appetite of the two gods is interesting:

A lip to earth, a lip to heaven,
and the birds of the heavens and the fish of the sea enter their
mouths.

(SS R II, 29f)

A similar phrase is used another time (I* AB II, 1f) of Mot or the underworld, and it is interesting to compare it with the description of the behaviour of the ungodly in Psalm 73. The functions of the two gods seem to be of such a nature that the description 'gracious' is best taken as a euphemism.

The text concerning 'Nikkal and the bridesmaids' is very fragmentary. It tells of the marriage of the moon-god Yariḥ with the daughter of 'the summer king', Nikkal, and is interesting for the glimpse it gives us of wedding customs at Ugarit. As some sort of bridesmaids we find the Kāthirāt, 'the skilful' (the same root as in the name of the god Kothar-wa-Ḥasis), who are also called 'the swallows, the daughters of Hilal (the full moon)'. At the beginning of the text occurs the prediction 'see, the young woman shall bear a son'. This shows that Isa. 7.14 contains a very old standing formula; it is noteworthy that the word for 'young woman' is the same in both texts (Ugaritic *ġlmt*, Hebrew *'almā*).

There are also two other longer cycles of an epic character; but there is still no general agreement to what extent they are to be regarded as myths or as something else. One, the Aqhat cycle, consists of three tablets. The arrangement of their contents is not completely clear because of their fragmentary condition. The most probable sequence of the story is as follows: a king called Daniel (probably the same as is referred to in Ezek. 14.14) is a righteous judge, who protects the cause of the widow and the fatherless. But he has no son. Finally, Baal intercedes for him with El, and El gives him a son who is given the name Aqhat. One day when Daniel is sitting 'in the gate and judging' (cf. the Bible) Kothar-wa-Ḥasis, the skilled craftsman, comes by, and Daniel invites him to a meal. As a reward for his hospitality he gives Aqhat a marvellous bow. During a hunt Aqhat meets the goddess 'Anat, who is filled with desire to own the bow, and offers Aqhat riches and immortality in exchange if he will relinquish it to her. But Aqhat answers: How can a mortal receive eternal life? I shall die like all other men. 'Anat is furious at this defiance, and having obtained El's permission to take vengeance, she sends the warrior Yatpan in the form of an eagle to slay Aqhat. But when Aqhat is gone, the vegetation withers away and Baal is inactive: there is no thunder, no rain, no dew, no springs. His sister Paghat bewails him, and sets out on an expedition of vegeance. She finds his tent, but is clearly overpowered by the wine that she is offered. Here the text as preserved ends, but it is very probable that the continuation told how Paghat was finally successful, and that either Aqhat returned to life, or Daniel got another son.

How is this narrative to be understood? It is clearly not a myth in the usual sense of the word, since those taking part are largely men. But nor can it be historical. What it relates is rather to be regarded as typical. The king is responsible for justice and righteousness, fertility depends on the king's son. The parallel between the fate of Aqhat and that of Baal is striking: each dies a violent death, each is avenged by his sister. Does this mean that the king or the king's son played the part of the dying and rising god in the cult? The text does not allow a firm answer to this question, but the close connection between Aqhat and Baal at any rate is established.

The third epic cycle is that which tells of King Keret (or Karit or Kuriti—the vocalization is, as always in Ugaritic, unknown). This too consists of three tablets, of which one is quite well preserved, both the others very fragmentary. It is not completely certain that the first tablet really contains the beginning of the story.

Keret, the son of El, is a righteous king who has lost his wife and his children. While he laments and weeps over this, El appears to him in a dream and tells him what he is to do: he is to offer sacrifice to him, and to start on an expedition of war to the land of Udum, and to request of its king Pabil the hand in marriage of his daughter Ḥurai,

> whose grace is as the grace of 'Anat,
> and whose beauty is as the beauty of 'Athtart,
> whose eyes are like sapphire stones,
> and whose eyelids are like bowls of onyx.
>
> (I K VI, 26–30)

(Note the similarity of this descriptive song to the Song of Solomon.)

Keret does as he is instructed, and Ḥurai becomes his wife, and thanks to the intervention of Baal he has 'seven sons, yea eight'. The youngest of these, Yasib, is suckled by the goddesses Athirat and 'Anat, and he will have the same strength as his father, and in fact outshine him.

Keret, however, becomes ill and feeble, and can no longer perform his kingly duties. El intervenes to heal him, and it looks as if he recovers, at least for a time. Yasib receives a revelation that he will have his father's place, and he reproaches his father harshly with failing to perform his royal duties: he has not cared for the right of the widow and the fatherless, he has not helped the oppressed, etc. 'Come down from your throne, so that I may rule.' This is followed by a curse uttered by Keret, in which he calls down the punishment of Horon and 'Athtart upon his rebellious son.

The continuation, which should have given us the solution of the intrigue, is unfortunately lost, and with it also the key to a definite understanding of the text. The historical interpretation, according to which the epic contains memories of warfare against cities to the south of Ugarit (but hardly Edom), has now been generally abandoned. According to another interpretation it is a 'sociological myth', i.e. a report whose purpose is to explain why Semitic and Hurrian elements (cf. the name of the queen Ḥurai) lived together in Ugarit; but this appears rather improbable. A third interpretation is the cultic view, which makes Keret the mythical prototype of the sacral king. Even if this interpretation perhaps goes too far, the fact remains that Keret appears the whole time as a sacral king, and that the epic is excellent evidence for the Ugaritic royal ideology, and shows both the social and the cultic and ritual functions of the king. The importance which is attached to the question of the continuation of the dynasty is also of interest.

Attention has been drawn to certain analogies between the Keret text and the biblical narratives of the patriarchs (warfare, the desire for descendants, the promise in a dream), and the account of David in 2 Samuel (especially the rebellion of Absalom). This shows in any case that historical recollections tend to be shaped in a certain pattern of definite motifs, and that the Keret text is just one literary deposit of a combination of a number of such motifs. But it hardly needs to be stressed that the main motif is the importance of the king and the dynasty for the continued existence of the community.

THE GODS OF THE ARAMAEANS

This heading avoids the word 'pantheon' for two reasons: (*a*) there does not appear to have been any organized pan-Aramaean pantheon, but rather different locally varying groups of deities, and (*b*) we cannot assume that the Aramaean group of gods remained the same from the period about 1100 when the Aramaeans first appear down to the centuries about the birth of Christ, from which our last witnesses to Aramaean religion come.

The Aramaic inscriptions have a number of deities in common with those of the Canaanites and Phoenicians. So, for example, the god El appears here also, although his character is difficult to determine. Most of our evidence consists in theophoric personal names, and it has been suggested that '*el* here is the word for 'god' in general, and does not refer to a particular deity. On the other hand, El is definitely an independent figure in the Zenjirli inscriptions, in which he is mentioned in second place after Hadad, and in the Sefire treaty in which we meet the combination El and 'Elyān (see above, p. 130).

Another god shared with the Phoenicians is 'the Baal of heaven', in Aramaic Be'elshemīn. He is mentioned on the Zakir stele together with *'lwr* (El-wer, probably = Hadad) and in Aramaic letters together with a god of heaven whose name is unfortunately lacking. In the Hellenistic period the worship of this Baal is richly attested, and it appears that he was favoured by the Seleucids. We have evidence for his cult from Hauran, Palmyra, and Dura-Europos, and in the fifth century A.D. Isaac of Antioch reports that he was worshipped in Edessa. These attestations unfortunately give hardly any important information on his nature, except that he is specially known in Palmyra as the merciful and gracious god. An Atarsamain, i.e. 'Athtar of heaven, is mentioned in Assyrian sources, but it cannot be determined if the analogy extends further than the second member of the name.

The foremost of the gods of the Aramaeans, however, is Hadad, the Adad of the Akkadians, whom we have found in the Ugaritic texts in the figure of Al'iyan Ba'al. He is the West Semitic storm and thunder god, who here has the part of a national god, who has founded the monarchy and places the king upon his throne. The Zenjirli inscriptions indicate that he hears prayers, and sends all good things, but is also a god who is wroth with those who are displeasing to him. The Sefire treaty calls down his wrath on those who break the treaty. Kings of Damascus in the biblical period have the name Bar-Hadad, 'the son of Hadad', and on a coin from Hierapolis from the period of Alexander the Great a priest-king is called 'Abd-Hadad, the servant of Hadad.

Hadad appears as a god of thunder with the epithet Rammān, 'thunder' (in the Bible Rimmon, 2 Kings 5.18, preserved also in the compound Hadad-Rimmon in Zech. 12.11). This last passage also speaks of a lament for the death of the god, which is otherwise not attested in respect of Hadad. It must be connected with a cult which emphasizes the fertility aspect of the god, of roughly the sort that we find at Ugarit.

When Lucian identifies Hadad with Zeus, it is again the aspect of thunder-god which stands out. On the other hand, Macrobius, who writes about A.D. 400, says that Adad who is 'the foremost and greatest god of the Syrians' and whose name means 'the only' (a misunderstanding or a reinterpretation?) is the sun, and that his statue is surrounded by rays directed downwards. It is clear that we have here a manifestation of the emphasis in Hellenistic culture on the sun and the sun-god as the most important deity, perhaps also a measure of influence from the Hittite sun-god. Hadad was worshipped as a sun-god in, for instance, Heliopolis (Baalbek). Even if there are points of contact between Adad and Shamash in Mesopotamia, and both gods are often mentioned together, there is no reason to assume that Hadad had the character of a sun-god from the beginning. The identification with Zeus and Jupiter, which is well attested in the Hellenistic and Roman period, also points in the direction of a thunder-god or a god of heaven.

The inscribed statue of Hadad from Zenjirli shows him in a standing position and with horns on his head. At a later date a Jupiter Dolichenus, who is portrayed standing on a bull, and with a lightning symbol in one hand and a double axe in the other, was worshipped in the neighbouring city of Doliche. Lucian tells us that the image of Hadad in the temple at Hierapolis rested upon bulls, and coins from the third century A.D. show him together with the goddess Atargatis sitting on a throne supported by two bull figures.[21] A Jupiter Damascenus (i.e. from Damascus) is portrayed standing flanked by two bulls and with an axe in his left hand. The connection of Hadad with the bull is therefore well attested; the other symbols suggest thunder and fertility features.

Hadad's consort was (at least in Hierapolis according to Lucian and at Damascus according to Justinus's epitome) Atargatis. The Aramaic form of the name, which is attested on a number of coins, is 'tr'th, 'Attar-'ate. Its first element is the Aramaic equivalent of the Canaanite 'Athtart ('Ashtart); opinions are divided on the second element, but it is probably a contracted form of the name 'Anat ('ant > 'att)[22] or possibly a less well known name 'Ate. She is a typical form of the great West Semitic goddess. She is identified by Lucian with Hera although 'she has something of the attributes of Athene, and of Aphrodite, and of Selene, and of Rhea, and of Artemis, and of Nemesis and of The Fates'. It could as well be said that she is the feminine essence of divine power.

It could be expected that Atargatis would have been a central figure in myths, but no myths about her are known. On the other hand, there are pictorial representations which show her attributes. Lucian describes her statue in the temple of Hierapolis: she sits on a throne supported by lions, in one hand she holds a sceptre, in the other a distaff, and on her head she has rays and a tower. Representations on coins confirm this description; other coins show her sitting on a lion or give a half length portrait of her.

We also learn that the dove is one of her attributes, and that fish were regarded as sacred for her sake.

One form of Atargatis was, it appears, the Derketo who according to report was pictured with a fish-tail. In her temple there was a lake with holy fish. It appears that this goddess is most closely connected with Athirat, who also had a connection with the sea. But we have seen that Atargatis also had holy fishes. Clearly fishes were regarded as in some way representing the life force and fertility.

Diodorus Siculus reports that Derketo had a daughter Semiramis by a handsome youth named Simios. For shame at her illicit love she then had the young man drowned (he was also called Ichthys, 'fish') and drove the girl out into the desert, where she was fed by doves. Finally, the goddess threw herself into the sea near Askalon. It is clear that there is a connection between this myth and the sacred animals of the goddess. It is also very probable that the myth expresses certain ideas about life and fertility. Semiramis— which is also the Greek name of a legendary Assyrian queen—is represented according to Lucian by a symbol or a sign (*sēmeion*) which stood between the statues of Hadad and Atargatis in the temple of the goddess and which had 'no form of its own, but recalls the characteristics of other gods'. Twice a year this symbol was carried in procession to a lake nearby. On the other hand, we know from an inscription from the island of Delos of a triad from Hierapolis consisting of Hadad, Atargatis, and 'Asklepios', in which Asklepios appears to stand for the young god. The similarity of the names *sēmeion* and Semiramis may remind us of Simios in the Derketo myth, and the identification with Asklepios makes us think of the Phoenician Eshmun, a name which again is quite like Simios. It may be wondered whether we have here traces of a young god Eshmun–Simios by the side of Hadad and Atargatis, but it must be admitted that this is a hypothesis, and that it is noteworthy that such a god is not more clearly attested either in literature or in the inscriptions. The late inscriptions from Hatra refer to a triad 'our lord, our lady and the son of our lord and lady', which could be later developments of the three deities discussed here.

The sun and moon-gods, Shemesh and Shahr, are mentioned in several inscriptions, including the Zakir inscription and the two Nerab inscriptions (in the latter case we have tomb inscriptions for moon priests; a measure of Babylonian influence can be traced in these inscriptions).

Finally, there is special interest in the Nabataean inscriptions from about the beginning of our era, which mention 'the god of a certain person', and sometimes identify him with Be'elshemin or Zeus. Alt[23] found here a parallel with the mention in the patriarchal narratives of the god of Abraham, Isaac, and Jacob, and the identification of him with Yahweh. The 'god of the man' in Sumerian religion is also phenomenologically comparable.

THE CULT

The regular cult of the gods took place partly in the open, partly in regular temples. In the former case the Old Testament speaks of worship 'on high places and under every green tree'. This alludes in part to the fact that trees and groves were regarded as holy and came to mark cultic places—in areas such as Palestine and large parts of Syria which were poor in trees this was natural, since places where trees grew were bound to acquire a reputation for having a special life force. In part it points to the cult places which were to be found on hills and mountains, so-called 'high places' (*bāmā*). On these cultic high places there was either a stone pillar (*maṣṣēbā*), which was a symbol for the male divinity—in most cases no doubt Baal—or a wooden pole (*'ashērā*) which was thought of as representing the female divinity, and finally also an altar for the offering of sacrifices. Stone pillars are well known through archaeological discoveries—sometimes several have been found on one site—while the asheras have not survived. In cases where temples were built a round elevation was often erected outside, which was meant to represent the high place. There are certain indications which suggest that the word *bāmā* may in a number of cases have meant a grave-mound; it is therefore possible that sacrifice was sometimes offered on grave-mounds with the dead in mind.

In respect of the massebah it is tempting to ask how it is connected with what Greek authors call *baitylos* or *baitylion*, which is called by Philo Byblius *lithoi empsychoi*, 'stones with souls in'.[24] Apparently these are meteoric stones, which were regarded as holy and among other things used to provide oracles. Remembering that the word is similar to the West Semitic bēt-'ēl, 'house of god', and that the name Bethel in Genesis 28 is connected with the erection of a massebah, several scholars have seen a connection here. On the other hand, there are also mentions of such *baityloi* in places where no Semitic language is spoken, even in Greece itself, and it would therefore be wise to be cautious about drawing conclusions. The assumption is now favoured that we have an older word which is neither Greek nor Semitic, which in the West Semitic area would naturally be interpreted secondarily as 'house of god'.[25]

We are on safer ground when we compare the word *maṣṣēbā* with the Arabic *nuṣb*, which is undeniably derived from the same root. This signifies erected stones, which were to be found on sacred places (*ḥaram*) and which were smeared with sacrificial blood. Genesis 28 tells how Jacob poured out oil upon the massebah he erected in Bethel. There is clearly a degree of parallelism here, but a question that is not solved by these observations is that of the relation between the stones and the deity: the facts at our disposal at the moment show a peculiar fluctuation between the idea that the god dwells in the stone and the idea that the stone represents the god or is an altar.

The regular temple buildings represent from an historical point of view a later stage, even though they do not replace the high places but only supplement them. From archaeological discoveries and representations on coins we know that a temple establishment generally consisted of an enclosure with an altar and a stone pillar together with the temple itself, which had an inner room in which the cultic image (or images) stood, and one or more outer rooms where apparently certain cultic activities took place. A number of temples display a ground plan similar to that of the temple of Solomon in Jerusalem. A similarity of detail is that two pillars flank the gates of the temple, but unfortunately it is unknown what the symbolism involved is. Lucian tells us that those in Hierapolis are phallic symbols, but the ornamentation on the pillars Jachin and Boaz in the temple of Jerusalem suggest rather vegetation symbolism, while the names seem to suggest a connection with the continuity of the royal dynasty. A detailed description of the temple of Atargatis in Hierapolis is given in Lucian's book *On the Syrian Goddess*. It was placed on a hill, surrounded by a double wall. The author distinguishes between 'the great temple' which is open to all, and an inner shrine, to which only certain priests have access. In the latter were statues of 'Zeus and

Hera', i.e. Hadad and Atargatis. He speaks also of other statues of gods in the temple, and of a throne for the sun-god, which was empty because the sun and the moon were not portrayed in images.

We are also given an idea of the significance of the temple by the Baal myth in the Ras Shamra texts. From this it appears that to make his authority valid a god needed a 'house' or palace, i.e. a temple. *Bait* or *bēt*, 'house', is the usual word for a temple. This shows clearly that the temple was treated in the first place as the dwelling of the god, or as his official residence. An Aramaic inscription from Zenjirli says that King Panammuwa built a temple and 'caused the gods to dwell in it'.[26]

On the high places and in the temples sacrifice was offered regularly. Lucian speaks of sacrifice twice a day, which agrees with the custom in the temple at Jerusalem. The Ras Shamra texts give descriptions of sacrifice for special occasions, and Punic inscriptions, the so-called sacrificial tariffs from Carthage and Marseilles, give prescriptions for the priest's share in different sacrifices. Lists of sacrifices are also found among the Ras Shamra texts, which specify what is to be offered on different occasions to different gods.

We have a detailed description of a sacrifice in the narrative in the Keret text of Keret's preparations for the campaign against Udum:

> He washed himself and made himself red,
> he washed his hand and his arm,
> His fingers, even up to the shoulder;
> he went in to the shelter of the folds,
> he took a sacrificial lamb in his hand,
> a kid in both of them,
> all his *nzl* bread,
> he took *mṣrr* of a sacrificial bird,
> he poured wine in a silver cup,
> honey in a gold cup;
> so he went up in the tower,
> he climbed up on the top of the wall,
> and lifted his hands towards heaven.
> He sacrificed to the bull El, his father,
> he served Baal with his sacrifice,
> the son of Dagon with his food.
>   (I K III, 53–IV, 8)

The terminology of sacrifice gives rise to some observations. In the Ugaritic texts we find apart from the general word *dbḥ*, which corresponds to the Hebrew *zebaḥ* (slain) sacrifice, such terms as *šlm kll* and *šrp*, of which the first two correspond etymologically to the Hebrew *šᵉlāmîm* (RSV peace offerings) and *kālîl*, whole offering, and the last corresponds not etymologically but materially to the Old Testament burnt offering. 'To sacrifice' is called *šqrb* or *šʿly*, literally 'to bring near' and 'to let rise', terms which also have their equivalents in Israelite sacrificial terminology.[27]

The Punic sacrificial tariffs mention three main types of sacrifices: *kalil*, *ṣewaʿat*, and *šelem kalil*. Two of these terms have linguistic equivalents in Hebrew, but this is not to say that the functions of the different sacrifices exactly correspond to those in Israelite sacrifice. *Kalil* should be a 'whole offering', i.e. one which was completely burnt on the altar. *Šelem kalil* is a peculiar combination, since the Hebrew *šᵉlāmîm* sacrifice is a sacrifice in which only a part is given to God and the rest is eaten in a sacrificial meal. The term *kalil* appears to contradict this, and it has therefore been thought that the meaning must be 'concluding sacrifice' or 'substitute sacrifice' or the like. As for *ṣewaʿat* it seems to have been some sort of sin offering or intercessory offering, which has material similarities with the Old Testament *šᵉlāmîm*, inasmuch as this was connected with a sacrificial meal, which created a table fellowship between the participants and the god. The Punic texts also mention *ʿolat*, which corresponds etymologically to the Hebrew word for burnt offering, and *minḥat*, which as in Hebrew seems to signify the unbloody, especially vegetable, offering.

The linguistic similarity of the sacrificial terms in the Ugaritic, the Old Testament, and the Punic texts is therefore striking, but the meaning and use of the terms seem to diverge more. The probable answer is that we are dealing with an inherited West Semitic stock of words, which in use developed local differences.[28]

In respect of the materials of the sacrifices, the texts give us clear information. The Ugaritic sacrificial lists mention cattle, sheep, kids, certain sorts of gazelle, various vegetable sacrifices, and drink offerings of wine and honey. The Punic sacrificial tariffs show in large measure the same elements: bulls, calves, rams, lambs, goats, kids, certain sorts of birds, pastry, and milk.

A special problem concerns human, or rather child, sacrifice.

The Old Testament tells repeatedly of how the Israelites at times of apostasy 'made their children go through fire' to Moloch following a Canaanite example. For a long time the word Moloch (so in Greek; in Hebrew *mōlekh*) was taken to be a disparaging distortion of the divine title *Melek*, 'king', and it was assumed that the reference was to child sacrifice to a god with this epithet. This was then connected with a piece of information in Diodorus Siculus, according to which in Carthage there was a statue of a god made of bronze on the outstretched hands of which children were placed, so that they fell into a fire which burned behind or under the statue of the god. Two inscriptions from the temple complex of the goddess Tinnit expressly mention such sacrifices, while others appear to allude to a possibility of replacing the child by a sacrificial animal (for example, a lamb). According to 2 Kings 3.27 King Mesha of Moab offered his first-born son as a burnt offering in a critical situation. Certain archaeological discoveries have also been interpreted as evidence for human sacrifice in Canaan. In the Ras Shamra texts, however, there is no mention of anything of the sort.

It is therefore clear that human sacrifice occurred at least in special situations. On the other hand, it is doubtful whether Moloch is a god. In Punic *mlk*, which according to Latin transcriptions is pronounced *molk*, is a general term for 'sacrifice' or 'offering', and the Old Testament instances can at least in many cases be interpreted as saying that men caused children to go through fire 'for or as a *mōlek* sacrifice'. In other instances at least the Old Testament writers have understood *mōlek* as a title of a god.

We have little information about other cultic usages, and in particular about the great annual festivals. Most of what can be said on this must be deduced indirectly. Much depends on the extent to which the Ugaritic texts can be regarded as cultic myths which reflect ritual events.

It is difficult to deny that the myth of Baal's death and return to life was in some way expressed in a cultic feast. Everything suggests that the myth stands in close relationship to the idea of the withering and renewal of the vegetation. Classical writers attest mourning rites for the death of the god Adonis; and it seems undeniable that Adonis is only a special form of Baal. Various details in the myth can be explained if they are seen in connection with a ritual presentation of the events. Especially striking is the section which deals with how 'Anat attacks and kills Mot:

She seizes Mot, the son of El;
with the sword she cleaves him,
with the shovel she throws him,
with fire she burns him,
with the mill she grinds him,
on the field she scatters him
his flesh (?) the birds eat,
the wild beasts devour his limbs.
(I AB II, 31–8)

These lines make no sense if they are supposed to refer to a god conceived in personal terms. But if we picture Mot in the rite as represented by a corn-sheaf, the passage at once becomes meaningful. And when we know that such rites were often carried out in connection with the beginning or end of the harvest with the sheaf of the first-fruits (cf. Lev. 2.14) or 'the last sheaf', it is even more probable that the Baal myth was part of a cultic drama which had the purpose of maintaining the course of the year and the cycle of the crops.

How we reconstruct in detail the course of the feast (or feasts) apart from this depends on how closely we may assume that myth and ritual were related to one another, and since there is no general rule to decide this, we must depend on hypotheses. We can, for instance, suppose that the king played the part of Baal in the ritual (there are certain parallels for this) and that he therefore underwent a symbolic death and 'resurrection'. Or we can suppose that Baal's fight against Yam or the duel of Baal and Mot was represented in a cultic 'mock battle'. It is conceivable that the appointment of 'Athtar 'Ariẓ in the absence of Baal reflects a custom of providing a 'substitute king' on critical occasions or in connection with certain rites in which the king runs (symbolic) risks. But in none of these cases do we have other evidence which directly attests that it happened in this way. The only small bit of evidence so far available is a bilingual inscription in Punic and Etruscan from Pyrgi in southern Italy, in which there is apparently a mention of 'the day on which the god was buried'.[29] Its distance in time and space, and the fact that in such a setting the possibility of syncretism must be allowed for, warn us to be cautious about our conclusions from this passage.

A description of a cultic feast with *hieros gamos* is probably found in the text about 'the gracious and fair gods'. It begins with a proclamation: 'I will tell of the gracious and fair gods . . .', and an invitation: 'Come and eat bread; come and drink foaming wine!' The king, the queen, and ten sorts of priests are invited to the feast. Then follows a song which seems to allude to the pruning of the vines:

> Death-and-decay sits
> with the sceptre of childlessness in one hand,
> and the sceptre of widowhood in the other.
> They prune him like a vine,
> they bind him up like a vine,
> they dig him up out of the vineyard like a vine.

If this translation is correct, it indicates that what is done to the vine happens at the same time to the king sitting on his throne, who clearly in some way represents what can happen to vines if they are not tended. Gaster draws the conclusions that we have a festival in connection with the pruning of the vines in June.[30]

In the passage that follows we hear that a kid is to be boiled in milk and mint in 'curdled milk'—this is to be repeated seven times —that Athirat and Raḥmaya ('mother' and 'maid') come, and that seats or thrones are placed before the gods. 'The sun makes their tendrils abound with . . . and grapes', the text says, and there is a mention of sacrifices 'for favours', perhaps sacrifices of firstlings. After this the myth begins, and in this the main theme is the conception and birth first of Shaḥar and Shalim ('the dawn' and 'twilight'), then of the gracious and fair gods, who first go off to the desert, and then eat and drink all the bread and wine which a peasant (?) has. The ending is lost, but it is clear that a popular feast like this cannot have ended on a negative note; it must in some way have ended in prospering the growth of corn and wine. The text as a whole gives us an indication of the religious customs which were connected with the different phases of viticulture, and it is interesting to see how the everyday work of the vineyard acquires 'mythological' interpretation. It is interesting that the custom of boiling a kid in milk is forbidden in the Old Testament (Exod. 23.19)—this is clearly a rejection of a Canaanite rite.

A recently discovered text seems to allude to a peculiar rite: 'Anat 'eats her brother's (Baal's?) flesh without a knife and drinks his blood without a cup.' It has been suggested that we have here an equivalent of the tearing apart of an animal which is regarded as representing the god in the Greek cult of Dionysus. Others think that it is Baal's male organ that the goddess eats, and that she then becomes pregnant.[31] In view of the fragmentary condition of the text it is, however, uncertain whether this interpretation is correct. It is possible that new material will throw further light on this question.

Some glimpses into the cult at Hierapolis are given us by Lucian in his book *On the Syrian Goddess* (chaps. 13, 48). He tells us that twice in the year water was fetched from 'the sea' (either the Euphrates, or a nearby lake) and poured out in the temple. At the head of the procession the so-called *sēmeion* (see p. 157) was carried. Lucian (chaps. 12f) connects this rite with the version of the flood story which he tells. According to this the earth was subjected to an inundation because of the sin of mankind, but Deukalion was saved with his family and a pair of every sort of animal in a ship. After the flood the water is supposed to have vanished into a cleft which opened up in the ground. It is over this cleft that the temple in Hierapolis, it was said, was built, and into it the water was poured out in the rite. It seems, however, probable that we are really dealing with a rain rite. Something similar occurred in the Jewish Feast of Tabernacles: water was brought from the spring Gihon, and poured out in the temple. A passage in the myth of the gracious and fair gods may possibly allude to a similar event: El goes down to the shore of the sea, and takes something handful after handful 'to the edge of the bowl'; the context, however, is uncertain.

Lucian tells us also that the statues of Hadad and Atargatis were carried yearly down to the beach of a nearby lake. He informs us that they came to see the holy fishes, and that Hera (Atargatis) came first, and then prevented Zeus (Hadad) from seeing them. It is usually assumed that we have here a washing of the images of the gods in preparation for the *hieros gamos*, but Lucian says nothing about this. He tells us further that the greatest sacrificial feast of the year is called 'the pyre' or 'the lamp' and takes the form of men cutting down tall trees, setting them up in the temple court, and hanging sacrificial gifts on them, after which it is all set alight, while the images of the gods are carried around the pyre.

References are found throughout the area to a sort of society or guild which celebrated a special cult together. The word is *mrzḥ*

(Hebrew *marzēᵃḥ*), and we meet it already in an Akkadian text from Ras Shamra, where there is a mention of the house of the members of the *ma-ar-zi-ḥi*. A recently published text tells how El at one such *mrzḥ* drinks to excess—perhaps this is a cultic myth of such a guild.[32] A Phoenician inscription from Sidon speaks of a certain man being garlanded on the fourth day of such a feast, a late Punic inscription speaks of such a group giving gifts to a temple.[33] Specially well-known are the Palmyrene cult societies with their banquets, which were regarded as a meal with the god. These sacral meals also had an important role among the Nabataeans in Petra.

The Ras Shamra texts also mention divinatory rites. When Baal is to return to life, 'Anat learns of it because El reveals himself to her in a dream, and announces the great news (I AB III, 8–13). Clearly the dream was regarded as a natural means of revelation. In the Keret text El shows himself in a dream to the mourning Keret and gives him instructions how he is to get himself a wife (I K I, 35ff). In the Aqhat text Daniel sacrifices for seven days, and passes a night in the temple; and although it is not completely clear how it happens, he learns that Baal has interceded for him, so that he will have a son (II D I, 1ff). This is clearly an incubation.

Once we also hear of interpretation of the stars: Aqhat's sister Paghat is addressed as 'she who knows the courses of the stars', while two other epithets perhaps refer to some sort of divination with the help of rain and dew (III D 5of). Recent excavations have also brought to light clay models of liver and lungs provided with inscriptions which show that they were used for extispicy, i.e. divination using the entrails of the sacrificial animal.[34]

Finally, as regards the cultic staff our information is noticeably thinner. The Ras Shamra texts mention *khnm*, in which we can recognize the Hebrew *kōhᵃnim*, priests. We hear also of a *rb khnm*, i.e. a high priest. In one case he also has the title *rb nqdm*, i.e high-*nōqēd* (to use the Hebrew form), and this word has generally been thought to describe a [shep]herd: Amos is called *nōqēd* (Amos 1.1; cf. 7.14), and King Mesha of Moab is said in 2 Kings 3.4 to have been a *nōqēd*, who gave lambs and rams as a tribute to the king of Israel. In Akkadian documents the *nāqidu* is a shepherd of the temple herds, and for this reason it can be assumed that the *nqdm* at Ugarit too were connected with the temple herds. As for *kōhēn*, this is attested as a title of priests also in a number of

Phoenician and Punic inscriptions; a high priest too is mentioned in one of these. Priestesses too, for example a *khnt* of Astarte, are mentioned. In Aramaic inscriptions, on the other hand, the usual word for a priest is *kmr* (*kōmer, kumrā*), a word which occurs a couple of times in the Old Testament (2 Kings 23.5; Hos. 10.5; Zeph. 1.4).

The Ugaritic texts also mention other categories of cultic servants. Next after 'the priests' come often *qdšm*, 'holy' or 'hallowed' ones, whose function is not immediately obvious. In the Old Testament the word *qᵉdēšîm* means the male practitioners of temple prostitution, while the feminine ones are described as *qᵉdēšōt*, temple prostitutes (in Ugarit they seem to be called *'inšt*, 'women'). We do not of course know whether the term had the same meaning in Ugarit, but we can safely assume that the institution existed, and had an important part to play in the fertility cult. The Old Testament prophets direct harsh criticism against the custom, for example Amos 2.7: 'son and father both go into the same prostitute'; Hos. 4.14: 'men go aside with harlots, and sacrifice with cult prostitutes'; Jer. 2.20: 'under every green tree you bowed down as a harlot'. Classical authors such as Herodotus, Strabo, and Lucian also attest that sacral prostitution was a custom in the whole north-west Semitic area in their time. Whether a bridegroom (?) of Astarte who is mentioned in a Phoenician inscription[35] is connected with this is uncertain but possible. Obviously sexual intercourse was thought of as promoting the powers of nature by the working of analogy: the powers which were set in motion in the area of the holy promoted corresponding powers in the land.

Other classes of temple staff which are attested in the Ras Shamra texts are the singers (*šrm*) and *'rbm*, 'the enterers', which can be compared with the Akkadian *ērib bīti*, 'he who enters into the house', as a description of a class of priests who obviously had the right of entering the temple or certain parts of it. Various specialists and their temple duties are mentioned in a Phoenician inscription from Cyprus.[36]

In certain cases special oracle priests or prophets are mentioned. The prophets of the Mari texts, who often appeared completely spontaneously with their message, have already been dealt with in connection with Akkadian religion (pp. 95f). In certain cases they are called *āpilu*, 'answerer', which seems to be a translation of a

West Semitic term, for example '*ōneh*.[37] In the Ras Shamra texts it is not so far possible to distinguish particular specialists in the giving of oracles. On the other hand, an early Aramaic inscription from Hamath gives an interesting description of an oracular process; it is King Zakir who speaks:

> And I lifted up my hands to Be'elshemin, and Be'elshemin answered me and [spoke] to me through seers (*hzyn*) and 'prophets' ('*ddn*) and (he) said to me: 'Fear not, for I have made you king . . . and I shall save you (from your enemies).'[38]

'Seers' corresponds linguistically too to the seers (*hōzeh*) who are mentioned in some older Old Testament texts, while the other term is not known from elsewhere (unless Oded in 2 Chron. 15.1, 8 can be taken as an instance).[39] The Mesha stone tells us twice that Chemosh spoke to the king, but gives no information how this happened. It is probable that some sort of oracle priest mediated the message.

An interesting piece of information is given by the Egyptian Wen Amon in his report of a mission he carried out in Phoenicia in the twelfth century B.C.: when the Phoenician king sacrificed to his gods, the god seized one of his men and placed him in a state of ecstasy, in the course of which he uttered an oracle which advised the king to pay the tribute which Wen Amon had been sent to ask for. This account shows the occurrence of ecstatic prophets of roughly the same sort as Saul encountered according to 1 Sam. 10.10f.

Obviously magical ceremonies and incantations also occurred among the West Semites, although direct attestations are rare. Two examples, however, are worth particular mention. A recently published text from Ras Shamra consists of a quite long incantation against snake-bite.[40] Like so many other similar texts, it is placed in a mythological context: it is an otherwise unknown goddess Paḥlat, who is the daughter of the sun-goddess, but who is also called 'the daughter of the spring, the stone, the heavens and the deep (*thm*)', who gives the rules for carrying out the incantation to Shapsh, who in turn is assisted by eleven other deities. In a mythological episode we hear how the god Ḥoron builds a 'city in the east', and plants there 'the tree of death'. Finally the formula against snakes follows.

Another incantation text is in Phoenician and comes from the seventh century B.C.; it was discovered in 1933 at Arslan Tash in northern Syria. It occurs on an amulet which on one side shows a picture of a sphinx and a wolf with a scorpion's tail which is devouring a child, on the other a god with a double axe. The text conjures a female demon, described as 'the flying one' and 'she who strangles lambs', to stay away because of the owner's covenant with all the gods.[41]

Magical efficacy can probably also be ascribed to the cursing formulas which are almost regularly to be found on grave inscriptions: if anyone destroys or robs this grave let him be punished by misfortune from the gods. In the Aramaic Sefire inscription, which contains the text of a state treaty between three minor princes, there are similar curses against any party to it who breaks the treaty. Certain magical rites seem to be involved here too; the text says:

> As this wax burns in the fire, so may Arpad (one of the countries participating) and [its many cities] burn. And may Hadad sow salt and cress in them so that they are no more mentioned. This tail and [. . .] are Mati'el (the prince) and his person. As this wax burns in the fire, so may Ma[ti'el burn in the fi]re, and as the bow and these arrows are broken asunder, so may Anahita and Hadad break [the bow of Mati'el] and the bows of his mighty men . . .[42]

We may therefore assume that the ideas and usages in this field were not basically different from those which we have met in Mesopotamia. The negative evaluations of magic and sorcery which are found here and there in the Old Testament reinforce this assumption, even though they do not allow us to draw conclusions about concrete details.

KINGSHIP

The West Semites never formed large kingdoms, but were organized mainly in a varying number of small states. But the heads of these as a rule had the title of king, and as far as our information goes they exercised sacral functions.

If we leave aside for the moment the Ras Shamra texts, however, the material is fairly thin. The Amarna letters, which otherwise give such valuable insights into the situation in Canaan in the fourteenth century B.C., must at this point be used with great caution. Certainly various utterances are found here about the king as divine, and as the giver of light and life, but the subject is the Egyptian king, and we must assume that the language has been influenced by the Egyptian court ceremonial. On the other hand, we do not get direct information about the sacral role of the Canaanite princes.

From the later inscriptional material we can in any case gather that the king received his position from the gods. Yeḥawmilk of Byblos declared that the goddess of the city, Ba'alat Gebal, has made him king,[43] and an Aramaic prince says that it is Be'elshemin who has given him his position.[44] Panammuwa of Ya'udi says that Hadad, El, Rakib-el, Shamash, and Resheph have given him the sceptre of prosperity (?).[45] (On the other hand, Kilamuwa of Zenjirli and Azitawadda of Karatepe say: 'I placed myself on the throne.')

It appears from several inscriptions that the king is responsible for the building of the temple.[46] A couple of times a king calls himself 'priest of Astarte',[47] but it is impossible to tell whether this is a rule or an exception.

The righteousness of the king appears as specially important in the inscription of Yeḥimilk from Byblos (tenth century B.C.): 'A righteous king and an upright king before the holy gods of Byblos he is.'[48] And another inscription from the same city from c. 400 B.C. says: 'May the lady of Byblos bless Yeḥawmilk, king of Byblos, and give him life and make his days and his years over Byblos long, for he is a righteous king.'[49] We see then that the prosperity of the king and of the land are dependent on the favour of the gods which the righteousness of the king obtains.

On the other hand, the expression ṣmḥ ṣdq in a Phoenician inscription from Cyprus (c. 275 B.C.)[50] probably does not mean 'righteous shoot', as it could literally be translated (cf. Jer. 23.5), but rather 'legitimate heir (to the throne)'.

We gather from a passage in the Kilamuwa inscription (c. 825) what is expected of a good king:

I was to one a father and to another a mother and to another again a brother. And him who had never seen a sheep I made the owner of a herd of sheep; and him who had never seen an ox I made the owner of a herd of cattle and the owner of silver and gold; and he who from his youth had not seen linen, was in my days dressed in fine linen. And I took the *mškbm* by the hand and they felt for me as the fatherless does for his mother.[51]

Although there is not necessarily a specifically religious content in these phrases, which perhaps have a propaganda purpose, they do in any case tell us much about the ideal of the king and the duties of the king.

King Zakir of Hamath applies to himself an epithet about which there has been much argument when he calls himself '*š* '*nh*, 'a humble man'. This has been compared with Zech. 9.9, but it has not so far been possible to establish what is the solid content of the expression, and why it was thought important enough to be mentioned in a victory inscription.

It has been asserted that King Mesha of Moab was called 'the son of Chemosh', but this is an over-hasty conclusion. The text of the Mesha stone has in fact a gap between *bn* (son) and *Kmš*, and this implies that Mesha's father had a name which was compounded with a divine name, for example 'Abd-Chemosh, the servant of Chemosh. Mesha is therefore 'the son of *x*-Chemosh'.

If we turn now to the Ugaritic texts, we again meet the question of the nature and function of the Keret and Aqhat texts: Are they mythological, or do they deal with actual kings? For our purposes the question is perhaps not so important, for we may assume that the kings of the myths were described in categories borrowed from real life. Nevertheless, a measure of uncertainty is inevitably involved in our conclusions.

If we look first at the Keret Epic, we find that King Keret is regarded as the son of El, and when he himself has a son, he is suckled by the goddesses Athirat and 'Anat. An ivory relief from the royal bed in the palace at Ugarit shows two male children sucking from the breasts of a goddess.[52] We know corresponding representations in Mesopotamia. The meaning is clearly that the king is the representative of El on earth, and nurtured on divine powers. He is therefore a mediator of divine power and blessing to the community, and when, as in the case of Keret, he is prevented by illness from fulfilling all his duties, the whole community suffers: the rain does not fall, the crops do not grow, and corn, oil, and wine fail in the land (II K III).

To what extent the king was regarded as divine is a matter of dispute. A recently found tablet, which contains a list of names of kings, all preceded by *'il,* 'god', may possibly suggest that the Ugaritic kings after death were treated as divine.[53]

No agreement has been reached on the meaning of Keret's war expedition to Udum to get himself a wife. Is this a symbolic theft of a bride which is part of the rites of the king's marriage, or is it to be understood more literally? A decision can be reached only on the basis of one's understanding of the Keret Epic as a whole.

We hear in the Keret text, as we do also in the Aqhat text, of the king's duty to protect the rights of the poor, the widow, and the fatherless—obviously an ideal for rulers which was dominant over the whole of the ancient Near East, apparently having a religious motivation.

Daniel in the Aqhat text is certainly not called king in so many words, but he is a righteous judge, and seems also in other respects to perform kingly functions. The wish for a son and heir is stressed just as strongly as in the Keret text, and it is realized through the intervention of El. The death of the son has the same consequences as the illness of Keret: rain and dew fail, and vegetation dies. One conclusion that can be drawn from this is that whether both texts are ritual texts or not, there is an intimate connection between the king in his god-given position, and the fertility of the land. Certain scholars draw the conclusion that the king in the cult played the part of the fertility god Baal in his death and resurrection. There is much to indicate that this may have been the case, but if the demand is made for explicit proof, it must be admitted that this is not available.

On the other hand, we receive an idea of the king's role in the cult from a couple of shorter texts. A fragmentary tablet contains at its beginning the words 'forgiveness for the soul' (*slḥ npš*), unfortunately without a clear context, and as it goes on gives directions for certain ceremonies in the month of Tishri, including a ritual washing of the king and various sacrifices.[54] This may well be an instance of an atonement ritual in which the king plays a leading part. A ritual bath in the sea on the fourteenth day of every month is mentioned in a recently discovered text.[55]

Another text,[56] which certainly had a ritual function, speaks of sacrifices to the gods because of sin, which was clearly understood as the cause of a defeat at the hands of enemies. The king is not mentioned explicitly, but it is reasonable to suppose that in such a case he acted on behalf of the people. In this context it may be mentioned that Rib-Addi of Byblos in one of the Amarna letters speaks of the gods being angry, and that for this reason he has confessed his sins before them. We see here a connection between the actions of the king as judged religiously, and the fate of the country.

GOD AND MAN
RELIGION AND MORALITY

To attempt to draw a comprehensive picture of how the West Semitic peoples thought of the relationship between god and man is impossible on the basis of the inscriptions, with their highly specialized and limited content, and the primarily mythological descriptions of the Ras Shamra texts. We must be content with some glimpses, which as far as they go are interesting enough.

Important information is given in the first place by personal names.[57] In many of them the deity is described as a relation: father, brother, kinsman (uncle), for example Abiba'al, 'my father is Baal', Ahiba'al, 'my brother is Baal', 'Ammiba'al, 'my kinsman is Baal'. It is indubitable that there is expressed here a feeling of close kinship and security. On the other hand, it is not clear to what extent the kinship was understood more literally. In a number of cases we may be dealing with tribal gods, which at the same time are regarded as the ancestors of the tribe.

A basic idea in many proper names is that the god is lord, for example Adon-Ba'al, 'Baal is lord', or exalted and mighty; Ba'alram, 'Baal is exalted'; Ahiram (Hiram), 'My brother is exalted'; Addirba'al, 'Baal is mighty'. In other cases these properties were expressed in relationship to man in the form of grace and help of various forms: Yehawmilk, 'Milk (the king) gives life'; Yatonba'al, 'Baal gives'; Mattanba'al, 'gift of Baal'; Ba'alšamar, 'Baal preserves'; Ba'alšama', 'Baal hears'; Ya'zan'el, 'El listens'; Ba'al-hilleṣ, 'Baal delivers'; Ešmun-ṣilleh, 'Eshmun gives success'; Ba'al-yahon, 'Baal is gracious'; Ešmun'azar, 'Eshmun helps', etc. Many personal names describe the man who bears them as servant (*'abd*) or maidservant (*'amat*) to a divinity: 'Abd-'Aštart, 'Abd-Melqart, Amat-Ba'al, etc. In some cases the word *kalb*, 'dog', occurs as an expression for man's dependence on the deity[58] (or is it the faithfulness of the dog that is the point?).

The name of the Phoenician king Ittoba'al signifies 'Baal is with him'.

If we now look at the rest of the content of the inscriptions, we can establish first that the prayer that the gods will give long life is very common.[59] It shows that life was thought of as being a gift of the gods, and that it stood within their powers to prolong or to shorten it. In this connection a strange expression is found in the Phoenician Eshmun'azar inscription, which says, 'I was snatched away (or, was cut off), not in my time', i.e. too early.[60] We think inevitably of the Akkadian expression about one who dies 'on the day which is not that of his destiny'. Unfortunately we do not hear any more about the cause.

Another assertion which is usual in the inscriptions is that a man has prayed to a deity who has also heard his prayer. 'I prayed to the lady of Byblos and she heard my voice . . . she heard my voice and treated me kindly.'[61] Eshmun 'heard his voice and cured him'.[62] To this can be added as in the Yeḥawmilk inscription a prayer for continued blessing and grace.[63] One of the Aramaic inscriptions from Zenjirli speaks of how the gods have given abundance and great things.[64] But the same inscription also calls down Hadad's curse on him who in any way commits a sin: 'may he not have pleasure in him, and whatever he prays for, may Hadad not give it him, and may Hadad pour out his wrath upon him [. . .] may he in his wrath give him nothing to eat and keep sleep away from him at night.'[65]

We find an unusual form of expression in an inscription from Carthage in which it is said: 'he who will take away this stone . . . over that man's spirit (*rūḥ*) shall Tinnit be judge'.[66] It is, however, not a question of a judgement of a dead man; 'spirit' is in the sense of life, i.e. the goddess shall end the life of the guilty man.

If we add to this expressions in Aramaic inscriptions which say that the gods give a good name and long life on account of the righteousness of the man concerned,[67] or that he is saved on account of his father's (!) righteousness,[68] we get a picture of a doctrine of reward, which presupposes that righteousness is rewarded with success and long life, while disobedience to the will of the gods is punished with misfortune, and that this reward extends also over several generations (just as in the Old Testament).

On the Mesha stone from Moab this principle is transferred to political history. King Omri of Israel 'oppressed Moab', because

'Chemosh was wroth with his land'. Mesha won the favour of the national god, and had the victory at his bidding both over Israel and over other enemies. In thankfulness he 'dedicated' (the same word that in the Old Testament is translated 'give over to destruction') his war-booty to Chemosh.

The Ugaritic texts confirm this picture. Here too sin seems to be treated as a cause of the devastations of the enemy (see above), and the demand for righteousness in the king may also be seen as expressing general ethical values. Ugaritic has at least two of the three words for sin which are usual in Hebrew: *pš'*, 'transgression, rebelliousness', and *ḥṭ'*, 'sin, slip' (a couple of Aramaic instances of the latter are also found). This suggests that the religious evaluation of 'sin' was similar to that which we meet in the Old Testament. It is interesting that in parallel to *pš'* we once have *g'n*,[69] 'pride, arrogance', which here too, as often in the Old Testament, is regarded as being the essence of sin: to set oneself up against God in self-sufficiency.

BELIEF IN AN AFTERLIFE

The Ras Shamra texts show that the rites of death and burial were in large measure the same as in Israel. When Baal is dead the mourning rites which El carries out are described: he steps down from his throne and sits on the ground, he takes off his head-covering and strews dust upon his head, he tears his belt asunder, he utters a loud lament, and gashes himself in the face and on the chest and arms. 'Baal is dead', he laments. 'What shall come then of the people of the son of Dagan? What shall come of the multitudes belonging to Baal? I will go down into the earth.' Then follows a banquet, a sacrifice for or to the dead. We know such sacrifices also through a pictorial representation on the sarcophagus of King Ahiram from Byblos, and from Aramaic inscriptions. Tombs in Ras Shamra had special equipment for sacrifices. It is not clear how these were understood, but an inscription speaks of the soul of Panammuwa eating and drinking with Hadad.[70] It looks as if the dead king together with the god takes part in the sacrifice. This either means that the king after his death was believed to become divine, or that there is a belief in an existence in a place of the dead comparable with the Sheol, or world of the shadows, known from the Old Testament.

The Ras Shamra texts have otherwise nothing further to say about a life after death. On the contrary, it is emphasized that death is mankind's reward, and that immortality belongs only to the gods. When 'Anat offers Aqhat new life like that of Baal, he rejects the possibility: 'I shall die the death of all men' (II D VI, 37). It is emphasized in the Keret text too that the gods do not die, and that there is something wrong with Keret's divinity when his illness threatens to lay him in the grave (II K II, 42ff).

There are also three fragmentary texts[71] from Ras Shamra which could be expected to throw light upon the ideas of a realm of the dead. They deal with beings which are either called *rp'm*, in form the same as the Hebrew *rephā'im*, meaning the inhabitants of the land of the dead (*še'ōl*), or *'ilnym*, which perhaps means 'divine beings' or 'spirits' of some sort. It appears from the texts, which are very badly preserved, that they are connected with threshing-floors and gardens, and that they receive sacrifice or take part in a banquet. We may be dealing with chthonic deities, concerned with the fertility of the earth, but it is not impossible that they are the spirits of the dead. Perhaps these two alternatives are not completely exclusive, since the dead and chthonic beings are often closely connected with one another. In any case it is clear that the same word *rp'm* occurs also in Phoenician inscriptions, where there are references to finding or not finding a resting place among them,[72] i.e. 'the shades', the spirits of the dead in the realm of the dead. It is interesting that in one case 'to be buried in a grave' and 'to get a dwelling place among *rp'm*' are treated as more or less equivalent expressions. It is clear that a proper burial was regarded as important for the continued existence of the dead, of whatever nature this may have been.

Abbreviations

AfO	*Archiv für Orientforschung*
ANET	J. B. Pritchard, ed., *Ancient Near Eastern Texts Relating to the Old Testament*. 2nd edn, Princeton 1955; 3rd edn with supplement, 1969
AOTU	*Altorientalische Texte und Untersuchungen*, ed. B. Meissner. Leiden 1916–17
BANE	G. E. Wright, ed., *The Bible and the Ancient Near East* (Albright Festschrift). London 1961
BHB	K. L. Tallqvist, ed., *Babyloniska Hymner och Böner*. Helsingfors 1953
BiOr	*Bibliotheca Orientalis*
Bottéro	J. Bottéro, *La Religion Babylonienne*. Paris 1952
BWL	W. G. Lambert, *Babylonian Wisdom Literature*. Oxford 1960
CHM	*Cahiers d'Histoire Mondiale*
ChS	P. D. Chantepie de la Saussaye, *Lehrbuch der Religionsgeschichte*, 4th edn. 2 vols. Tübingen 1924–5
CRAIB	*Comptes rendus de l'Academie des inscriptions et belles lettres*
CRRA	*Comptes rendus des rencontres assyriologiques* (No. 2, Paris 1951; No. 3, Leiden 1954)
CT	*Cuneiform Texts from Babylonian Tablets etc. in the British Museum*. London 1896–
Dhorme	E. Dhorme, *La Religion Assyro-babylonienne*. Paris 1910
Divinità	S. Moscati, ed., *Le Antiche Divinità Semitiche* (Università di Roma—Centro di Studi Semitici, Studi Semitici 1). Rome 1958
Fiore	S. Fiore, *Voices from the Clay*. Norman, Oklahoma 1965
HbOr	*Handbuch der Orientalistik*. Leiden
HBS	S. N. Kramer, *History Begins at Sumer*, 2nd edn. London 1961
Int. Adv.	H. Frankfort and others, *The Intellectual Adventure of Ancient Man*. Chicago 1946
JAOS	*Journal of the American Oriental Society*

JCS	*Journal of Cuneiform Studies*
JNES	*Journal of Near Eastern Studies*
KAI	H. Donner and W. Röllig, *Kanaanäische und Aramäische Inschriften*. 3 vols. Wiesbaden 1962–4
KG	H. Frankfort, *Kingship and the Gods*. Chicago 1948
MAW	S. N. Kramer, ed., *Mythologies of the Ancient World*. Chicago 1961
MVAG	Mitteilungen der Vorderasiatisch–ägyptischen Gesellschaft
NF	Neue Folge (=New Series)
NS	New Series
OECT	S. Langdon, ed., *Oxford Editions of Cuneiform Texts*. Oxford and Paris 1923–30
Oppenheim	A. L. Oppenheim, *Ancient Mesopotamia*. Chicago 1964
Or	*Orientalia*
PAPS	*Proceedings of the American Philosophical Society*
RA	*Revue d'Assyriologie*
RoB	*Religion och Bibel*
RSO	*Rivista degli Studi Orientali*
Römer	W. H. P. Römer, *Sumerische 'Königshymnen' der Isin-Zeit* (Documenta et Monumenta Orientis Antiqui, vol. 13). Leiden 1965
Saggs	H. W. F. Saggs, *The Greatness that was Babylon*. London 1962
SAHG	A. Falkenstein and W. von Soden, *Sumerische und Akkadische Hymnen und Gebete*. Zurich and Stuttgart 1953
SM	S. N. Kramer, *Sumerian Mythology*. Philadelphia 1944. Rev. ed., New York 1961
SDK	I. Engnell, *Studies in Divine Kingship*. Uppsala 1943. Reprinted, Oxford 1970
Sum.	S. N. Kramer, *The Sumerians*. Chicago 1963
SVT	Supplement to *Vetus Testamentum*
TuL	E. Ebeling, *Tod und Leben nach den Vorstellungen der Babylonier*, I. Texte. Berlin and Leipzig 1931
UT	C. H. Gordon, *Ugaritic Textbook*. Analecta Orientalia 38. Rome 1965
VT	*Vetus Testamentum*
ZA	*Zeitschrift für Assyriologie*

Notes

The notes are primarily intended to give the evidence for details which do not occur in the usual textbooks, and also to indicate where the quotations are taken from. It must be emphasized that apart from this completeness has not been aimed at.

CHAPTER 1

1. *SAHG*, pp. 12f.
2. R. D. Biggs, 'The Abū Ṣalābīkh Tablets. A Preliminary Survey', *JCS* 20 (1966), pp. 78ff.
3. T. Jacobsen, 'Formative Tendencies in Sumerian Religion', *BANE*, pp. 268ff; 'Ancient Mesopotamian Religion: the Central Concerns', *PAPS* 107 (1963), p. 474, n. 3.
4. S. N. Kramer, *Sum.*, p. 145.
5. A. Falkenstein, ed., *Sumerische Götterlieder*, vol. 1 (Abhandlungen der Heidelberger Akademie der Wissenschaften, Phil.-Hist. Kl. 1959, I) (Heidelberg 1959), No. 1, pp. 19ff; Kramer, *Sum.*, pp. 120f.
6. *SAHG* No. 12, p. 78.
7. *SAHG* No. 17, p. 90.
8. *SAHG* No. 22, p. 109.
9. Å. Sjöberg, *Der Mondgott Nanna-Suen in der sumerischen Über-lieferung* (Stockholm 1960); M. Lambert, 'La Littérature Sumér-ienne', *RA* 55 (1961), p. 180.
10. Kramer, 'Sumerian Literature, a General Survey', *BANE*, p. 255 with n. 59. For the picture on the seal see Saggs, pl. 50a.
11. *SAHG* Nos. 42, 43.
12. Jacobsen, 'Early Political Development in Mesopotamia', *ZA*, NF 18 (1957), p. 108, n. 34. *PAPS* 107, p. 476, n. 6, interprets the name as 'lady of the date-clusters' (AN; *sissinnu*). I. J. Gelb, 'The Name of the goddess Innin', *JNES* 19 (1960), pp. 72–9, argues for the form Innin.
13. *SAHG* No. 18, p. 93.
14. *SAHG* No. 7. Cf. also the hymns in Falkenstein, 'Sumerische religiöse Texte', *ZA* NF 18 (1957), pp. 18ff.
15. Kramer, *SM*, pp. 82f; Falkenstein, review of Kramer, *SM*, *BiOr* 5 (1948), p. 166; Falkenstein, 'Zur Chronologie der sumerischen Literatur', *CRRA*, No. 2, p. 15.
16. So understood in Akkadian, *māru kēnu*. Jacobsen: 'he who gives life to the young'.

17. So Falkenstein. Saggs, p. 382 (after Jacobsen, *ZA* NF 18 (1957), p. 108, n. 34): 'the one great source of the date-clusters'.

18. A. Moortgat, *Tammuz: der Unsterblichkeitsglaube in der altorientalischen Bildkunst* (Berlin 1949).

19. Even this, however, is uncertain.

20. A criticism by Kraus is in *CRRA*, No. 3, pp. 69ff.

21. J. J. A. van Dijk, *La Sagesse suméro-accadienne* (Leiden 1953), pp. 65–85; Kramer in a review of H. Frankfort and others, *The Intellectual Adventure of Ancient Man, JCS* 2 (1948), pp. 6of.

22. Kramer, 'Cuneiform Studies and the History of Literature: The Sumerian Sacred Marriage Texts', *PAPS* 107 (1963), pp. 497–9.

23. Three further texts of this type in *PAPS* 107, pp. 493ff.

24. Kramer, *Sum.*, pp. 153–5.

25. Kramer, *Sum.*, pp. 156–60.

26. Falkenstein, *CRRA*, No. 3, pp. 41–65.

27. Jacobsen, 'Towards the Image of Tammuz', *History of Religions* 1 (1961–2), pp. 189–213.

28. Damu is also a god of healing, E. Bergmann, 'Untersuchungen zu syllabisch geschriebenen sumerischen Texten', *ZA* NF 22 (1964), pp. 34, 36.

29. Jacobsen, *PAPS* 107, p. 476, n. 8; p. 477, n. 9; p. 478, n. 16.

30. *PAPS* 107, pp. 478f, n. 16.

31. *PAPS* 107, p. 476, n. 7. Cf. also the text on the suffering of Lillu (Mululil), *BHB* No. 85, p. 135.

32. Å. Sjöberg, 'Replik', *Svensk Exegetisk Årsbok* 31 (1966), p. 137; Kramer, *Bulletin of the American School of Oriental Research* 183 (1966), p. 31.

33. *PAPS* 107, pp. 476f, n. 8.

34. Jacobsen, *History of Religions* 1, pp. 192f, 203f.

35. *CT* xv. 26 as given in *PAPS* 107, pp. 477f; also *SAHG* No. 34, pp. 185f.

36. *History of Religions* 1, pp. 193f.

37. H. Zimmern, *Sumerische und Babylonische Tamuzlieder*, No. 5.

38. *History of Religions* 1, pp. 199f; cf. *SAHG* No. 35.

39. 'Farmer's almanac', Kramer, *Sum.*, pp. 340–2.

40. *SM*, pp. 80ff; *Sum.*, pp. 151ff; cf. also Jacobsen, 'Sumerian Mythology: a Review Article', *JNES* 5 (1946), pp. 146f. Earlier edition by S. Geller, 'Die sumerisch-assyrische Serie: Lugal-e ud Me-lam-bi Nir-gal', *AOTU* 1:4 (1917), pp. 255–362.

41. *Wörterbuch der Mythologie*, ed. H. W. Haussig, 1, Götter und Myther im vorderen Orient (Stuttgart 1965), p. 115.

42. *SAHG* No. 32, A ix–x.

43. *PAPS* 107, p. 482; cf. *Int. Adv.*, pp. 203–7; *BANE*, p. 270.

44. *Sumerian Texts of Varied Contents*, ed. E. Chiera (University Chicago Oriental Institute Publications 16, Cuneiform Series (Chicago 1934), 1, i, pp. 15–18.

45. T. J. Meek, 'Some Explanatory Lists and Grammatical Texts', *RA* 17 (1920), p. 122, iii and iv, 5–8. Both quoted in *Int. Adv.*, p. 204.

46. *SM, HBS, MAW, Sum.*
47. Jacobsen, 'Sumerian Mythology: A Review Article', *JNES* 5 (1946), pp. 128–52; M. Lambert and R. Tournay, '"Enki et Ninhursag", A propos d'un ouvrage recent', *RA* 43 (1949), pp. 105–36.
48. *AOTU* 1:4, pp. 307ff.
49. Jacobsen, *JNES* 5, pp. 138ff.
50. J. van Dijk, 'Le motif cosmique dans la pensée sumerienne', *Acta Orientalia* (Copenhagen) 28 (1964/5), pp. 1–60.
51. I. Bernhardt and S. N. Kramer, 'Enki und die Weltordnung', *Wissenschaftliche Zeitschrift der Friedrich-Schiller Universität Jena, Gesellschafts- und Sprachwissenschaftliche Reihe* 9 (1959–60), pp. 231–56; Falkenstein, 'Sumerische religiöse Texte', *ZA* NF 22 (1964), pp. 44–113.
52. *HBS*, pp. 162f (Amer. edn, p. 109).
53. *SAHG*, p. 133.
54. *SM*, pp. 64–8.
55. Kramer, *HBS*, pp. 208–13 (Amer. edn, pp. 144–9); *Sum.*, pp. 147–9, 282f.
56. Lambert and Tournay, *RA* 43 (1949), pp. 105–36.
57. Kramer, *Sum.*, p. 285; Falkenstein, *CRRA*, No. 2, p. 16.
58. Oppenheim, p. 203.
59. Kramer, *SM*, pp. 82f; *Sum.*, p. 171; cf. Falkenstein, *CRRA*, No. 2, pp. 15f.
60. Kramer, *HBS*, pp. 114–18 (Amer. edn, pp. 70–5); *Sum.*, pp. 162f.
61. Kramer, *Sum.*, pp. 163f; *ANET*, pp. 42–4.
62. Kramer, *SM*, pp. 98–101; *Sum.*, p. 164; cf. Falkenstein, *CRRA*, No. 2, p. 17.
63. On temples see H. J. Lenzen, 'Mesopotamische Tempelanlagen von der Frühzeit bis zum zweiten Jahrhundert', *ZA* NF 17 (1955), pp. 1–36; F. R. Kraus, *CHM* 1 (1953–4), pp. 518–46.
64. Kramer, 'Hymn to the Ekur', *RSO* 32 (1957), pp. 95–102, especially p. 101.
65. J. van Dijk, 'La fête du nouvel an dans un texte de Šulgi', *BiOr* 11 (1954), pp. 83–8; H. Ringgren, 'Hieros gamos i Egypten, Sumer och Israel', *RoB* 18 (1959), pp. 37ff.
66. *BiOr* 11, p. 86.
67. *SAHG* No. 18, pp. 96f.
68. *BiOr* 11, p. 86.
69. A. M. van Dijk, 'La découverte de la culture littéraire sumérienne et sa signification pour l'histoire de l'antiquité orientale', *Orientalia et Biblica Lovanensia* 1 (1957), p. 14.
70. Kramer, *PAPS* 107, pp. 501ff.
71. Kramer, *Sum.*, p. 254.
72. *SAHG* No. 18, pp. 97–8.
73. J. van Dijk, *La Sagesse suméro-accadienne*, pp. 31ff.
74. J. van Dijk, 'Une insurrection générale au pays de Larša avant l'avènement de Nūradad', *JCS* 19 (1965), pp. 21f.
75. Kramer, *Sum.*, p. 140; B. Landsberger, *Der Kultische Kalender der*

Babylonier und Assyrier (Leipziger Semitistische Studien, vol. 6) (Leipzig 1915), *passim*.

76. *PAPS* 107, p. 476, n. 7.
77. *PAPS* 107, p. 477, n. 8.
78. *Sum.*, pp. 142f; *ANET* pp. 455–63; *SAHG* No. 38.
79. *SAHG* No. 37, and note Kramer, 'Literary Texts from Ur, VI, Part II', *Iraq* 25 (1963), pp. 171f.
80. Kramer, *Sum.*, p. 208.
81. Kramer, *Sum.*, pp. 62–6; Falkenstein, 'Fluch über Akkade', *ZA* NF 23 (1965), pp. 43–124.
82. Falkenstein, op. cit., pp. 48f, asserts that the Gutians were a standard element in such laments, and that in any case the curse on Agade does not directly reflect an historical reality. It is anti-Akkadian in tendency, and Inanna is praised for the destruction of Akkad.
83. M. Witzel, *Tammuz-liturgien und Verwandtes*, Analecta Orientalia 10 (Rome 1935).
84. Cf. Landsberger, *Der Kultische Kalender*, pp. 5f: the absence of the god is a 'fiction'; a number of these occasions of lamentation depend on an historical tradition. The problem has recently been treated by J. Krecher in the introduction to his *Sumerische Kultlyrik* (1966), especially pp. 46ff, but without any definite conclusions being reached.
85. *SAHG* No. 31.
86. *SAHG* No. 24.
87. *SAHG*, p. 26.
88. Falkenstein, *Die Haupttypen der sumerischen Beschwörung, literarisch untersucht* (Leipziger Semitistische Studien NF 1) (Leipzig 1931), pp. 83ff.
89. Falkenstein, op. cit., pp. 92ff.
90. Jacobsen, 'Early Political Development in Mesopotamia', *ZA* NF 18 (1957), pp. 91–140.
91. D. O. Edzard, 'Enmebaragesi von Kiš', *ZA* NF 19 (1959), p. 23.
92. Falkenstein, 'La cité-temple sumérienne', *CHM* 1 (1953–4), p. 795.
93. Römer, p. 153. On the royal hymns in general, see also W. W. Hallo, 'Royal Hymns and Mesopotamian Unity', *JCS* 17 (1963), pp. 112–18.
94. E. Sollberger, 'Deux pierres de seuil d'Entemena', *ZA* NF 16 (1952), p. 15.
95. Römer, p. 11.
96. J. van Dijk, *JCS* 19 (1965), p. 15.
97. Römer, p. 56; Falkenstein, 'Sumerische religiöse Texte', *ZA* NF 16 (1952), p. 65.
98. Sjöberg, 'Den sumerisk-babyloniske konungens gudomliga härstamning', *RoB* 20 (1961), pp. 14–29; cf. Falkenstein, *CHM* 1, p. 796.
99. *ZA* NF 16, pp. 74f.
100. Sjöberg, *RoB* 20, p. 24, and in a review of Römer, *Or* NS 35 (1966), pp. 288f.

101. Sjöberg, *RoB* 20, p. 25.
102. Römer, pp. 55f.
103. Römer, p. 57.
104. Römer, pp. 24ff, 214; Falkenstein, *ZA* NF 16, p. 65.
105. *ZA* NF 16, p. 65.
106. *ZA* NF 16, pp. 78–80; cf. Römer, pp. 25f, 36, 39, 45, 49 and G. Castellino, 'Urnammu, Three Religious Texts', *ZA* NF 19 (1959), pp. 121f.
107. H. Schmökel, 'Geschichte des alten Vorderasiens', in *HbOr* 11: (Leiden 1957), p. 27; Kramer, *Sum.*, pp. 317ff.
108. Kramer, *Sum.*, pp. 83f.
109. Kramer, *Sum.*, pp. 87f; cf. D. O. Edzard, *Die 'Zweite Zwischenzeit' Babyloniens* (Wiesbaden 1957), pp. 95f. Text with translation in Falkenstein, 'Das Gesetzbuch Lipit-Ištars von Isin', *Or* NS 19 (1950), pp. 103ff.
110. Römer, p. 26.
111. Römer, p. 213; cf. p. 35.
112. Römer, p. 213.
113. Römer, pp. 33f.
114. Römer, pp. 51f.
115. Römer, pp. 213f.
116. Jean, *La religion sumérienne*, pp. 216f.
117. Oppenheim, pp. 210, 213.
118. Kramer, *Sum.*, p. 157; *MAW*, pp. 111f.
119. Römer, p. 45.
120. Kramer, *Sum.*, pp. 124f.
121. 'Man and his god', cf. below.
122. Kramer, *HBS*, pp. 167–71 (Amer. edn, pp. 114–18); *Sum.*, pp. 126–9.
123. Kramer, *Sum.*, pp. 129ff.
124. Kramer, *Sum.*, pp. 130f; G. Castellino, 'Urnammu, Three Religious Texts', *ZA* NF 18 (1957), pp. 9–12, 17–57.
125. Kramer, *Sum.*, pp. 210–17; cf. p. 132.
126. Kramer, *Sum.*, pp. 197–205, 132f.
127. Kramer, *Sum.*, pp. 146f; cf. p. 133.
128. Kramer, *HBS*, pp. 222, 229–37 (Amer. edn, pp. 157–69); *Sum.* pp. 153–5; cf. pp. 133f.
129. Kramer, *Sum.*, pp. 129f; Saggs, pp. 372ff.
130. Cf. R.-R. Jestin, 'La conception sumérienne de la vie post-mortem', *Syria* 33 (1956), pp. 113–18 (this interpretation seems somewhat speculative).

CHAPTER 2

1. Kramer, 'Sumero-Akkadian Interconnections: Religious Ideas', *Genava* NS 8 (1960), p. 277.
2. Bottéro, p. 22.
3. Cf. Jacobsen, *PAPS* 107, pp. 482f; see also E. Bergmann, 'Unter-

suchungen zu syllabisch geschriebenen sumerischen Texten', *ZA* NF 23 (1965), p. 35.
4. See Oppenheim, in V. Ferm, ed., *Forgotten Religions (Including some Living Primitive Religions)* (New York 1950), pp. 66f.
5. Bottéro, pp. 54ff.
6. Oppenheim, p. 177.
7. *Genava* NS 8, p. 276.
8. *BHB* No. 63, pp. 103f.
9. *BHB* No. 71, p. 116.
10. Oppenheim, p. 195.
11. *BHB* No. 75, p. 119.
12. *BHB* No. 72, pp. 116f.
13. *BHB* No. 79, p. 122; *BWL*, pp. 121–38.
14. Saggs, p. 333.
15. *BHB* No. 31, p. 62.
16. *BHB* No. 25a, p. 46.
17. *BHB* No. 29, p. 60.
18. Saggs, p. 335; cf. E. Dhorme, *Les religions de Babylonie et d'Assyrie*, Mana I: 2 (Paris 1945), p. 97.
19. *BHB* No. 2, pp. 17f.
20. *BHB* No. 1, p. 17.
21. *BHB* No. 57, pp. 97f.
22. Similar ideas in *CT* 24, pl. 50: 'Ninurta is Marduk as the god of plantation; Ilbaba is Marduk as the god of dominion and council; Nabu is Marduk as the god of destinies; Sin is Marduk as the god who illuminates the darkness; Shamash is Marduk as the god of justice; Adad is Marduk as the god of rain.' Cf. Fiore, p. 49. See also B. Hartmann, 'Monotheistische Stromingen in de Babylonische Godsdienst', *Nederlands Theologisch Tijdschrift* 20 (1966), pp. 328–38.
23. *ANET*, pp. 103f.
24. *BHB* No. 87, pp. 138f, and more fully Zimmern, *Sumerisch-babylonische Tamuzlieder*, No. 1.
25. Oppenheim, p. 177.
26. H. Gressmann, ed., *Altorientalische Texte zum Alten Testament* (Berlin and Leipzig 1926), p. 130; S. G. F. Brandon, *Creation Legends of the Ancient Near East* (London 1963), p. 70.
27. In English translation A. Heidel, *The Babylonian Genesis* (Chicago 1942), and *ANET*, pp. 60–72. Important discussions in Jacobsen, *Intellectual Adventure*, pp. 168ff; Brandon, *Creation Legends of the Ancient Near East*, pp. 90ff.
28. English translations in A. Heidel, *The Gilgamesh Epic and Old Testament Parallels* (Chicago 1946), and *ANET*, pp. 72–99.
29. Kramer, *HBS*, pp. 253–74 (Amer. edn, pp. 189ff).
30. Laessøe, *BiOr* 13 (1956), pp. 89ff. Text in *ANET*, pp. 104–6; cf. Fiore, pp. 193ff. New edition, with new material from *CT* 46 (1965), W. G. Lambert and A. R. Millard, *Atra-ḫasis, The Babylonian Stor: of the Flood* (Oxford 1969).

31. *ANET*, pp. 101–3; Fiore, pp. 216ff.
32. E. Reiner, 'The Etiological Myth of the "Seven Sages"', *Or* NS 30 (1961), pp. 1–11.
33. *ANET*, pp. 114–18; Fiore, pp. 211ff.
34. *ANET*, pp. 111–13, Fiore, pp. 208ff.
35. On the reading see Landsberger, 'Einige unerkannt gebliebene oder verkannte Nomina des Akkadischen', *Wiener Zeitschrift für die Kunde des Morgenlandes* 57 (1961), pp. 1ff.
36. Jacobsen, 'The Myth of Inanna and Bilulu', *JNES* 12 (1953), p. 167, n. 27; p. 168, n. 29: a personified thundercloud (dubious).
37. F. Gössmann, *Das Era-Epos* (Würzburg 1956); Fiore, pp. 207f; Oppenheim, pp. 267f.
38. Oppenheim, pp. 51, 187.
39. Saggs, p. 355.
40. G. Widengren, *The King and the Tree of Life in Ancient Near Eastern Religion*, Uppsala Universitets Årsskrift 1951: 4 (Uppsala 1951), ch. 1.
41. The letter is to be found in L. Waterman, *Royal Correspondence of the Assyrian Empire, Part II* (Ann Arbor 1930) (University of Michigan Humanistic Series, vol. xviii), pp. 157f; on its interpretation see S. Smith, 'Notes on "the Assyrian Tree"', *Bulletin of the School of Oriental Studies* 4 (1926–8), p. 72, in which all the (justified) question-marks in his previous article, 'Miscellanea', *RA* 21 (1924), p. 84, have disappeared. On the rites discussed see Saggs, pp. 388f.
42. S. Langdon, *Babylonian Penitential Psalms*, OECT vi (Paris 1927), p. 37; cf. F. Willesen, 'The Cultic Situation of Psalm LXXIV', *VT* 2 (1952), pp. 292ff. A ritual for the repair of a temple in *ANET*, pp. 339–42.
43. Oppenheim, p. 106.
44. S. A. Pallis, *The Babylonian Akitu Festival* (Det Kgl. Danske Videnskabenes Selskab, Historisk-filologiske Meddelelser, xii, 1) (Copenhagen 1926); Falkenstein, 'akiti-Fest und akiti-Haus', in *Festschrift Johannes Friedrich*, ed. R. von Kienle and others (Heidelberg 1959), pp. 147–82.
45. *ANET*, pp. 331–4.
46. W. G. Lambert, 'The Great Battle of the Mesopotamian Religious Year: the Conflict in the Akitu House', *Iraq* 25 (1963), pp. 189f.
47. Pallis, pp. 260ff.
48. Earlier translation by Zimmern, *Zum babylonischen Neujahrsfest* ii (1919); cf. Hooke, *Babylonian and Assyrian Religion*, pp. 111–13; a new treatment by W. von Soden, 'Gibt es ein Zeugnis dafür, dass die Babylonier an die Wiederauferstehung Marduks geglaubt haben?', *ZA* NF 17 (1955), pp. 130ff; another fragment in *ZA* NF 18 (1957), pp. 224–34.
49. K 3476, Pallis, op. cit., pp. 213ff; Hooke, op. cit. p. 113.
50. *Keilschrifttexte aus Assur religiösen Inhalts*, ed. E. Ebeling (Wissenschaftliche Veröffentlichungen der Deutschen Orient-Gesellschaft, vol. 34) (Leipzig) No. 307; Ebeling, *TuL*, No. 7.

51. R. Frankena, *Tākultu, De sacrale Maaltijd in het Assyrische Ritueel* (Leiden 1953).
52. K. F. Müller, *Das Assyrische Ritual*, MVAG 41 : 2 (Leipzig 1936).
53. Frankena, op. cit. pp. 6off; English summary, pp. 132ff.
54. *ANET*, pp. 342f.
55. Detailed presentation with several examples in Saggs, pp. 302ff.
56. E. Meier, *Die assyrische Beschwörungssammlung Maqlu* (AfO Beiheft 2) (Graz 1937); E. Reiner, *Šurpu* (AfO Beiheft 11) (Graz 1958).
57. R. C. Thompson, *The Devils and Evil Spirits of Babylonia*, vol. I (London 1903); B. Meissner, *Babylonien und Assyrien* II (Kulturgeschichtliche Bibliothek I 4) (Heidelberg 1925), pp. 216–21.
58. Saggs, p. 307.
59. Saggs, pp. 307f.
60. Saggs, p. 311.
61. Saggs, pp. 311f.
62. See J. Laessøe, *Studies on the Assyrian ritual and series bit rimki* (Copenhagen 1955); cf. Jacobsen, *PAPS* 107, pp. 480f.
63. On divination in general, see Oppenheim, pp. 206–27, with notes.
64. A. Haldar, *Associations of Cult Prophets among the Ancient Semites* (Uppsala 1945), pp. 1–21.
65. Oppenheim, p. 208.
66. Oppenheim, pp. 212ff.
67. Oppenheim, p. 209.
68. Oppenheim, pp. 224ff.
69. Oppenheim, p. 221; Haldar, op. cit. pp. 21ff.
70. W. von Soden, 'Verkündung des Gotteswillens durch prophetisches Wort in den altbabylonischen Briefen aus Mari', *Die Welt des Orients* I (1947–52), pp. 397–403; G. Dossin and A. Lods, 'Une tablette inédite de Mari, interessante pour l'histoire ancienne du prophétisme sémitique', in *Studies in Old Testament Prophecy* (Robinson Festschrift), ed. H. H. Rowley (Edinburgh 1950), pp. 103ff.
71. Both of these in *ANET*, pp. 450f.
72. *ANET*, pp. 451f; several examples in A. K. Grayson and W. G. Lambert, 'Akkadian Prophecies', *JCS* 18 (1964), pp. 7–30; cf. W. W. Hallo, 'Akkadian Apocalypses', *Israel Exploration Journal* 16 (1966), pp. 231ff.
73. F. R. Kraus, 'Ein Sittenkanon in Omenform', *ZA* 43 (1936), pp. 77–113.
74. F. M. T. de L. Böhl, *Der babylonische Fürstenspiegel* (Mitteilungen der Altorientalischen Gesellschaft 11 : 3) (1937), esp. pp. 7f; Lambert, *BWL*, pp. 110ff.
75. Saggs, p. 359; Frankfort, *KG* p. 237.
76. Oppenheim, p. 98.
77. A collection can be found in I. Engnell, *SDK*, pp. 178ff.
78. R. Labat, *Le caractère religieux de la royauté assyro-babylonienne* (Paris 1939), pp. 45ff (at least as Frankfort interprets him, *KG*, p. 406, n. 21; Labat expresses himself very cautiously).
79. See G. Widengren, 'Det sakrala kungadömet bland öst- och västsemiter', *RoB* 2 (1943), pp. 69f; *The Ascension of the Apostle and*

the *Heavenly Book*, Uppsala Universitets Årsskrift (1950:7), pp. 19f.
80. *ANET*, p. 119.
81. Dhorme, p. 156; Frankfort, *KG*, p. 239.
82. *ANET*, p. 315.
83. Frankfort, *KG*, p. 300.
84. Dhorme, p. 168.
85. Dhorme, p. 169.
86. Frankfort, *KG*, pp. 227, 229.
87. Fiore, p. 70.
88. Oppenheim, p. 151.
89. Fiore, pp. 73f.
90. Frankfort, *KG*, pp. 309f.
91. Engnell, *SDK*, p. 44; Widengren, *Religionsphänomenologie* (Berlin 1969), pp. 367f.
92. Waterman, *Royal Correspondence of the Assyrian Empire* I, pp. 2f; Engnell, *SDK*, pp. 43f; Widengren, op. cit., p. 367.
93. Dhorme, p. 173.
94. Frankfort, *KG*, pp. 407f.
95. Frankfort, *KG*, p. 310.
96. Saggs, p. 370.
97. Saggs, pp. 361ff, bibliography, pp. 523f; J. Gray, 'Royal Substitution in the Ancient Near East', *Palestine Exploration Quarterly* 87 (1955), pp. 180–2.
98. Our information comes from the Babylonian priest Berossus, who is quoted by Athenaeus, *Deipnosophist* 14, 44 (p. 639c) and from Dio Chrysostom, *Oratio* IV, 66f (Loeb edn, p. 198), who speaks of a Persian feast.
99. Dhorme, pp. 184f.
100. Oppenheim, pp. 201f, 204f; cf. also Fichtner and Jeremias, *MVAG* (1922), p. 2.
101. Dhorme, pp. 195f.
102. Dhorme, pp. 199ff.
103. Dhorme, pp. 254ff.; *BHB* 84a and b, p. 134.
104. *BiOr* 13 (1956), p. 144 (in a review by W. G. Lambert of E. Ebeling, *Literarische Keilschrifttexte aus Assur* (Berlin 1953)).
105. O. Ravn, *Illustreret Religionshistorie* (ed. J. Pedersen, Copenhagen 1948), p. 179.
106. Dhorme, p. 202.
107. Dhorme, p. 214.
108. *ANET*, pp. 434–5.
109. *BHB* No. 98b, p. 157; *ANET* p. 427; Lambert, *BWL*, p. 105.
110. Dhorme, p. 217f.
111. E. A. Speiser, 'Authority and Law in Mesopotamia', in *Authority and Law in the Ancient Orient*, *JAOS* supplement 17 (1954), p. 12; B. Landsberger, 'die babylonischen Termini für Gesetz und Recht', in *Symbolae ad Iura Orientis Antiqui Pertinentes Paulo Koschaker dedicatae* (Studia et documenta ad jura orientalis antiqui pertinentes 2) (Leiden 1939), pp. 220f.

112. G. Widengren, *RoB* 2 (1943), p. 75.
113. Cf. above, n. 56. This passage is also found in I. Mendelsohn, ed., *Religions of the Ancient Near East* (New York 1955), pp. 212f; cf. Dhorme, pp. 226f.
114. *ANET*, pp. 426f (II, 12ff); Lambert, *BWL*, pp. 101, 103.
115. Dhorme, p. 231.
116. *BHB* No. 91, p. 143.
117. *BHB* No. 97b, p. 152.
118. *BHB* No. 91, pp. 142f.
119. *BHB* No. 34, p. 67.
120. *BHB* No. 26, p. 54.
121. G. Widengren, *The Accadian and Hebrew Psalms of Lamentation as Religious Documents* (Stockholm 1936).
122. See B. Albrektson, *History and the Gods* (Coniectanea Biblica, Old Testament Series 1), (Lund 1967).
123. *ANET*, pp. 434–7; Lambert, *BWL*, pp. 21–62. A fragment with a similar theme in J. Nougayrol, 'Une version ancienne du "juste souffrant"', *Revue Biblique* 59 (1952), pp. 242ff; W. von Soden, 'Zu einigen altbabylonischen Dichtungen', *Or* NS 26 (1957), pp. 315–19.
124. B. Landsberger, 'Die babylonische Theodizee', *ZA* NF 9 (1936), pp. 32ff; *ANET* pp. 439–40; latest edn, *BWL*, pp. 63–89.
125. *ANET*, pp. 437–8; *BWL*, pp. 139–49.
126. Oppenheim, p. 274.
127. Ebeling *TuL*, pp. 1–9, re-edited by W. von Soden, 'Die Unterweltsvision eines assyrischen Kronprinzen', *ZA* NF 9 (1936), pp. 1–31; *ANET*, pp. 109f.
128. Bottéro, p. 105.

CHAPTER 3

1. M. J. Dahood, 'Ancient Semitic Deities in Syria and Palestine', *Divinità*, p. 74.
2. *KAI* 4. 4; Dahood, op. cit., p. 66.
3. S. Mowinckel, *Palestina før Israel*, p. 136.
4. M. Tsevat, 'Additional Remarks to "the Canaanite God Šälaḥ"', *VT* 4 (1954), p. 322.
5. H. S. Nyberg, 'Studien zum Religionskampf im Alten Testament', *Archiv für Religionswissenschaft* 35 (1938), pp. 329–87; M. Dahood, 'The Divine Name 'Êlī in the Psalms', *Theological Studies* 14 (1953), pp. 453–7.
6. *De Dea Syria* 6.
7. J. G. Frazer and T. H. Gaster, *The New Golden Bough* (New York 1959), p. 288.
8. *KAI* 66; cf. p. 21.
9. D. B. Harden, *The Phoenicians* (London 1962), p. 86; F. Jeremias in ChS I, p. 638.
10. F. Vattioni, 'Il dio Resheph', *Instituto Universitario orientale di Napoli Annali*, NS 15 (1965), pp. 39–74.

11. *Palais Royal d'Ugarit* II, 162; C. Virolleaud, 'Les Nouvelles Tablettes de Ras Shamra (1948–49)', *Syria* 28 (1951), p. 25; J. Gray, *The Canaanites*, p. 126.
12. Groupe linguistique d'études Chamito-sémitiques: *comptes Rendus* (Paris), 9, pp. 50f.
13. J. B. Pritchard, ed., *The Ancient Near East in Pictures* (Princeton 1954), pl. 457.
14. Cf. W. C. Graham and H. G. May, *Culture and Conscience* (Chicago 1936), pp. 81ff.
15. Dahood, *Divinità*, p. 87.
16. Discussion in Dahood, op. cit., pp. 85ff.
17. Ringgren, *Word and Wisdom*, pp. 174ff; A. Caquot, 'Le dieu 'Athtar et les textes de Ras Shamra', *Syria* 35 (1958), pp. 45–60.
18. *KAI*, p. 96.
19. A. Caquot, 'La Divinité Solaire Ougaritique', *Syria* 36 (1959), pp. 90ff.
20. Cf. the numerical progression, for example in Prov. 30.18–31; Amos 1.3, 6, 9, 11, 13; 2.1, 4, 6.
21. *The Syrian Goddess*, tr. H. A. Strong and J. Garstang (London 1913), p. 70.
22. *KAI*, pp. 295f, with literature.
23. 'The God of the Fathers', *Essays in Old Testament History and Religion* (Oxford 1966), pp. 1–77, esp. pp. 32ff.
24. R. Largement in *Histoire des Religions*, ed. M. Brillant and R. Aigrain, IV, n.d. (1957), pp. 230f.
25. See the article 'Baitylia' in *Der Kleine Pauly* I, ed. K. Ziegler and W. Sontheimer (Stuttgart 1964), coll. 806–8.
26. *KAI* 214.19.
27. Eissfeldt, *HbOr* VIII: 1, p. 89.
28. On this see R. Dussaud, *Les origines cananéennes du sacrifice israelite* (2nd edn, Paris 1941); H. Ringgren, *Israelite Religion* (London 1966), p. 176.
29. Published by M. Pallottino and others, 'Scavi nel santuario etrusco di Pyrgi: relazione preliminare della settima campagna, 1964, e scoperta di tre lamine d'oro inscritto in etrusco e in punico', *Archeologia Classica* 16 (1964), pp. 49–117; cf. S. Moscati, 'Sull'iscrizione fenicio-punica di Pyrgi', *RSO* 39 (1964), pp. 257–60, and G. Garbini, 'Considerazioni sull'iscrizione punica di Pyrgi', *Oriens Antiquus* 4 (1965), pp. 35–7.
30. T. H. Gaster, *Thespis* (2nd edn, New York 1961), pp. 407ff.
31. M. C. Astour, 'Un texte d'Ugarit récemment decouvert et ses rapports avec l'origine des cultes bacchiques grecs', *Révue de l'histoire des religions* 164 (1963), pp. 1–15; E. Lipinski, 'Les conceptions et couches merveilleuses de 'Anath', *Syria* 42 (1965), pp. 45–73.
32. C. Virolleaud, 'Les nouveaux textes mythologiques de Ras Shamra', *CRAIB* (1962), pp. 111f.
33. *KAI* 60.1, 69.16, and p. 73.
34. C. Virolleaud, 'Les nouveaux textes alphabétiques de Ras-Shamra',

CRAIB (1962), pp. 93f, and C. Schaeffer, 'Nouvelles fouilles et découvertes à Ras Shamra–Ugarit xxive campagne, automne 1961', ibid., p. 202.
35. *KAI* 44.2 (*mtrḥ*).
36. *KAI* 37.
37. A. Malamat, 'Mari and the Bible: some Patterns of Tribal Organization and Institutions', *JAOS* 82 (1962), p. 149.
38. *KAI* 202.11–15.
39. *KAI*, p. 208; A. Haldar, *Associations of Cult Prophets* (Uppsala 1945), p. 75, n. 1.
40. Virolleaud, *CRAIB* (1962), pp. 105ff.
41. *KAI* 27.
42. *KAI* 222A. 35ff.
43. *KAI* 10.2.
44. *KAI* 202A. 3.
45. *KAI* 214.2f; cf. also 224.24f: the gods have restored the dynasty.
46. *KAI* 14.15ff; cf. 10.3ff (altar).
47. *KAI* 13, 1 and 2.
48. *KAI* 4.6.
49. *KAI* 10.8f.
50. *KAI* 43.11.
51. *KAI* 24.10–13.
52. J. Gray, *The Canaanites*, pl. 9.
53. Virolleaud, *CRAIB* (1962), p. 97.
54. Gordon, *UT* 9; Gray, op. cit., p. 137.
55. Virolleaud, *CRAIB* (1962), p. 97.
56. *UT* 2. According to A. Caquot, 'Un sacrifice expiatoire à Ras Shamra', *Revue d'histoire et de philosophie religieuses* 42 (1962), pp. 201–11, the text is to be understood as a ritual for an expiatory sacrifice.
57. Cf. Jeremias in ChS 1, pp. 634f.
58. *KAI* 8.
59. *KAI* 4.3; 5.2; 6.2; 10.9, etc.
60. *KAI* 14.2f.
61. *KAI* 10.2f, 8.
62. *KAI* 66.1f.
63. *KAI* 10.8ff.
64. *KAI* 214.11.
65. *KAI* 214.22ff.
66. *KAI* 79.10ff.
67. *KAI* 226.2.
68. *KAI* 215.2.
69. II D VI 43.
70. *KAI* 214.17, 21f, and p. 220.
71. *UT* 121–4.
72. *KAI* 13.8; 14.8.

Bibliography

SUMERIAN RELIGION

C.-F. Jean, *La religion sumérienne*. Paris 1931.
  In many respects out of date, but with instructive and for its period full quotations.
S. N. Kramer, *Sumerian Mythology*. Philadelphia 1944. Rev. edn, New York 1961.
  A description of the contents of the myths with translation of selected parts.
S. N. Kramer, *From the Tablets of Sumer*. Indian Hills 1956.
  Reprinted with the title *History Begins at Sumer*. London 1958, 2nd edn 1961. New York 1959.
S. N. Kramer, *The Sumerians*. Chicago 1963.
  Popular presentation of the culture, literature, and religion of the Sumerians with good references to the literature.

BABYLONIAN AND ASSYRIAN RELIGION

P. Dhorme, *La religion assyro-babylonienne*. Paris 1910.
  A treatment which is still in many respects unsurpassed, especially in matters of 'the inner side' of the religion.
B. Meissner, *Babylonien und Assyrien* I–II. Heidelberg 1920–25.
  A detailed description of all sides of Babylonian and Assyrian culture.
E. Dhorme, *Les religions de Babylonie et d'Assyrie*, in Mana, Introduction à l'histoire des religions, 1: 2. Paris 1945.
  A more modern but not always so perceptive a presentation as the same author's earlier work. Good documentation.
J. Bottéro, *La religion Babylonienne*, in the series Mythes et Religions. Paris 1952.

S. H. Hooke, *Assyrian and Babylonian Religion*. London 1953. Reprinted Oxford 1962.
Popular but not completely up-to-date treatment.

H. W. F. Saggs, *The Greatness that was Babylon*. London 1962.
Modern factual picture of Assyrian and Babylonian culture, with good chapters on religion and literature.

A. L. Oppenheim, *Ancient Mesopotamia*. Chicago 1964.
Modern, stimulating interpretation of important sides of Babylonian culture, rich in ideas.

J. Klima, *Gesellschaft und Kultur des alten Mesopotamien*. Prague 1964.
Emphasis on material and economic culture, but intellectual life is also given attention.

S. Fiore, *Voices from the Clay*. Norman, Oklahoma 1965.
Primarily culture and literature.

SUMERIAN AND BABYLONIAN TEXTS

K. Tallqvist, ea. and tr., *Babyloniska hymner och böner* (ed. J. Aro). Helsinfors 1953.
A good selection with a perhaps not entirely up-to-date Swedish translation.

A. Falkenstein and W. von Soden, *Sumerische und Akkadische Hymnen und Gebete*. Zurich 1953.
A representative selection in an excellent translation.

J. B. Pritchard, *Ancient Near Eastern Texts related to the Old Testament*. Princeton 2nd edn 1955; 3rd edn with supplement 1969.
A rich and many-sided selection, also from other parts of the ancient East.

WEST SEMITIC RELIGION

F. Jeremias, 'Kanaanäer, Syrer und Phönizier', in Chantepie de la Saussaye, *Lehrbuch der Religionsgeschichte*, I. 4th edn. Tübingen 1925.
A presentation which in its time was excellent, and is still in many respects useful.

R. Dussaud, 'Phéniciens, Syriens' in Mana 1:2. Paris 1945.
A solidly reliable but somewhat brief presentation.
J. Starcky, 'Palmyréniens, Nabatéens et Arabes du Nord avant l'Islam' in *Histoire des religions*, ed. M. Brillant and R. Aigrain. Vol. 4. Paris n.d. [1957].
R. Largement, 'La religion Canaanéenne', ibid.
O. Eissfeldt, 'Kanaanäisch-ugaritische Religion' in *Handbuch der Orientalistik* VIII:I. Leiden 1964.
Up to date but extremely brief.
J. Gray, *The Canaanites*. London 1964.
General cultural history, with good pictorial material; devotes very considerable attention to religion.
D. B. Harden, *The Phoenicians*. London 1962; rev. edn, 1963.
Of the same type as the previous book.

The following specialized works should also be mentioned:

R. Dussaud, *Les origines cananéennes du sacrifice israélite*. 2nd edn. Paris 1941.
M. H. Pope, *El in the Ugaritic texts*. SVT 2. Leiden 1955.
J. Gray, *The Legacy of Canaan*. SVT 5. Leiden 1957; 2nd edn, 1965.
A. S. Kapelrud, *Baal in the Ras Shamra Texts*. Copenhagen 1952.
A. S. Kapelrud, *The Ras Shamra Discoveries and the Old Testament*. Oklahoma 1963: Oxford 1965.

Index

Index

lamentations 15f, 31f, 52, 76, 79, 108,
  117f
laws, lawgiving 40
lecanomancy 94
Leviathan 149
life, bread of 75, 108; herb (plant)
  of 35, 72, 104, 108; tree of 78f,
  104; water of 35, 75, 108
Lilitu 89
Lipitishtar 3, 40
Lotan 148f
lots, casting 94
love, goddess of 10, 60f, 141
Lucian 126, 136, 156f, 159f, 165
ludlul bēl nimēqi 118, 120
lugal 36f

madonnas 59
magic 34f, 90f, 168f
maḫ priest 25
maḫḫu priest 80, 86
maḫḫū prophet 80, 95f, 167f
Mama 74
Maqlū 90
Marduk 55, 65-7, 69-71, 83-8, 101,
  103, 119f
Mari 3, 49, 95f, 124, 137, 167
Martu, myth of 23
marzēaḫ 165f
mašmašu 80, 86, 90
massebah 158f
Mekal 138
melammu 53, 99, 111
Melqart 138f
mes 5, 8, 20f, 37, 43
mēšaru 58, 103, 112f
Milkom 139
mirror of princes, Babylonian 98
'mirror of sins' 113
Moloch 162
monotheistic tendencies 57, 66
moon-god 8, 56f, 144
morality 42-6, 107-20, 173-5
Moses' birth legend 100
Mot 134, 143, 144, 148-50, 162-5
mother-goddess 4, 141
mountain, sacred 78, 86f, 133
mystery cults 60
mythologies 18-24, 68-76, 144-54

Nabonidus 57, 100, 105
Nabu 67, 84, 86, 102
nakedness, ritual 25, 81
namburbē 93, 123
Nammu 19f

Nanna 5, 8f, 38, 40, 56
Nanshe 17, 44
nature religion 128
Nazi 17
Nergal 63, 122, 137, 139
Nerigal 17
new moon (feast) 30
New Year Festival 25, 30, 67f, 83,
  106-8, 120
Nikkal 57, 144, 151
Ninazu 17
nindingir priest 25
Ningal 57, 100
Ningirsur 17, 24, 30, 37, 39
Ningishzida 14
Ninḫursag 6, 8, 22, 37
Nininsina 17
Ninki 56
Ninlil 14, 30, 34, 37, 40, 47, 55, 62,
  97, 101f
Ninmaḫ 8, 20
Ninsuna 37
Nintu 8
Ninurta 16-18, 22, 62, 86f
Nisaba 17, 39, 97
nōqēd 166
Numushda 23
Nusku 17, 63

Oannes 55
omens 43, 93-5, 98, 166
oracle priests 43, 80, 93, 168
oracles 43, 62, 93-7, 105f, 168

Paghat 152
Paḥlat 168
pantheon 128f, 154
paradise myth 21f
Pazuzu 89
'pessimistic dialogue' 120
Philo Byblius 126, 129f, 134, 141,
  144, 158
pickaxe, poem of the 21
plant of birth 75; of life 35, 72,
  108
Plutarch 128
prayer 45f, 110, 116f, 174
presence of god in image 77f, 159
priesthood 25, 79-81, 166f
priestly titles of king 36f, 79, 105f
prophets, ecstatic 95f, 167f
prostitution, temple (or sacred) 25,
  81, 167
proverbs 46
psalms 52, 107, 117

Biblical References